# Values and Ethics in Coaching

**SAGE** was founded in 1965 by Sara Miller McCune to support the dissemination of usable knowledge by publishing innovative and high-quality research and teaching content. Today, we publish over 900 journals, including those of more than 400 learned societies, more than 800 new books per year, and a growing range of library products including archives, data, case studies, reports, and video. SAGE remains majority-owned by our founder, and after Sara's lifetime will become owned by a charitable trust that secures our continued independence.

Los Angeles | London | New Delhi | Singapore | Washington DC | Melbourne

# Values and Ethics in Coaching

Ioanna Iordanou
Rachel Hawley
Christiana Iordanou

Los Angeles | London | New Delhi
Singapore | Washington DC | Melbourne

Los Angeles | London | New Delhi
Singapore | Washington DC | Melbourne

SAGE Publications Ltd
1 Oliver's Yard
55 City Road
London EC1Y 1SP

SAGE Publications Inc.
2455 Teller Road
Thousand Oaks, California 91320

SAGE Publications India Pvt Ltd
B 1/I 1 Mohan Cooperative Industrial Area
Mathura Road
New Delhi 110 044

SAGE Publications Asia-Pacific Pte Ltd
3 Church Street
#10-04 Samsung Hub
Singapore 049483

Editor: Susannah Trefgarne/Amy Jarrold
Editorial assistant: Edward Coats
Production editor: Rachel Burrows
Marketing manager: Camille Richmond
Cover design: Lisa Harper-Wells
Typeset by: C&M Digitals (P) Ltd, Chennai, India

**Library of Congress Control Number: 2016938548**

**British Library Cataloguing in Publication data**

A catalogue record for this book is available from the British Library

ISBN 978-1-4739-1955-6
ISBN 978-1-4739-1956-3 (pbk)

At SAGE we take sustainability seriously. Most of our products are printed in the UK using FSC papers and boards. When we print overseas we ensure sustainable papers are used as measured by the PREPS grading system. We undertake an annual audit to monitor our sustainability.

The first step in the evolution of ethics is a sense of solidarity with other human beings.

Albert Schweitzer (1875–1965),
French-German Nobel Peace Prize laureate,
physician and theologian

# Contents

# About the Authors

**Dr Ioanna Iordanou**: I am a senior lecturer in Human Resource Management and Coaching and Mentoring at Oxford Brookes University, where I am incredibly fortunate to be part of a superb team of colleagues who make up the International Centre for Coaching and Mentoring Studies. As part of my role, I teach modules on Coaching and Mentoring, Management and Leadership, Adult Learning and Social Science Research. My passion lies in researching coaching and mentoring, and embedding the study and practice of coaching skills in undergraduate curricula. I derive great energy and pleasure from learning with and from my students and this is the principle underpinning my pedagogic practice. A historian by trade, I thoroughly enjoy tracing the roots of coaching and mentoring practices in the long-forgotten apprenticeships of the pre-Industrial period. I hold an MA, PhD, a Certificate and a Diploma in Coaching from the University of Warwick.

**Rachel Hawley**: I am a coach, researcher, consultant and lecturer, with teaching experience in the fields of healthcare leadership and management. I hold an MSc in Coaching and Mentoring from Sheffield Hallam University. I have over twenty-five years of experience in working with a wide range of organisations in the UK public sector at local, regional, national and European levels, where public, learner and staff engagement has extensively underpinned my experience. I am so grateful to the team at the Sheffield Mentoring and Coaching Research Unit, who helped to make my journey of learning for coaching and mentoring such an adventure, igniting my curiosity to continue to learn and write on this topic. I am indebted to my dad, Eric, who, without either of us knowing, first taught me the value of values. Reflecting my passion for collaborative practices, I am currently undertaking my Doctorate in Professional Studies at Sheffield Hallam University on leadership for engagement.

**Christiana Iordanou**: I am a licensed psychologist and dramatherapist, offering my services in Athens, Greece. I hold an MSc in Sport and Exercise Psychology from Loughborough University and an MSc in Developmental Psychology from Lancaster University. Having faith in the healing and cathartic power of art, particularly drama, I completed a four-year postgraduate professional training course in Dramatherapy at the AEON Dramatherapy Institute in Athens, and further postgraduate training in Group Analytic Psychotherapy from the University of Athens Medical School, First Department of Psychiatry. I have extensive experience working with individuals dealing with various mental health difficulties, young children and their parents, and young athletes. I am indebted to my clients for giving me the opportunity to accompany them on their personal journeys to healing and self-actualisation. My passion for continuing professional development in my field has led to my desire to pursue a PhD. I am currently a doctoral researcher at the Department of Psychology at Lancaster University. For this, I have been awarded a fully funded scholarship by the Faculty of Sciences and Technology.

# Foreword

*David Clutterbuck*

Both coaching and mentoring claim their historical roots in the *Odyssey*, mentoring directly, coaching indirectly. Athena, the Goddess of Wisdom, helps Odysseus – and his son, Telemachus – reflect upon their experiences to acquire insight and wisdom of their own. She leads them to explore and question their values, to achieve self-honesty in comparing their espoused values with their behaviours, and to better understand the effects of their actions upon others. In the book *Telemachus* by the French cleric François Fénelon, the learning dialogue is given even greater emphasis.

A metaphor I find helpful in explaining coaching and mentoring is that they connect two contexts. One context is the person's internal world: their sense of identity, their perception of their strengths and weaknesses, their values and their personal narrative. The other context is the external world: what is happening around them, and the subtle and not-so-subtle influences on them and other people that shape their views of what is possible, probable and inevitable. Coaching is a conversation that links these two contexts – and the narratives that go with them – by raising awareness and exploring with curiosity where values, ideas and narratives reinforce, overlap and conflict.

Human beings have a remarkable talent for self-delusion and for not noticing (we unconsciously filter out most of the stimuli that arise within and around us). Surveys have shown that the majority of people in gaol consider themselves to be more ethical than the average person inside or outside of prison. Most men (and women) in the Western world consider themselves to be better-than-average drivers. Our desire to feel morally correct is deep-rooted, to the extent that we appear to have an in-built moral equilibrium. If we do something unkind or illicit, we tend to compensate with an act of kindness that resets the balance. And vice versa!

Ethical behaviour in the workplace is influenced by many subtle factors of which we are scarcely aware. Fill someone's working hours with figures and targets and they become less humane, less people-focused and less ethical in their reasoning and decision-making. Given that organisational roles tend to be more figures-driven as people rise in the hierarchy, it is perhaps not surprising that we see ethical issues occurring so often in executive coaching conversations.

Unethical behaviour is also closely associated with obsessive goal pursuit, whether in business or climbing Mount Everest. The scandals in business have been paralleled by equally unacceptable revelations in sport. What both of these examples reveal is that ethical behaviour is easily undermined when the systems and unconscious values within which people operate condone and encourage behaviour. Our capacity for moral self-deception becomes apparent at organisational or societal levels just as readily, if not more so, than at individual levels. Codes of practice, while helpful in setting out desired behaviours, can become tools of unethical or immoral behaviour when they are observed to the letter, rather than the spirit.

A company lawyer told me recently:

> I have worked for this company and for one of its biggest competitors. The difference between the two was that the previous company expected decisions to be made on the basis of *What can we legally or practically get away with?* or *How close to the wind can we sail?* This company asks: *How can we ensure we are both legally and morally unassailable?* There's no question which is better to work for!

Coach education needs to pay far more attention to ethical awareness, ethical competence, ethical resilience and ethical maturity. First, coaches must develop these qualities in themselves, developing their self-awareness and being honest about how they create narratives that protect their moral self-images. For example, my colleague Doug McKie and I have started to collect coaching taboos – the issues that coaches avoid confronting about themselves and their practices. We may collude with the coachee in numerous ways by failing to challenge their own self-narratives – such as the fiction that they are truly engaged with their self-development, when they are simply using coaching to tick the box showing that they have 'done' self-development this month.

Coaches also require the skills to help clients develop ethical awareness, ethical competence, ethical resilience and ethical maturity. That includes helping the client both to recognise how the organisation's social systems inhibit ethical behaviour and to acquire the resources to challenge actual ethical failings or environments, which heighten the chances of unethical practice happening and becoming embedded.

All three of these contexts – coach, client and organisation – provide rich sources for reflection and dialogue within supervision. Indeed, if a coach supervisee isn't regularly bringing up ethical issues for discussion, this may well be a sign to the supervisor that there is something missing in the coach's reflections on their practice.

This book provides both a theoretical base and a wide range of clues, hints and tips on how to incorporate ethical thinking into coaching practice in all three contexts. I hope that some of these make every reader feel a little uncomfortable and less certain of their own moral rectitude – for it is in this discomfort that our journey towards ethical maturity begins.

# Acknowledgements

We thoroughly enjoyed researching and writing this book, but it would not have come into existence had it not been for the valuable contribution of several individuals who shared our passion, enthusiasm and zeal for values and ethics in coaching. We would like to take this opportunity to thank them.

First and foremost, we wish to thank our visionary commissioning editor, Kate Wharton, who embraced this book from its inception and offered inexhaustible support and encouragement throughout the writing process. Her infectious enthusiasm provided the driving force for the realisation of this project. In parallel with Kate, Bob Thomson, Christian van Nieuwerburgh and David Clutterbuck offered vital reinforcement at the launch of the project and continued to bestow their faith and support all the way through to completion. For this, we are immensely grateful.

The process of writing a book is like a journey: it is more enjoyable when you share it with others, in one way or another. Similarly in our journey, we have been incredibly fortunate to have enjoyed the 'company' of a number of colleagues and friends, who offered invaluable support through their constructive criticism, feedback and unique reflections on our writings. We particularly wish to thank David Clutterbuck, Stella Jones-Devitt, Andrew McDowell, Pat McCarry, Paul Stokes and Christian van Nieuwerburgh for their powerful contributions to the book. Jo Stephenson kindly shared with us her personal experience, which is reflected in a 'Story from practice' in Chapter 2; for this, we are immensely grateful. A special mention is due to the colleagues from the International Centre for Coaching and Mentoring Studies at Oxford Brookes University. In particular, we wish to thank Tatiana Bachkirova, Elaine Cox, Judie Gannon, Peter Jackson, Juliette Koning, Carmelina Lawton Smith and Adrian Myers. We have benefited beyond measure from their support, suggestions and feedback but any errors of fact or interpretation in this book are our own doing; they bear no responsibility whatsoever for those.

In SAGE we found a committed, supportive and ethical publisher. We particularly wish to thank Laura Walmsley, Susannah Trefgarne, Amy Jarrold, Rachel Burrows and Edward Coats for their tireless support, constructive feedback and ceaseless positive attitude from inception to completion of the book. We consider ourselves incredibly fortunate to be part of such a supportive publishing family. On this note, we would like to express our sincere gratitude to Lisa Harper for capturing so fittingly the core message of this book through the cover design – that ethical issues in coaching are rarely black or white but, rather, several shades of grey – and to the numerous anonymous reviewers who offered extensive constructive feedback at various stages of writing. Their comments have most certainly strengthened the reliability of our arguments.

It would be remiss of us not to acknowledge the invaluable contributions of our students and our clients, who have given us the opportunity to reflect critically on our own values and ethics as human beings and as professional practitioners. It is our learning with them and from them that laid the groundwork for this book.

We would like to extend a special 'thank you' to Andrew Armatas, Clinical and Coaching Psychologist, for being a wonderful mentor and friend, and for showing us in practice what ethical coaching is all about.

Last, but by no means least, we owe our most sincere gratitude to our close family and friends, who have shared in our enthusiasm and passion for this book. Importantly, they endured with admirable patience endless hours of writing even during family holidays, the occasional midnight phone call for chapter reflections and edits, and the numerous momentary outpourings of stress and panic, especially when the finish line was in sight. In particular, we wish to thank Chris Moran, Simon, Tom and Amelia Hawley, and Ben, who remains Rachel's inspiration. Without their love, support and patience, this book would simply not have been accomplished.

# Introduction

One of the most valuable aspects of coaching is its interdisciplinary nature. As we assert in the book, the fact that coaching draws from so many different disciplines – such as management, education, counselling, psychotherapy and other behavioural and social sciences – means that it has built a knowledge base that is rich in theoretical and practical applications. This variety has rendered coaching a valuable intervention in many contexts, including business, education, sports and healthcare. This diversity in theoretical perspectives and professional contexts sits against a rich historical narrative. However, this breadth goes hand in hand with a certain degree of complexity and confusion. This is particularly pertinent when it comes to addressing ethical issues in coaching. Accordingly, and in order to include and explore the diverse ethical issues that may arise in coaching from a variety of perspectives, we wanted this book to be as interdisciplinary as possible. It is for this reason that the book's authoring team is made up of individuals who come from three distinct professional backgrounds: management and organisation studies, healthcare leadership, and psychology. Despite this diversity, we are joined by common experience in the discipline of coaching and a mutual passion for an ethical coaching practice.

In February 2016, the Association for Coaching (AC) and the European Mentoring and Coaching Council (EMCC) announced the creation of the Global Code of Ethics (GCoE). Premised on four distinct sections – terminology, working with clients, professional conduct and excellent practice – the GCoE was primarily produced to promote excellence in coaching and mentoring by raising standards of practice. The aim is to provide: 'appropriate guidelines, accountability and enforceable standards of conduct for all our members' (AC, 2016). This is an extremely positive step forward, as lack of independent regulation still holds great implications for the professional credibility of coaching. In this respect, we welcome the prospect of a commonly driven code of ethics that underpins the practice of the coach. Such an initiative, however, begs a significant question – can a well-defined list of explicit guidelines cater for the diversity of people and, in consequence, ethical issues that coaches encounter in their daily coaching practice?

Let's take a few minutes to reflect on this question. Imagine that you are in an individual coaching session with:

- A white middle-class man
- A Buddhist monk
- The CEO of your organisation
- A Muslim woman wearing a burka
- The employee you directly line-manage
- A white working-class man
- An Afro-Caribbean woman
- A middle-aged Indian man with a terminal condition
- A gay man
- An Asian adolescent in a wheelchair
- A refugee
- A Catholic priest.

We can keep adding to the list but this is not the point of this imaginary scenario. How do you think you would work with these different types of individuals? Would you treat everyone in the same manner or do certain categories call for variations in your behaviour? We would expect most coaches to acknowledge that they see no issue with coaching individuals from different backgrounds and with diverse needs, reverberating the oft-quoted dictums: 'I treat everyone as equal' or 'I treat everyone as I want to be treated.' Yet, a little self-reflection will show that characteristics of, say, ethnicity, religion, sexuality – even of professional and social status – matter and can affect the way in which we view and behave around others.

Let's reflect some more on these imaginary clients. With whom might you feel more at ease? Is there any category that you might find particularly challenging? Upon reflection, you might feel more at ease with people who share a similar identity with you. Or you might affirm that you feel at ease with everyone regardless of cultural or other differences between you and them. But would you feel the same if, say, the balance of 'power' shifted and placed you in the coachee's role while one of them was the coach? These reflections bring to the fore two more important questions: To what extent does a shared (or equal) positioning in the world increase or limit the possibilities of how we work with others? Does a position of 'power' change the way in which we view and work with other people (see Pelham, 2016: 90–6)?

The answers to these questions will vary and depend upon our individual values that are shaped by the culture in which we grow up. The nuanced idiosyncrasies that we bring into the coaching practice, either as coaches or as coachees, are too numerous to be somehow encompassed by a single, unified code of ethics. This is because the coaching practice is immersed in a plethora of ethical issues that different people view in different ways. For example: Does a coach need formal qualifications in order to practise coaching? How important is supervision? Can a manager be a coach for her subordinates?

These are a handful of the ethical issues that coaching practitioners face in their everyday practice. To recognise and address such ethical issues, coaches use a variety of approaches. For example, some base their ethical decisions on their intuition or their professional idealism. Others rely primarily on the codes of ethics of the professional membership bodies that they have joined, such as the AC, the EMCC or the International Coach Federation (ICF). Indeed, independent professional bodies' codes of ethics, just like the Global Code of Ethics, purport to provide a platform on which to build an ethical coaching practice. Yet, to date, there has been no systematic guidance that can help coaches navigate the complex landscape of ethical coaching practice.

This is the main objective we wish to achieve in this book. Through plentiful practical examples and interactive activities, the book explores and explains a variety of ethical issues that may emerge in coaching. It does so by presenting a series of real-life case studies that showcase a plethora of complex moral and ethical issues in practice. These are based on interdisciplinary theoretical knowledge and evidence-based research. Through the analysis of such real-life scenarios, this book encourages you to consider the basic principles of values and ethics in coaching and reflect on how your own values and ethics affect your coaching practice. Against this imaginative and conceptual backdrop, discussions throughout seek to contextualise personal, cultural and professional values within different settings where coaching takes place. In each chapter, we offer some practical suggestions that, we hope, will help you become a more consciously ethical practitioner. Please note that through these discussions we are not seeking to offer solutions; rather, we wish to stimulate the kinds of conversations and conditions that enable ethical issues to be unsurfaced.

Ultimately, this book is the first dedicated guide to some of the most fundamental issues concerning the ethical practice of coaching. It is aimed at anyone with an interest in coaching, in practice, education and research settings. It will, therefore, be of use not only to professional coaches, but also to learners, leaders, managers and educators, in the public, private, independent and voluntary sectors. Overall, the book explores the pressing issue of values and ethics in coaching practice in an accessible narrative, illustrating an array of contextual issues and complexities that challenge, inspire and reassure.

## What we shall be covering

Part I of the book explores the meaning and nature of the terms 'ethics' and 'values', encouraging you to consciously reflect on your personal values. It then welcomes you to consider how your personal values might affect your personal and professional relationships and attitudes towards others. It also attempts to place this conscious understanding of one's values into the canvas of one's professional practice. Issues like cultural and organisational values are dealt with in this part too.

Part II delves into the key ethical issues that coaches face while practising, from contracting and being a reflective practitioner, to ending the coaching relationship. Some of the key ethical issues discussed are: contracting and confidentiality; boundaries of competence and appropriateness; formal qualifications vs long-lasting experience; and supervision, evidence-based practice (EBP) and continuing professional development. This part pays particular attention to the different and context-specific ethical issues that arise in the variety of coaching contexts. It supports the view that adopting a stance of critical enquiry into our coaching practice and the contexts in which it is situated enhances our potential of becoming more ethical practitioners.

Part III focuses on some of the most distinct coaching contexts that are bound to raise a variety of ethical and moral dilemmas – namely, business, sports, coach training and education, and healthcare. These are discussed through the lens of real-life case studies that bring to the fore a plethora of such issues.

The book concludes by inviting you to reflect on what you have learned through your reading journey, and to consider the next step towards developing and maintaining an ethical coaching practice. It also offers some tangible suggestions on how we can all support the creation of a common ethical mindset, as the basis for a positive professional culture that places values and ethics at the forefront of the coaching practice.

## How to use the book

We wanted to make this book as interactive and engaging as possible. Our intention was not to produce a mere practitioner's manual but, rather, a practice companion that will encourage you to reflect on your learning through your book-reading journey. To achieve this goal, we have included several interactive features in the book that we hope you will find useful. These are specifically designed to help you hear your voice, as well as the voice of the authors and other coaching practitioners who have contributed to this book. These features are the following:

## Activity

This is where you are asked to participate in an activity that is designed to help you capitalise on your learning so far.

## Pause for reflection

We use this feature quite extensively in this book, as we consider reflection to be a powerful learning and development tool. The 'Pause for reflection' gives you the space to reflect on your learning, allowing you to combine what you have learnt with what you already know. We encourage you to make use of this feature as much as possible.

## From principles to practice: practitioner's reflection

In this feature we host the reflections of colleagues who kindly accepted our invitation to share some of their own learning. This derives from their professional experiences on ethical issues they have encountered in their practice. This feature is premised on our firm belief that a common ethical mindset stems from open communication and joint reflection on ethical issues that arise in our daily coaching practice. We hope that you will find the practitioners' reflections a helpful resource for further reflection.

## Suggested reading

At the end of every chapter, we suggest some texts that we have found particularly thought provoking on several subjects that are relevant to values and ethics in coaching. We trust that you will find some or all of these sources as helpful as we have.

Ultimately, the chapters that you read and the activities that you engage in are a product of collaborative conversations with each other, our colleagues, students, clients and our editing team, but, as the authors of this book, we take full responsibility for our views and any error of fact or interpretation in the book. We hope that by actively engaging with the diverse features in this book, you will join in the conversations as well. It is through continuous conversations, where we share our experiences of ethical issues, that we can bring our professional values and ethics to the forefront (rather than the background) of our coaching practice.

We hope that you enjoy reading this book!

# Part I

## The Nature of Values and Ethics

# 1

# What are Values and Ethics?

## Chapter aims

- To explore the origins and meanings of the terms 'values' and 'ethics'.
- To introduce ways in which personal values and ethics can impact on the coaching practice.
- To familiarise coaching trainees and coaches with the codes of ethics of professional coaching associations.
- To discuss and dispel the myth of a universally accepted ethical code of practice.

## Chapter overview

In this chapter, we discuss the meaning of the words 'values' and 'ethics', offering a brief philosophical overview of the origins of these concepts. We then explore some of the key ethical issues that are relevant to the coaching practice. We place particular emphasis on the unregulated landscape in which coaching is situated and which is partly accountable for the lack of coherent ethical guidelines that could underpin the coaching profession. We also look at the distinct ethical codes that have been developed by prominent professional coaching bodies. We conclude the chapter by highlighting the significance of understanding your values and constantly reflecting on their impact on your development as a coach and your coaching practice.

## Key words

values, ethics, ethical conduct, professional coaching associations

## Introduction

In the course of your coaching training, practice and even accreditation, you will often come across phrases like 'personal values', 'professional ethics' and 'ethical' and 'unethical' practice. We like to think that most coaches ground their coaching practice on a set of values that aim to support clients in achieving their goals. Yet, it is inevitable that during our coaching practice, we will be placed in a position of having to make ethical decisions, wondering what is morally right or wrong. Such decisions will involve issues ranging from the gravely serious to the mundane. If you have developed a warm and trusting relationship with your client, for instance, would you consider having dinner with her after the coaching session? If your coaching client has revealed to you that she illegally claims benefits that she is not entitled to, do you report her? Or do you carry on coaching a client who shows clear signs of mental illness but does not wish to admit it and is keen to continue the coaching process?

Such ethical questions are central to coaching. In fact, they are central to any professional activity that involves supporting other people, in one way or another. This book will help you explore issues of values and ethics that you might face in your own coaching practice. It will do so by delving into the nuanced differences of the different applications of coaching. But, before we embark on this journey of exploration, we invite you to consider the meaning, *your* meaning, of the terms 'values' and 'ethics'.

---

## Pause for reflection

Take a few minutes to reflect on the following questions. You can even consider jotting down your answers:

- What is your own definition of the word 'values'?
- What is your own definition of the word 'ethics'?

## What are values?

The *Oxford English Dictionary* defines 'values' as: 'principles or standards of behaviour; one's judgement of what is important in life'. Values dictate what is actually important to us. Many a time they equip us with the drive and motivation to do something. Importantly, values determine how we feel after having taken a particular decision. Contrary to skills (which can be learnt and cultivated), values are inherent and, while they can be consciously explored, they cannot be easily altered.

The word 'value' has different meanings that are all grounded in basic personal preferences and choices of importance. From a numerical perspective, if you believe that the value of your car is £10,000, it means that you will preferably choose to exchange it for a sum of money only if it is equal to £10,000 or higher. From a personal perspective, when you say to a friend 'I value your opinion', it means that this friend's opinion is important to you and that you choose to take it into consideration. From a cultural perspective, the priorities set within the community or society in which you live are bound to affect your choices. In a democratic state, for instance, personal freedom will take precedence over, say, rigid religious directives or social cohesion that might be more pronounced in other societies. The environment in which you are reared, be it family, school or the local community, will most probably have a strong influence on the values and the value system you adopt.

A value system is a set of personal and cultural values evolved and accepted by a person, community or society as a standard moral code that guides one's behaviour. This set of values is not easily changeable and, at times, we can even define it using a specific term: 'I am a socialist', 'I am a Christian', 'I am a European.' For most of us, such beliefs and attitudes are imprinted in our inner being and dictate how we make decisions for what is morally right or wrong. In fact, they influence the way in which we think, judge and act, and shape our overall conduct in life. In other words, our value system shapes the identity we develop within a society. When we talk about 'Christian values', 'American values' or 'working-class values', we are talking not only about the values of an individual but also about the set of values shared by an entire community. Different circumstances and traditions will influence the diverse criteria that communities and cultures use to prescribe their preferences and choices.

## Values in coaching

This plethora of culturally based values that can be held by an individual is bound to penetrate professional contexts, including that of coaching. Consider, for instance, the following scenarios:

- Due to unforeseen circumstances, you have been forced to reschedule an appointment with a client three times. You finally manage to agree on a specific day and time. But, then, your 8-year-old son informs you that his school's play, in which he is participating, happens to be taking place on that particular day and time. Do you reschedule your appointment with your client yet again?
- An employee you directly line-manage has started to show clear signs of deteriorating performance due to a personal family crisis. Your own line manager suggests that you take the role of your employee's coach in order to support her during this tremulous time. Do you accept?
- You are appointed as a coach in a high-profile organisation. Your responsibility is to coach managers who are facing the prospect of dismissal. The organisation's human resources (HR) manager directly asks for your input as to who should be laid off. Do you offer your views?
- A good friend has decided that she needs coaching for personal and professional purposes. She knows that you are very successful in your job and asks you to be her coach. Do you consent? If so, do you charge a fee?

The choice you make in any of these scenarios will primarily depend on the set of consequences that are more preferable to you. In your view, is maintaining client satisfaction more important than your child's play? Do you think that one should keep their personal and professional life separate? Is it your duty, as a coach, to determine who can succeed or fail in a professional context? Can someone assume the role of a good friend's coach? If so, is it acceptable to charge money for the service provided? The course of action that you take to address such ethical dilemmas will be determined by your values. These may be either inherent or you have chosen to adopt them as part of a professional code of ethics.

---

## Pause for reflection

Take some time to consider the scenarios listed above:

- What choice would you make?
- What personal values would you base your decision on?

---

As we have already ascertained, values are a set of personal principles that guide our behaviour and, by extension, our coaching practice. While you are reflecting on these hypothetical dilemmas, you may notice that values can, at times, be conflicting. You may feel, for instance, that your strong work ethics do not allow you to reschedule your appointment with your client but, as a parent, you feel that it's your obligation to be present at your child's play. Indeed, these are difficult decisions exactly because they involve balancing contrasting values. How we deal with such contrasting values and how we choose to make one set of values override another is something that we will keep coming back to in this book.

## A brief philosophical overview of values

As we have already established, values are, in one way or another, associated with choice of action. They dictate not what we do but what we feel we *ought* to do. You see, you can always consider the positive and negative consequences of a situation before deciding on a course of action. But your sense of what you *ought* to do will help you determine which set of consequences you prefer. This observation takes us all the way back to the Scottish Enlightenment and one of its most prominent exponents, the Scottish philosopher and historian David Hume (1711–76).

### Contributions from philosophy: David Hume

In his *A Treatise of Human Nature* (2007 [1739]), David Hume attempted to explore the psychological basis of human nature and argued that feelings, rather than reason, dictate human behaviour. In stark contrast to the contemporaneous Cartesian notion of 'I think, therefore I am', Hume promulgated the view that: 'Morals excite passions, and produce or prevent actions. Reason itself is utterly impotent in this particular. The rules of morality, therefore, are not conclusions of our reason' (ibid.: 458).

It follows that, for Hume, human beings are inherently more interested in how things ought to be, rather than what they actually are. Additionally, Hume saw no causal relationship between an *ought* and an *is*. He could not believe that what we *ought* to do derives from what we actually *do* (ibid.: 420). The question of how *ought* can be derived from *is*, also known as the *ought-to* problem or Hume's Law, has become one of the central questions of ethical theory. For our purposes, what is important to take from Hume's thinking is that, when it comes to making ethical decisions, what guides our actions is not what we know but how we feel about it.

How we feel about an action is influenced by the environment in which we are reared. This is made up of the society in which we are brought up and by the specific societal subgroups in which we take part. Such subgroups include gender, age group, ethnic or geographical community, occupational group, and political party and class, among others. Inevitably, we tend to subscribe to several of the values our society espouses. In other words, our values are shaped by what Michel Foucault termed 'the regime of truth' of our society.

---

### Contributions from philosophy: Michel Foucault

Michel Foucault argued that: 'every society has its own regime of truth, its "general politics" of truth: that is, the types of discourse which it accepts and makes function as true' (Foucault, 1980: 131). This 'regime of truth' will most probably influence the development of our value system.

---

These societal values tend to change and evolve, as we move from subgroup to subgroup. Have your political or religious values changed as you moved from one age group to another? Has the priority of your values altered if you have moved from one country to another? Taking time to reflect on these questions, we might realise how a particular societal consensus influences our values and, most importantly, how tacitly ongoing this process is. Beckett and Maynard explicate this change through a series of examples, some of which are the following:

- *Sexual behaviour*: Sixty years ago in Britain, premarital sex was, generally speaking, socially unacceptable, while same-sex relationships were only decriminalised in 1967. While these attitudes are now considered anachronistic in most European countries, in some other parts of the world such beliefs remain unaltered. In fact, there are still countries where same-sex sexual relationships are subject to legal sanctions, including the death penalty.
- *Corporal punishment*: While half a century ago it was acceptable to discipline a child by means of corporal punishment at school, in most European societies nowadays even a smacking of the hand can lead to a lawsuit.
- *Freedom of expression*: In today's digital world of social media and freely available pornography, we can surmise that freedom of expression has come a long way. Still, devastating events like the killings of the *Charlie Hebdo* employees in Paris in January 2015 could suggest otherwise. So can the long list of assassinated journalists, compiled by UNESCO on a yearly basis (see the organisation's website).

- *The sanctity of life*: Although most societies assign an inestimable value on human life, there is no consensus regarding what justifies taking a life. The death penalty, for instance, is still considered an appropriate form of punishment in several states in the USA, while it is no longer acceptable in Europe. Moreover, while abortion and euthanasia are contentious practices in many societies, both are more openly discussed. In fact, in some societies, like in Britain, abortion is legal and state-provided. (2013: 15–16)

Undoubtedly, other examples of recent changes in what society deems morally *right* or *wrong* will come to mind, and the more you think about them the more radical differences you will find amongst contemporary societies and cultures. Consider, for example, attitudes towards the role of men and women in society, single or same-sex parenthood, or prostitution. In March 2015, for instance, 1 in 20 UK-based students were reported to have sought employment in the sex industry for financial benefit, and the numbers are likely to increase (Sagar et al., 2015). Where do you stand on sex work as a means of tackling the mounting costs of a university degree? What matters most – the end or the means?

It follows, then, that just because you grew up in a society that has instilled in you certain commonly accepted values, this does not mean that your personal values will not, at times, clash with the former. It is inevitable that, in both personal and professional contexts, you may find yourself disagreeing with other people as to what constitutes 'right', 'appropriate' or even 'normal' behaviour. You may also realise that even deeply rooted, widely accepted values can collide. Consider, for instance, potential contradictions in the following conflicting values – loyalty vs honesty, competition vs cooperation, freedom of information vs national security, confidentiality vs safety, equality vs individuality, and tradition vs novelty.

## Pause for reflection

- Do you have any conflicting values that may affect your coaching practice?
- Have you found yourself in a position where you have had to compromise one value for another?

As a social being and as a professional, you will more often than not struggle with conflicting values – personal, professional, societal, even organisational – when it comes to taking decisions and proceeding to action. This becomes more complicated when your occupation involves working closely with people and helping them with personal or professional issues. The practical application of your values in the form of decisions and actions is bound to be guided by rules and codes of conduct. These rules of conduct can be summed up in one term, *ethics*.

## What are ethics?

According to the *Oxford English Dictionary*, 'ethics' are: 'moral principles that govern a person's behaviour or the conducting of an activity'. Ethics, therefore, refer to a person's decisions and actions, as dictated by their beliefs and values. Put more simply, ethics is the practice that determines what is good or bad, right or wrong (de Jong, 2010). In comparison to values, ethics do not merely relate to 'our general notions of what is important, but to actual rules, codes, and principles of conduct' (Beckett and Maynard, 2013: 20). In other words, ethics can be seen as the practical application of values. In coaching, according to de Jong (2010), ethical principles determine the virtue of helping others, focusing on the needs and interests of the client, honouring trust and confidentiality, and promoting individual autonomy. But this is a lot easier said than done. Let's unpack this with a hypothetical example.

## Story from practice

Irene is an experienced coach who was recently employed by a governmental organisation to coach Mike, a senior manager who has been struggling to adjust to the organisational changes that the newly appointed CEO imposed. During their penultimate coaching session, Mike reveals to Irene that he wittingly took advantage of the company's travel expenses policy to claim more money than he was actually entitled to. With one coaching session to go before she completes her work in that organisation, Irene is faced with a great ethical dilemma. Does she maintain her client's confidentiality, a value that underpins her professional ethics, or does she report Mike (and, if so, to whom?), respecting the organisational (and societal) values of honesty and justice? Questions to consider:

- What is Irene's responsibility to Mike? To the organisation?
- How can Irene address this issue without violating Mike's confidentiality?
- What could Irene do to prevent this kind of ethical dilemma arising in the future?

The way in which Irene will respond to this ethical challenge will depend on which of her values take precedence over others. Clear contracting at the outset of the coaching relationship – a topic that we will discuss in detail in Chapter 3 – can help anticipate such ethical challenges. Still, while the process of exploring this issue can be unpleasant, it can also provide an excellent opportunity for learning, both for the coach and the coachee. Irene can invite Mike, for instance, to explore the reasons that led to his misconduct and what he considers to be the best course of action henceforth, from an ethical perspective. In this way, the exploration of ethical behaviour can be a powerful learning tool for both the coach and the coachee.

## A brief philosophical overview of ethics

Historically, ethics can be traced back to the work of ancient Greek philosophers such as Socrates (*c.*470–399 BC), Plato (*c.*428–*c.*348 BC) and Aristotle (384–322 BC). Ethical behaviour for them depended on different factors. While for Socrates moderation was a key determinant of what is right or wrong, Plato advocated the denial of any bodily pleasure. He believed that happiness, known as *eudaimonia* in Ancient Greek, could be achieved by living a life of virtue, *arete*. So did Aristotle, but the two disagreed on what constituted virtue. For Plato, virtue was a product of knowing what is good. Knowing what is good – that is, wisdom – implied doing what is good. This, according to Plato, was sufficient to achieve *eudaimonia*. For Aristotle, knowledge of what is good was inadequate in the pursuit of *eudaimonia* without also practising good (Crisp, 2013). The historical ruminations over these early philosophic views on good paved the way for the development of moral philosophy.

Moral philosophy is primarily concerned with what is 'right' or 'wrong' behaviour; it has produced a variety of ethical models to answer this question. In the Western world, primarily in Europe and North America, deontological ethics and utilitarian ethics have been the two prevailing ethical models. *Deontological* ethics are premised in the doctrines of Immanuel Kant (1724–1804), who situated reason at the core of morality. In essence, deontological ethics derive from one's sense of duty and obligation and are grounded in a set of universal beliefs about the nature of reality. *Utilitarian* ethics are based on the writings of David Hume, Jeremy Bentham (1748–1832) and John Stuart Mill (1806–73). Contrary to deontological ethics, utilitarian ethics focus on the maximisation of utility for the benefit of society. Whether an action is right or wrong is judged by an evaluation of its positive and negative consequences. In the final analysis, the deontological approach sees human beings as ends in themselves, while the utilitarian approach considers them as means to an end (Bond, 2015: 47).

Several other ethical approaches have sprung up, primarily as a result of the competition, if not restriction, of the deontological and utilitarian ethics. A revival of Aristotle's ethics generated *virtue* ethics. Virtue ethics dictate that it is not duties, obligations or consequences that determine the 'rightness' or 'wrongness' of an action, but the virtues that enable an individual to grow and develop (see, for instance, Hursthouse, 1999). *Ethics of care* is a feminist approach to ethics that recognises the female experience of living with the dependency of others, for instance children (Gilligan, 1993). It is closely related to virtue ethics and, in practice, it accentuates the 'rightness' or 'wrongness' of an action as an implication of interconnectedness. As Koggel and Orme (2010: 109) prosaically summed up, ethics of care 'emphasizes the importance of context, interdependence, relationships, and responsibilities to concrete others'.

Of course, where there is more than one person involved, the question of power will inevitably arise. If a physician and a patient disagree on the significance of the patient's physical symptoms, who is right? The one with the expert knowledge or the one with the direct experience? More pertinently nowadays, consider how in several capitalistic societies the financial promiscuity of banks is tolerated by governments, compared to the financial promiscuity of individuals. This takes us back to Karl Marx's (1818–83) ideas of values and morals being dictated by the most powerful in a society. When we think in this way, we are bound to ask the question: 'Whose interest would this serve?' This approach has been termed *ethics of power and structure* (Becket and Maynard, 2013: 23).

All of these approaches to ethics (and several others that we have not discussed) depend on various factors and cannot easily converge into one coherent and universal ethical approach that every one of us can employ. This postmodern doubt of the possibility of producing a universally distinct ethical system has generated *discourse* or *narrative ethics* (see, for instance, Habermas, 1990; and Newton, 1997). This approach is grounded in a postmodern assertion that a universally distinct ethical system may not be possible. In essence, it may be more practical to explore what kind of ethics is more appropriate for any particular context, rather than to attempt to impose a universal code that everyone must adhere to. This issue is particularly pertinent in professional contexts, where a morally 'right' or 'wrong' action is dependent on a variety of conflicting factors – including knowledge, culture and pluralistic values – which may be in conflict with each other.

Ethics in professional contexts, otherwise known as *professional ethics*, is a subsidiary area of moral philosophy. Professional ethics is a rapidly growing discipline, which is informed by several strands of social sciences and the law. The core focus of professional ethics is the application of a set of values that dictate ethical professional conduct and constitute 'an integral part of professional identity' (Bond, 2015: 47). The most elaborately developed type of professional ethics are *medical ethics*. This is due to the long history and ethos of the discipline of medicine, which necessitated the combination of ethical and technical issues in the training and practice of physicians.

---

### Contributions from philosophy: Thomas Percival

The first modern code of medical ethics was crafted by the English physician Thomas Percival (1740–1804). His *Medical Ethics, or a Code of Institutes and Precepts, Adapted to the Professional Conduct of Physicians and Surgeons* was initially produced as a pamphlet in 1794, and expanded in 1803 (Waddington, 1975).

---

Professional codes like Percival's medical code of ethics have had an immense influence on the development of ethical standards of practice in other relevant 'helping' professions like counselling and psychotherapy (Bond, 2015). These are grounded in deeper societal values that pertain to issues of trust and confidence, power and status, even conflict of interests. As Brennan and Wildflower (2014: 432) appositely claimed, these codes have gradually created a consensus of morally acceptable behaviour that transcends professional activities and encompasses all aspects of human interactions. 'It is', they argued, 'in the nature of being a professional that one functions with a particular level of consciousness of the effect of one's behaviour' (ibid.).

## Ethics in coaching

Over the last two decades, the use of coaching as a developmental tool has increased exponentially, primarily in North America, Europe and Australia, and more recently in Asia and Africa. A recent study initiated by the International Coach Federation found that coaching is a $2 billion-per-year industry employing 47,500 professionals globally, and that the number of coaching programmes and professionals entering the field is constantly on the rise (PricewaterhouseCoopers (PwC), 2012). This rapid success brings with it a certain degree of notoriety (Brennan and Wildflower, 2014). Unlike relevant 'helping' professions like medicine, nursing, social work or counselling and psychotherapy – all services that are subjected to the regulatory scrutiny of professional associations or the government – coaching continues to remain largely unregulated. As a result, ethical standards of professional practice are primarily self-imposed and no coach is obliged to comply with any specific codes of ethics, if he or she does not wish to do so.

So, how do coaches make decisions when it comes to ethical issues or dilemmas? In most cases intuition, as dictated by one's value system, seems to be the coach's first port of call. Passmore (2009: 8) put it very appositely when he claimed that:

> Most coaches are in most cases ethical pluralists, who hold to a few solid principles, but for most of what they do they consider the circumstances of the situation and consider the motives and situations of the characters involved to help them reach a decision about the course of action to follow.

But are 'a few solid principles' adequate to safeguard ethical practice? Despite this unregulated landscape of coaching, or (better put) because of this landscape, the existence of a code of ethics for practice has been deemed essential (Brennan and Wildflower, 2014). This is because a code of ethics can provide a set of guidelines against which coaches and clients can measure a coach's performance and evaluate their practice for continuous development and improvement. Additionally, as coaching is still not recognised as a legitimate, stand-alone profession, a code of ethics will allow it to move away from what Grant and Cavanagh termed 'pseudo-credentialising mills' (2004: 2). Indeed, in 2008, the Global Convention on Coaching (subsequently named the Global Coaching Community – GCC), a symposium of coaching scholars and practitioners from around 40 countries, prioritised the issue of ethics as of paramount significance to the legitimisation and preservation of the coaching profession (GCC, 2008). This is not to say that coaching has been in existence with no standards of ethical practice whatsoever. Several professional coaching bodies have produced their own codes of ethical practice which coaches can adopt, should they choose to. Let's look at them.

## Professional coaching associations and their codes of ethics

A code of ethics is a list of guidelines that signposts what is to be expected from a practitioner of a particular profession (Gert, 1988). In essence, it is a set of standards of conduct that dictate what is considered morally acceptable behaviour within a particular field of practice and/or organisation (Brennan and Wildflower, 2014: 431). But, before we proceed further with our discussion, we wish to be clear about terminology. In particular, we think that it is important to distinguish between the terms 'code of conduct' and 'code of ethics'. The *Collins English Dictionary* defines a code of conduct as 'an agreement on rules of behaviour for a group or organization'; and a code of ethics as 'an agreement on ethical standards for a profession or business'. We adopt these definitions in this book and we refer to conduct as the actual behaviour; and ethics as the general guides that influence that behaviour.

When you join a professional coaching body, you agree to enter a community of practice with mutual obligations towards its members and the overall profession (Khurana and Nohria, 2008). It also means that you agree to comply with its professional and ethical standards. By extension, your membership implies that you accept to be held accountable for ethical conduct and, as a result, to be subjected to the organisation's complaints procedure, in case of breech of its code of ethics. Pursuing accreditation from such an institution, in addition to mere membership, can be an onerous process, but of course it has several benefits. This includes the opportunity to claim publicly that you operate under the aegis of one such association. It also enhances your status and credibility as a practitioner of this relatively young, emerging profession (Carlo and Prior, 2003; de Jong, 2010).

In the field of coaching, the most well-known professional associations are the:

Africa Board for Coaching, Consulting and Coaching Psychology (ABCCCP)

Association for Coaching (AC)

Association for Professional Executive Coaching and Supervision (APECS)

European Mentoring and Coaching Council (EMCC)

International Association of Coaching (IAC)

International Coach Federation (ICF)

Worldwide Association of Business Coaches (WABC)

Recognising the relevance of coaching in the fields of counselling and psychotherapy, several psychological professional associations have established special interest groups in coaching psychology. Some of these are the:

American Psychological Association (APA)

Australian Psychological Society (APS)

British Association for Counselling and Psychotherapy (BACP)

British Psychological Society (BPS)

Joining a professional coaching body and agreeing to comply with its professional and ethical standards is a matter of ethics. Considering the pros and the cons, what are your thoughts on the merits of joining a coaching body?

---

### Activity

Write a list of the professional values that underpin your coaching practice. Then, go online and find the professional coaching body that you are a member of or that operates in your country. Within its website, locate their ethical code of conduct, which is usually freely available to download. Have a read through it (it's usually no more than one page long). Can you find similarities with your own professional values?

---

While the different professional coaching bodies operate independently from each other, if you carefully go through their 'codes of ethics' or 'codes of conduct', you will most certainly trace several similarities. These, of course, will be dictated by the societal values in the community within which you operate.

Brennan and Wildflower (2014: 431–2) conducted an expansive survey of several professional bodies' codes of ethics across various related professions. They found that there is a degree of consistency in the ethical principles that underpin professional practice, the most common of which are:

1. Do no harm: Do not cause needless injury or harm to others.
2. Duty of care: Act in ways that promote the welfare of other people.
3. Know you limits: Practise within your scope of competence.
4. Respect the interests of the client.
5. Respect the law.

If one looks at the 'code of ethics' documents of professional coaching associations like the ICF, EMCC, AC, IAC, APECS, WABC and ABCCCP, at first glance they appear quite similar. A brisk analysis of the first three, the ICF, EMCC and AC, for instance, shows that they all place great significance on a coach's qualifications and expertise, continuing professional development and supervision, respectful practice that promotes the profession, adhering to codes of ethics, confidentiality and boundary management, as well as contracting and conflicts of interest.

A more nuanced examination, however, reveals critical differences in the priorities they place on what constitutes ethical conduct. While the ICF makes it perfectly clear that sexual relationships with clients or sponsors are frowned upon, the AC does not seem to refer to this issue. The EMCC places strong emphasis on maintaining professional responsibility, especially towards confidentiality and provision of follow-up coaching, after the termination of the coaching relationship. It is also the only body that seems to place emphasis on respecting the variety of different approaches to coaching. The ICF makes particular reference to ethical issues of further compensation for the coach through third parties that could be perceived as personal, professional or monetary benefits. It also mentions the significance of conducting and disseminating research in an ethical manner. Finally, the AC specifies the need for indemnity insurance and places particular emphasis on issues of diversity and equality that are only implicit in the other two bodies' codes of ethics.

All of the differences in both wording and emphasis between these associations are bound to cause confusion (Brennan and Wildflower, 2014). Moreover, if coaches opt for membership in more than one of these organisations, ethical dilemmas may arise as to which guidelines should take precedence (Passmore and Mortimer, 2011). To mitigate the potential risks of such inconsistencies, in 2011 the ICF and EMCC joined forces with the European Union (EU) in an attempt to produce a shared code of conduct as a benchmark for ethical practice in coaching and mentoring. This pursuit lays the groundwork for the development of self-regulation in both coaching and mentoring and, in this respect, it is registered on the dedicated EU database for self-regulated initiatives in Europe (Brennan and Wildflower, 2014: 433). A few years earlier, a group of these bodies (the ICF, AC, APECS and EMCC) commenced a process of agreeing on the First UK Statement of Shared Professional Values (Association for Coaching, 2008).

According to the agreement statement, the shared professional values are the following:

- Every coach, whether charging fees for coaching provided to individuals or organisations or both, is best served by being a member of a professional body suiting his/her needs.
- Every coach needs to abide by a code of governing ethics and apply acknowledged standards to the performance of their coaching work.
- Every coach needs to invest in their ongoing continuing professional development to ensure the quality of their service and their level of skill is enhanced.
- Every coach has a duty of care to ensure the good reputation of our emerging profession.

The same statement contains the following guiding principles that underpin the First UK Statement of Shared Professional Values:

## Principle One: Reputation

Every coach will act positively and in a manner that increases the public's understanding and acceptance of coaching.

## Principle Two: Continuous Competence Enhancement

Every coach accepts the need to enhance their experience, knowledge, capability and competence on a continuous basis.

## Principle Three: Client-Centred

Every client is creative, resourceful and whole and the coach's role is to keep the development of that client central to his/her work, ensuring all services provided are appropriate to the client's needs.

## Principle Four: Confidentiality and Standards

Every coach has a professional responsibility (beyond the terms of the contract with the client) to apply high standards in their service provision and behaviour. He/she needs to be open and frank about methods and techniques used in the coaching process, maintain only appropriate records and to respect the confidentiality a) of the work with their clients and b) or their representative body's members' information.

## Principle Five: Law and Diversity

Every coach will act within the laws of the jurisdictions within which they practise and will also acknowledge and promote diversity at all times.

## Principle Six: Boundary Management

Every coach will recognise their own limitations of competence and the need to exercise boundary management. The client's right to terminate the coaching process will be respected at all times, as will the need to acknowledge different approaches to coaching which may be more effective for the client than their own. Every endeavour will be taken to ensure the avoidance of conflicts of interest.

## Principle Seven: Personal Pledge

Every coach will undertake to abide by the above principles that will complement the principles, codes of ethics and conduct set out by their own representative body to which they adhere and by the breach of which they would be required to undergo due process.

*Source*: Association for Coaching (www.associationforcoaching.com).

Let us clarify here that codes of ethics cannot guarantee a solution to every ethical problem a coach is faced with in practice. Their role is to provide the catalyst for moral thinking and to function as a quality assurance mechanism (Bailey and Schwartzberg, 1995). In other words, while codes can provide the 'scaffolding' that underpins the profession (Duffy and Passmore, 2010), they cannot control it (Bond, 2015). Importantly, no unified code of ethics can alleviate the challenges of making ethical decisions. For this reason, scholars and practitioners have proposed the development of ethical decision-making frameworks as a potential avenue for making ethical decisions (see, for instance, Duffy and Passmore, 2010; Passmore and Mortimer, 2011). The word 'framework', however, can imply intellectual and practical complication, and may not be appealing to every practitioner. The nuanced idiosyncrasies of distinct communities and societies also preclude any attempt to customise and generalise ethical conduct. Echoing our colleagues' concerns regarding possible negligence when coaches do not consciously set out their ethical guidelines to clients (Passmore and Mortimer, 2011; Spence et al., 2006), we emphasise the significance of consciously exploring and reflecting on individual values and ethics and their impact on one's coaching practice.

## Conclusion

Our ethical behaviour as coaches is our own responsibility. Ethical dilemmas – what van Nieuwerburgh (2014: 172) calls 'ethical moments of choice' – will inevitably arise in all aspects of our personal and professional lives. If treated appropriately, ethical dilemmas can enhance our personal and professional development. This is because they alert us to what is morally right or wrong. As a practitioner, if you catch yourself worrying over specific decisions you have to make in your practice, this is generally wonderful news. A right level of worry is indicative of your commitment to your clients and your will to provide them with a service that is right and appropriate for them. Moreover, a healthy dose of worry enables you to be humble and involved in your coaching practice and facilitates the development of your professional maturity. So don't be reluctant to open up yourself to conflict and confusion. Doing the right thing may not always feel right, and this feeling of 'wrong-ness' – what Passmore and Mortimer (2011: 212) call *cognitive dissonance*, echoing Festinger's (1957) seminal theory – can spawn further reflection, learning and development. The key to success is to maintain a conscious and recurrent ethical thinking, and to continuously reflect on your values and how they can influence the decisions that you make in your coaching practice. This will be the focus of the following chapter.

## Chapter summary

- Ethical decisions involve what is morally right or wrong.
- Values are a set of personal principles that guide our behaviour and, more often than not, they clash.
- Ethics are moral principles that determine whether our actions are 'good' or 'bad', 'right' or 'wrong'.
- In coaching, ethical standards of professional practice are self-imposed and no coach is obliged to comply with any specific codes of ethics.
- Several professional coaching associations have produced their own codes of ethics that have both similarities and differences in their ethical priorities.
- Codes of ethics do not ensure best practice in coaching, as they cannot guarantee a solution to every ethical problem a coach is faced with in practice.
- Constant exposure to ethical issues in practice and conscious reflection on them will help you develop your ethical maturity.

---

### Suggestions for further reading

We hope that you will find this book helpful in your exploration of your personal, professional, even organisational values and how they interact with your coaching practice. We also acknowledge that the writing of this book not only has been grounded in other colleagues' previous work, but it is also affected by our own beliefs, principles and values as authors. We therefore recommend that you expand your horizons by reading more widely on the subject. To facilitate this process, we will offer a few relevant recommendations at the end of every chapter.

For a practical application of ethics in professional contexts, we recommend:
Banks, S. and Galagher, A. (2009) *Ethics in Professional Life*. Basingstoke: Palgrave Macmillan.

For a useful introduction in ethics as a subject of philosophical study, see:
Deigh, J. (2010) *An Introduction to Ethics*. Cambridge: Cambridge University Press.

For an insightful overview of the influence of ethics in helping professions, we recommend:
Bond, T. (2015) *Standards and Ethics for Counselling in Action*, 4th edn. London: Sage Publishing.

For a brisk overview of ethics in coaching, see:
Brennan, D. and Wildflower, L. (2014) 'Ethics in coaching', in E. Cox, T. Bachkirova and D. Clutterbuck (eds), *The Complete Handbook of Coaching*, 2nd edn. London: Sage Publishing, pp. 430–44.

# 2

# Understanding Personal and Professional Values

## Chapter aims

- To engage in a critical dialogue for understanding our personal and professional values as individuals and as coaches.
- To explore how values affect our behaviours and attitudes in coaching relationships.
- To explore approaches for raising awareness of values for an ethical coaching practice.
- To engage in activities that support the development of a reflective coaching practice.

## Chapter overview

In this chapter, we aim to encourage readers to reflect on their own experiences and engage in a critical self-dialogue in order to understand, more consciously, their personal and professional values in the context of their coaching practice. We are committed to the view that coaching with a good understanding of our personal and professional values can enhance ethical maturity and, thus, open up new opportunities for supporting clients. Activities are designed to help you reflect on personal and professional values and beliefs. The chapter constitutes a metaphorical mirror. It is based on the premise that you are how you coach. We think about how our values shape our identity and impact on the coaching relationship. We consider how we come to make decisions ethically, as 'a way of being'. In doing this, we move beyond the definitions of values and ethics to explore how these affect our attitude and behaviour within our coaching practice.

## Key words

personal and professional values, reflective practice, critical consciousness, behaviours

## Through the looking glass: understanding your values

Words such as 'good', 'bad', 'right' and 'wrong' are often used when we discuss elements of one's coaching practice. Terms are used interchangeably, sometimes with little or no agreement, and the overtone often pertains to values and ethics. In this book, we view the coaching practice as a 'way of being' (Rogers, 1980; see also van Nieuwerburgh, 2014: 150–1). In the context of helping people, the term 'way of being' was first introduced by the influential humanist psychologist Carl Rogers, the founder of the person-centred approach to psychotherapy. His approach was premised on two fundamental beliefs: that people are their own best experts; and that people have the ability to realise their full potential (Rogers, 1980). Rogers' work has been claimed to be the cornerstone of the coaching practice and, despite the passing of time, it still influences the way coaches see and work with clients (Thomson, 2009: 139, 151–60).

Coaching as a 'way of being' presupposes taking a step back from the process in order to develop greater understanding of ourselves within the coaching relationship. This entails understanding our values and, importantly, how we see our clients through them. Do we believe that they hold the solution to their problem, what Simon Western (2012) calls the *celebrated self*? Or do we feel that they need our rescue, the *wounded self*? The lens we use to view our clients will determine our faith in our clients' ability to find their own solution. This process necessitates developing deeper understanding of our values as coaches, in order to experience coaching as a 'way of being'. This cannot be taught in traditional ways. Instead, as van Nieuwerburgh suggests, it can 'only be learned by people for whom it is important'. Once coaches recognise the importance of this coaching stance, they can utilise coaching conversations, especially the stories told in them, in order to understand the clients' values (2014: 10).

We all have a story to tell. What is your story? Stories, whether written or told, individual or collective, are increasingly recognised for their value in opening windows into the emotional world of individuals, offering a powerful tool for enquiry (Vogel, 2012). Books such as the children's tales *Alice's Adventures in Wonderland* and *Through the Looking-Glass* resonate, as we begin to explore our own values. 'What is the use of a book,' thought Alice, 'without picture or conversations?' (Carroll, 1954 [1865]: 1). Coaching, indeed, offers a marvellous opportunity for learning through conversation. Bolton (2014: xx) reminds us that 'wise Alice knew that texts have to capture hearts, imagination and spirit, as well as mind,' in order to communicate effectively. We are drawn to the idea that illuminating narrative that is expressed in prose, poetry, even pictures, can help us to discover hidden meanings and become more adventurous as we explore our own values. In this chapter, we use activities based on narrative and arts-based approaches to facilitate the process of exploring personal and professional values (Bochner and Ellis, 2003).

## Activity

First, take a few minutes to think of an ethical choice that you have had to make in your coaching practice:

- Recall and record the options you had and then the choices you made.
- Consider what values influenced your decisions. Repeat these steps several times.
- As you build a list of values, look for commonalities in these.

## What are your personal values?

Understanding our values is an ongoing journey of discovery and learning. So often we think we know our story well, yet as we explore our personal and professional values more closely, we tend to discover new insights. We also become more aware of how these influence our coaching practice. Indeed, the dialogic nature of the coaching practice, which is premised on conversation and discourse in order to construct meaning (Alred et al., 1998), is the cornerstone of the learning that ensues in coaching. This approach to learning is in stark contrast to the dominant linear learning that has been imposed by the intellectual movements of the last 200 years (Garvey and Williamson, 2002). We consider the learning that is generated in coaching to be non-linear, simply because it is the product of interaction with others. Against this backdrop, our learning about our values can be seen as 'socially constructed, so that we create rather than discover ourselves' (Alred et al., 1998: 14).

## From principles to practice: practitioner's reflection

### Rachel Hawley, author of *Values and Ethics in Coaching*

As a coach who has spent many years working in the UK National Health Service (NHS), it was perhaps unsurprising that the core values that I brought into my coaching training showed congruence with the values of the NHS: integrity, commitment, mutuality (everyone counts). As I reflected on my values over time through coaching and supervision, new insights emerged. For example, I realised that in an organisational setting, the perspective we have on the past is created by the holders of power and those who dominate the narrative. At that stage in my coaching journey, I began to see that the organisation and wider culture of the NHS were shaping me and my practice. According to Bruner (1985), people shape meaning from the past through metaphor and stories, just as I have done. Developing understanding of my personal and professional values was a significant step in my coaching journey towards ethical maturity in practice.

So, what are your values?

## Activity

Take an A4 piece of paper and entitle it 'My Values and Ethics'. Write down a list of your deeply held values; Ideally, at least five. Consider what is morally right or wrong for you. Do not be surprised if you find that some of these contradict each other. The important thing is to put them onto paper. You can keep these for further reflection and for supervision purposes. We advise that you periodically revisit this list to see how your ethical maturity develops. Do any of these principles change? If so, in what way? Can you recognise any of the triggers for change?

Do you feel that, after this activity, you have a clearer understanding of your personal values? How did you come to develop them? The process of development 'is like a journey from the familiar to confusion, adventure, great highs and lows, towards a world where nothing is different but all is transformed' (Daloz, 1986: 3). Coaching is fundamentally a process of development through learning about our beliefs and values, both as coaches and coachees. Done well, it harnesses the potential for personal and professional development through greater self-awareness for the coach. To achieve self-awareness of the kind we describe in this chapter, one way is to use the metaphor of a mirror. In the following section, therefore, we use this metaphor to stimulate a critical reflection on the values that have shaped your coaching practice. Are they the same as your personal ones?

## What are your professional values as a coach?

Having explored your personal values, we now invite you to start considering your professional values as a coach. As we have observed, values are the bedrock of ethical decision-making. They shape everything we do, not only in the coaching relationship but beyond, in our day-to-day lives. Indeed, they underpin human agency. Similarly, in our coaching practice every decision we make is influenced by our values and beliefs. A critical question that arises then is the following: are we consciously aware of our values or not? When we enter a coaching session as the coach, we bring a particular attitude. Our attitudes are premised on our beliefs. In essence, our attitude is the 'mental filter through which we experience the world' (Keller, 2007: 12) and it is bound to influence the coaching relationship and the ethical issues that emerge in it. Values and attitudes sit hand-in-hand. Thus, we need to explore them more consciously, in order to understand our decisions and actions as coaches.

---

### Pause for reflection

- Take a moment to reflect on your coaching practice. Think about the things that really matter to you as a coach. Which do you feel more proud of? What are the situations that you find most challenging?
- Now write down the five primary values that you hold as a coach, whatever the nature of the situation you may find yourself in.

---

Understanding our (personal and) professional values is a worthwhile pursuit, as it enables us to understand our coaching clients better. In the absence of this self-awareness, we are more likely simply to respond to the behaviours that we observe on the surface. Understanding our values, however, enables us both to become more aware of the underlying ethical issues that may be hidden under the surface, and to build the necessary skills to permeate the relationship more deeply, in order to address these. So, how can we bring these underlying ethical issues to the surface? Asking good questions, in the right way and at the right time, can help us to do this.

Coaching questions are central to the coaching relationship. In his poem 'The Elephant's Child', Rudyard Kipling (1902) wrote these often-quoted lines:

> I keep six honest serving-men
>
> (They taught me all I knew);
>
> Their names are What and Why and When
>
> And How and Where and Who.

The six serving-men questions provide a useful framework for thinking about coaching questions. Asking good questions during the coaching practice allows the coach to create a reflective space for the coachee. In this space, the coachee is given the opportunity to engage in a wider and deeper exploration of personal values and ethics. This powerful tool of questioning can also be used by coaches who turn the mirror on themselves, in order to reflect on their professional values. Looking in a metaphorical mirror and asking questions about our values is a process that can generate further insights into how we deal with ethical dilemmas in our professional practice. Consider asking yourself questions like: Tell me about what happened next? What else did you notice that was going on? Was there anything else that you were feeling at the time? As you become more seasoned as a coaching practitioner, we wonder if you notice the predominance of certain questions (like, for instance, *how*, *what* and *who*) over others, for example *why*, that can at times lead to defensive attitudes, rather than reflective exploration through interaction.

## Activity: the mirror

You have now compiled two separate lists of values: your personal and your professional ones. You should, ideally, have at least five in each list. Now imagine that you have a mirror in front of you. Do your personal and professional values match? In other words, does the reflection of the coach in the mirror match you, the person who is looking in it? If not, how is the coach in the mirror different from you, the person in front of it? What is it that creates the difference?

Remember, we cannot ignore the impact that our personal values have on our professional coaching behaviours in practice. What have you found through your reflections? Are you how you coach?

Our personal and professional values are intrinsically linked, often subconsciously. They are connected to how we view ourselves in relation to others in the world. In other words, our personal and professional values are an inherent part of our identity. Identity is not a rigid entity but an ongoing and dynamic phenomenon. This is because our values are influenced by the context in which we situate ourselves, and this has the potential to create disparity between our personal and professional values. The issue of context is a significant factor in the development of an ethical coaching practice, and we will discuss this in detail in Chapter 7. For the time being, however, let's delve further into the importance of understanding how our values and ethics can directly influence our coaching practice.

## What factors influence our values and our coaching practice?

The way we view the world determines the principles and values that we adopt to function in it. This is shaped by our position in society, since we are 'inextricably intertwined' with the environment in which we are brought up (Lago and Smith, 2010: 3). By extension, our view of the world is shaped by our interaction with others in our daily lives: family, friends, colleagues, clients. Indeed, as Heidegger (1962) argued, being in the world means being with others. It follows, therefore, that we are all part of a great whole that is determined by our relationships with others. It goes without saying, then, that how we practise as coaches is not only influenced by our culturally shaped values; it is also determined by how we interpret our clients' and employers' culturally shaped values. It is significant, therefore, that we comprehend the diverse institutional, social and political contexts in which coaches, clients and employers find themselves (Proctor, 2014: 88–9).

Let's examine this further. As we discussed in Chapter 1, the values that we have adopted as members of a particular social group inform the choices that we make in life and work. Yet, the institutional context in which we operate as professionals, for example the culture of the organisation we work in, can differ from other contexts in which we act and make choices. In consequence, the rules of conduct that govern our behaviour at work change, as do the values and principles that underpin our actions in it. Beckett and Maynard (2013: 80) offer some pertinent examples of such value changes. These are the following:

- While consensual sexual relationships between adults are a generally accepted human behaviour, determined by several social parameters, they can be frowned upon in certain professional contexts.

In educational settings, for instance, sexual relationships between teachers and students, even when students are of consenting age, are generally disfavoured.

- Although murder is generally considered unethical, within the realm of law, legal professionals have a moral obligation to defend individuals who have committed such crimes.
- Whereas a stringent manager may set prohibitive work targets for her employees, she may adopt a more laid-back attitude towards her children's academic achievements.
- While in our personal life the driving forces behind our decisions and actions can be our dreams and aspirations, at work the primary driver is our responsibility to our employer and/or clients.

All these examples demonstrate that there are several external factors that may interfere with your personal and professional values and principles as a coach. One such factor can actually be the organisational culture of your employer, as we observed above. If you are a coach working in the corporate world, you may have worked in organisations that impose pressures that do not necessarily constitute best practice, especially when performance targets are involved. As Green (2009: 116) appositely observed, 'the practices of performance management and managerial target-setting more often than not lead to perverse initiatives which distort professional judgement.' Still, the judgement that you will be called on to exercise may be determined by the organisation's set of values. Such values may be different to your personal ones and, we believe, you might find it helpful to be consciously aware and reflective of them.

Government policy can also have an impact on the principles that underpin your coaching practice. Consider, for instance, the possibility of favouring a more directive style of coaching in your work. You have just been offered a coaching role within the UK healthcare sector where, over the last decade, a raft of national policy has placed increasing emphasis on inclusivity. This emphasis aims at fostering partnerships between professionals and patients, replacing the 'doing to people' approach with the 'doing with people' approach. 'Doing with people' seems to be more congruent with the principles of coaching. How would you feel about this? Do you change and adapt the way in which you coach? This potential shift, of course, goes beyond a specific coaching style. It ultimately relates to the way in which you see your clients and their ability to find and pursue solutions for themselves. Thus, if you are employed in the public sector, certain values imposed by governmental policies are bound to impact, directly or indirectly, on your coaching practice.

Let's take this a step further now. What happens if your personal values are diametrically opposed to the ones that the society in which you live and work dictate? If, for instance, you are morally against extra-marital relationships, can you effectively coach a client who reveals that they have embarked on one? Let's consider an actual real-life scenario.

---

## Story from practice

Judith has been a life coach for over a decade. She loves her work and has enjoyed relative success over the years. She is a caring individual with very rigid religious beliefs, as she was brought up a devout Catholic with strict views about the institution of marriage. As such, she finds it difficult to accept same-sex relationships as an outcome of freedom of choice for people. It is not surprising, then, that her daughter's recent coming-out as a homosexual woman not only took her by surprise, but also spawned an internal struggle of principles. Recently, Judith took on a new client who has been struggling at work. After a few coaching sessions, the client reveals to Judith that she is considering leaving her husband, suspecting the emergence of what she believes to be supressed homosexuality. This is all too familiar – if not familial – for Judith, and she feels this internal struggle re-emerging. Questions to consider:

- How might Judith deal with this internal struggle?
- How much should her personal beliefs influence her relationship with her client?
- Considering Judith's background and family circumstances, do you think it unethical for her to continue working with the client?

---

The above story clearly shows that the way we see the world may differ from the way society generally sees it. When we make an ethical decision based on our view of the world, we not only have a say on what we consider to be right or wrong for us; we also indirectly decide on what we want the world to become as a result of that decision (Poole, 1972: 145). In the case of Judith, if she decides to proceed with her coaching client, this will have an impact on her client's world, as well. It is, therefore, essential to be able to understand how we view the world, how others view it, and where these different views converge or collide. In consequence, Judith needs to seriously consider what is more important for her as a coach and for her client as a coachee. This is not an easy process but the learning that ensues from it is incredibly valuable.

**Pause for reflection**

What factors have an impact on the principles that underpin your coaching practice? Consider, for instance:

- Your value system.
- The corporate culture of the organisation in which you coach.
- Government policies that influence your professional domain.
- Commonly accepted societal imperatives.

## How can understanding values enable ethical coaching?

We begin this section by considering how our understanding of our personal and professional values can help to address ethical moments of choice in order to make the best possible decision under the circumstances we find ourselves in. As a coach, whether novice or seasoned, you will inevitably encounter some challenging moments where you have to make an ethical choice. We borrow the term 'ethical choice' from de Jong (2010) and van Nieuwerburgh (2014) as an alternative term to that of 'ethical dilemma'. This is because 'dilemma' adds a negative flavour to critically important moments in the coaching conversation, while 'ethical choice' shifts this perspective. This helps us to focus on those moments during the conversation, when the coach is faced with an ethical issue or question and needs to make the best choice in order to respond appropriately and ethically.

Take time to observe and reflect on ethical moments of choice in your own coaching practice from a coach and/or coachee perspective. How aware are you of these moments? How easy is it to recognise them? How do you manage such tensions? How do your personal values help or hinder your choices?

**Story from practice**

Jo entered the coaching profession with a psychotherapeutic background and has faced several ethical moments of choice as a coach. The most pronounced challenge has been understanding the boundaries between coaching and therapy and developing her awareness of when she brings therapeutic approaches into the coaching relationship. This has not been an easy process. By committing to the practice of critical self-reflection, over time, she has become more aware of the boundaries of her coaching role. As part of this process, she engages in critical reflection of her professional values as a coach and her personal beliefs about the therapeutic relationship. Learnings are hard to undo. As a result, she has been able to locate and impose the boundaries between coaching and counselling. Becoming more consciously aware of *who* she is in the relationship – counsellor or coach – enabled Jo to draw on the most relevant skills. This increased awareness has certainly brought a deeper understanding of the diverse skills and tools at her disposal and their suitability within her coaching practice. For example, when addressing an ethical moment of choice, Jo is better able to consider the distinct options she has – to coach or counsel – and their consequences, in order to take the right decision.

Significantly, Jo discovered that building time for reflection into her coaching practice has helped her to develop ethical maturity. This is an ongoing process, part of which is done in a disciplined manner by consciously developing a reflective self-evaluation tool that is made up of the following questions:

- What went well? Why?
- What didn't go well? Why?
- How can I be better next time? What do I do differently?
- What do I need now?

After utilising this tool as a way of supporting her own reflective practice, Jo now encourages those she leads and coaches to undertake this activity and bring their reflections to their supervision to work collaboratively. This has definitely marked a fundamental shift for Jo, a move from 'doing' as a coach to 'being' as a coach. Questions to consider:

- What is Jo's responsibility for understanding her personal and professional values?
- How can Jo address the complexities of understanding her personal and professional values?
- What could be done to embed this kind of awareness in future coaching practice?

In testament to Jo's experience and in agreement with Kemp (2001), we advocate the significance of finding the time and space to reflect on one's personal and professional values before, during and after the coaching practice. Put simply, being an ethical coach is about making the right choices. The very act of reflecting helps to unfold existing values in order to facilitate the process of ethical decision-making. Let us then go on to explore the role of reflection in the following section of this chapter.

## The role of reflective and reflexive practice in coaching

Although reflective practice is recognised as important, as yet there is generally little literature on the theories and principles of reflection that inform its application in coaching. In this section we explore two relevant and distinct terms – reflection and reflexivity – in order to consider their relevance to an ethical coaching practice. Let's start with reflection.

Reflection is the in-depth consideration of events, situations, words and actions in order to achieve a deeper and clearer understanding of them and how you view yourself through them. Reflection is the cornerstone of a reflective practice. When you ask yourself questions such as 'What do I think about this situation or experience?' you are, in practical terms, working towards becoming a reflective practitioner. Such attitude helps to reconsider things and develop deeper understanding about yourself and others. It is important to keep in mind here that this new understanding is a product of your own interpretation, filtered through your values. We encourage you, therefore, to bring your reflections to supervision, in order to subject them to 'quality assurance' through dialogue and conversation.

Reflexivity is a process that delves into a deeper level of reflection. In essence, it is the 'questioning of taken-for-granted assumptions, frames, and mental models' (Yanow and Tsoukas, 2009: 1341). Within the context of coaching, as a coach you may be asking yourself questions such as 'Who is the *me* that interprets this situation or experience in such a way, and why?' Reflexivity, therefore, invites and enables the exploration of our reflections on a deeper level. We see reflection and reflexivity as the two ends of a spectrum and we will discuss this further in Chapter 6.

Both reflection and reflexivity are essential for developing and maintaining an ethical coaching practice. We consider that together these concepts form a firm foundation for understanding our personal and professional values. As we engage in understanding our personal and professional values in this chapter, we focus primarily on reflective practice. In Chapter 6, we move along the continuum to explore further reflexive practice and how it can help us develop ethical maturity.

Bolton (2014) identifies a number of principles that underpin reflective practice, including trust, self-respect and positive regard. Clutterbuck (1998) highlights the importance of reflecting both *in* and *on* the coaching practice, that is, reflecting in the moment of being in the coaching relationship, not only in action (see, for instance, Argyris, 1982; Schön, 1984, 1987) but also afterwards – *ex-post* action (see, for instance,

Polanyi, 1962). The latter can take place during supervisory conversations. Clutterbuck (1998) also illuminates the difference between the creation of personal reflective space as a solitary experience, and dyadic reflective space, where our personal reflections benefit from our dialogue with others. We shall now turn to exploring approaches that can enhance our reflection on our values and ethics in both personal and dyadic spaces.

# Reflective approaches for understanding our values

In this section, we explore some approaches that can be used to reflect on our values. We hope that these approaches will help you reflect on how your values can have a direct impact on your coaching practice.

## Using stories and writing for reflection

As the importance of ethics in coaching has seen limited empirical exploration, there is no systematic view on what are the best approaches to explore our values. Developing self-awareness takes commitment and courage. Inspired by the writings of Gillie Bolton (2014), who takes her readers on a creative journey of self-discovery and knowing, we believe that storytelling can open up the path to self-awareness. Stories can be used to illuminate the iterative nature of understanding our self and our values. Imagine for a moment that today is a new chapter in your life. How would this chapter begin? How would you relate it in a story? Bolton (2014) shows us how, by capturing and relating the story of an event, such as an ethical moment arising in a coaching session, we can explore it further and revisit it over time. Indeed, stories allow us to explore events more deeply and view them from different perspectives. Storytelling, thus, can lead to a richer kind of learning of the self.

Reflective writing is another useful way of exploring our practice and the ethical issues that can arise in it (see, for instance, Wright, 2012). During the writing of this book, we had many inspirational conversations with coaching learners and practitioners who advocated the instrumentality of reflective writing for coaches. A particular conversation with Professor David Megginson illuminated the significance of reflective writing as a means for understanding ourselves and others who are part of the coaching relationship. A fervent believer in the usefulness of reflective writing, Megginson explained that: 'working with self while writing is pretty much a part of me. It allows me to think and write about an event from different perspectives.' So, if done well, reflective writing offers us the space to explore an event, not only from our own perspective, but from those of others too. However, this does not mean that we can fully understand the world of others, as we only see them through our eyes and the words we put on paper. It is important, therefore, to adopt an attitude of welcoming the challenge of views, beliefs and assumptions. Thinking critically is one way to develop such ability.

## Thinking critically

Thinking critically is about 'making sense of the world through a process of questioning the questions, challenging assumptions, recognising that bodies of knowledge can be chaotic and evolving; ultimately with the aim of continually improving thinking' (Jones-Devitt and Smith, 2007: 7). In this chapter, we introduce a range of reflective approaches that can facilitate the understanding of our self and our values. A danger, though, is to think of these as recipes or linear steps, as if there is only one right way. Rather, since we are all unique, we need to develop individual approaches for understanding our values. Thinking critically can help us do this.

Ethical issues vary according to the perspective of the coach, the values of individual coachees, and the different contexts in which coaching takes place. As coaches, we need to think critically and question fundamental assumptions (Bolton, 2014: 46), since almost every action we make is based on assumptions. Too often there can be an unintended gap between our espoused values as coaches and our behaviours in practice (Brookfield, 1987). As a result, the latter can cause misunderstandings that may impact on the coaching relationship. In day-to-day practice, for instance, it is possible that we make an ethical decision, the intention of which is not understood by our clients. Consider, for instance, a coach with a psychotherapeutic background who decides to refer a coachee to a mental health professional for a deeply rooted emotional issue that she feels falls beyond her professional remit as a coach. While the client may feel dissatisfied, frustrated, even betrayed at times, thinking critically over the issue allows the coach to better understand the boundaries and limitations of her role. Indeed, thinking critically about our ethical decisions and actions affords the opportunity to critically explore and challenge assumptions. This brings us back to the importance of questioning that can activate our critical thinking mechanism. In other words, thinking critically mobilises a shift from the descriptive to the analytical. This shift has the potential of offering greater insights into our values and ethics as coaches.

## Embracing creativity: using arts-based activities

Using arts-based activities can assist us in our coaching practice and our reflections on it. Increasingly coaches use creative approaches, such as art, to enhance their self-awareness and sharpen their understanding of others. Taylor and Ladkin (2009: 58) suggest that, if we aim to view and represent our experiences as an object of art, it 'can contain contradictions (logical and/or moral) as well as unrealized possibilities that are not constrained by logic or limitations of our current lives. In this way, art making enables us to draw upon, and subsequently reflect on, a deep well of "unconscious stuff".' Let's explore this in practice. An arts-based session led by Whitaker and Rhodes (2004) illuminates how creating and wearing masks can assist us to be more aware of the metaphorical 'masks' we put on during our coaching practice. We can begin to notice the different masks of coaching that we assume in different contexts of our practice.

---

### Activity: what does an ethical coach look like?

Whitaker and Rhodes (2004) use masks to look beyond our instinctive behaviour, in order to allow for a deeper exploration of our practice. They show how masks can deepen our understanding of ourselves within our coaching practice.

For this activity, you will need to use: a) two plain masks, which may be an actual or a drawn mask; b) art and craft materials such as glitter, shapes, pipe-cleaners, etc.; and c) coloured pens or crayons.

Decorate your mask in such a way that shows how you see yourself as a coach now. Then, consider how you'd like to be as a coach. What would your new mask look like?

Question to consider: What do you aim to do and to be as a coach?

---

Rachel engaged with this exercise during a Coaching and Mentoring Research Day at Sheffield Hallam University. The way she decorated her mask revealed aspects of her coaching practice that she had not seen before. In particular, her decoration showed a connectivity between two dimensions in her own practice: formal vs informal coaching, and coaching vs mentoring. This gave rise to her emerging philosophy – 'making every conversation count' (Hawley, 2012, 2015), which we will discuss further in Chapter 11. What did you learn about your values and ethics through this activity?

# Creating shared space for understanding values and ethics

Reflection, reflexivity, critical thinking and creativity are only some of the ways in which we can explore and gain greater understanding of the values that underpin our coaching practice. Some of these activities, however, may at times need more structured environments to be conducted with method and further support. There are several such spaces for coaches. Here, we briefly discuss supervision and continuous professional development.

## Supervision and self-care

Supervision is paramount for an ethical coaching practice, as it offers a space for reflection and critical thinking. Indeed, as Johns (2013) argues, reflection should be subjected to supervision in order to help prevent meaning from being distorted. Supervision provides the opportunity to discuss in depth issues that arise in your coaching practice and cause concern. For example, can you recall a coaching relationship in which you may have struggled? Did you find it hard to remain focused in the session? Were you tired? Did the coaching conversation raise particular ethical issues for you? What did you notice? What strategies do you use at such times? To what extent are the strategies you use effective and how do you measure effectiveness?

These questions, which lend themselves to critical exploration in supervision, remind us of the wonderfully titled article, 'Pas de deux: Learning in Conversation' (Alred et al., 1998). In this article, the authors describe the kind of 'learning that occurs through revisiting and re-examining recurring issues in coaching, to arrive at new perspectives and new commitments to act in new ways' (ibid.: 308). Regular supervision sessions provide a space for these kinds of learning conversations. The learning that emerges from supervision is a result of collaboration and mutual understanding and appreciation of individual values and beliefs.

As you may have noticed, supervision is not compulsory in contemporary coaching practice, although it holds a prominent role in the ethical codes of the major professional coaching bodies. We would like to encourage practising coaches, regardless of knowledge and expertise, to consider the instrumentality and value of such a marvellous learning process. Supervision is conducive to the coach's self-care, offering a protected space for the exploration of issues, concerns and critical questions. All in all, supervision is one of the ways in which we can pursue continuous professional development.

## Continuous professional development

To engage in professional development as coaches, and in the wider context of change, we must first begin by recognising and accepting the need for change to take place. Change, of course, is not new. Over 2500 years ago, the philosopher Heraclitus argued that: 'Everything flows and everything is constantly changing. You cannot step twice in the same river, for other waters are constantly flowing on.' It follows that change, according to Heraclitus, is a natural process that we can embrace and harness its potential. One of the systematic ways of doing so within the context of coaching is continuous professional development (CPD).

Continuous professional development, that we will discuss in detail in Chapter 4, is a process through which individuals take control of their own learning and development by engaging in ongoing reflection and action (Megginson and Whitaker, 2003). It provides 'an opportunity to soar like an eagle or helicopter and look at our career progress from a wider perspective' (ibid.: 5). It challenges us to make time for regular personal reflection and review. It reminds us that we have a responsibility for developing ourselves rather than putting the onus onto our manager or others in the organisation. Ultimately, continuous professional development, in combination with supervision and reflective practice, form an important part of the journey towards understanding our personal and professional values and are conducive to the development of ethical maturity, which is instrumental for an ethical coaching practice.

## Developing ethical maturity

A person's individual maturity determines their ability to understand others, a crucial attribute of ethical behaviour (Laske, 2006). As we have seen, values and ethical behaviours are not solely the product of family-, school- or community-accepted principles that are passed on from one generation to the next. Much as these are significant factors, the development of values and ethical behaviour is a gradual process that occurs while individuals grow and collect more experiences. This leads people to construct richer meanings of themselves, their relationships with others and the world within which they live (Kegan, 1982). In consequence, the development of ethical behaviour is congruent with the development of one's personal maturity (Kohlberg, 1981).

Within the coaching practice, the practical experience that you acquire as you become increasingly and systematically exposed to ethical moments of choice can enhance your capacity, competence and confidence in developing ethical maturity. Your conscious awareness of your personal and professional principles and values, combined with

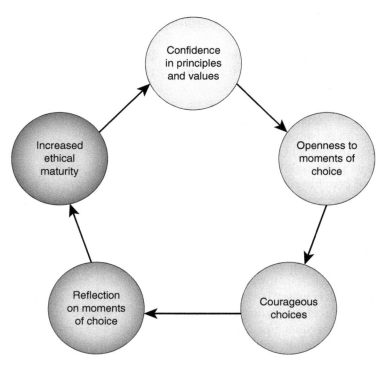

**Figure 2.1** Virtuous cycle of ethical maturity

*Source*: Christian van Nieuwerburgh (2014: 178).

systematic reflection on practice, can enhance ethical maturity even further (van Nieuwerburgh, 2014: 178). This process can be augmented in supervision, where the coach is subjected to the 'hypothetical testing of dilemmas', consciously fine-tuning his or her ethical stance by 'recurrent ethical thinking' (Duffy and Passmore, 2010). Van Nieuwerburgh has graphically represented this process as the 'virtuous cycle of ethical maturity' (2014: 178), as shown in Figure 2.1.

Being consciously aware of your principles and values and reflecting on them will allow you to approach any ethical issues that arise in your practice with confidence and competence. This will enable you to not shy away from the ethical issues, but to address them in a way that respects your clients and your practice. While supervision is not yet a mandatory requirement for coaches, we consider it to be a fundamental way of harnessing the potential for building ethical maturity. This is because supervision enables us to discuss and reflect on such issues and use them as an opportunity for learning, even a celebration of continuing ethical maturity (van Nieuwerburgh, 2014: 179). This will cultivate confidence in the coaching practice, and the virtuous cycle can continue.

We have found that the following steps are congruent with the 'virtuous cycle of ethical maturity'. Coaches who wish to reflect on their values and, in consequence, develop their self-awareness may find them useful. These steps are:

- Building critical consciousness of ethical issues and moments of choice through self-awareness.
- Understanding the context of the coaching relationship.
- Developing understanding and appreciation of the coachee's values and beliefs.
- Adopting an approach of 'doing with' clients rather than 'doing to' clients.

## Conclusion

We hope that reflecting on your personal values has taken you on 'a creative adventure, right through the glass to the other side of the silvering' (Bolton, 2014: 116), perhaps gaining new insights into yourself and your coaching experiences from a range of perspectives. A commitment to understanding our self and our values within the wider context of coaching is key to taking ethical responsibility in the coaching relationship. There is no single theory that accounts for the entire journey of values and ethics in coaching. As outlined in Chapter 1, there is little agreement amongst practitioners and scholars about what the most appropriate values are that underpin an ethical coaching practice. In the simplest of ways, understanding self and personal values in the coaching relationship can open up the path towards developing ethical maturity and an ethical coaching practice. In the next part of the book, we will focus on specific ways in which we can develop and maintain an ethical coaching practice that is premised on sound knowledge of the intellectual and practical underpinnings of coaching.

## Chapter summary

- It is important to strive to consciously understand our personal and professional values.
- Understanding our personal and professional values is a purposeful process that can be viewed as a continuum, from reflection to reflexivity.
- Reflective coaching practice focuses on what *I* think about an ethical issue. As we move towards reflexive practice, we begin to ask who the *me* is that thinks about this ethical issue and the choices I make.

- Ongoing reflection on ethical issues that arise in the coaching practice helps build ethical maturity.
- Reflection, critical thinking, supervision and continuous professional development are some of the ways that can fine-tune our ethical maturity.

## Suggestions for further reading

For inspiring reflections on individual values, we recommend:

Covey, S. (2004) *The 7 Habits of Highly Effective People: Powerful Lessons in Personal Change*. London: Simon and Schuster.

Rose, N. (1999) *Governing Soul: Shaping of the Private Self*, 2nd edn. London: Free Association Books.

For the reader who is interested in reflective practice and critical thinking, we recommend:

Bolton, G. (2014) *Reflective Practice: Writing and Professional Development*, 4th edn. London: Sage Publishing.

For a deeper exploration on the use of art for greater self-awareness, take a look at:

Cameron, F. (1994) *The Artist's Way: A Course in Discovering and Rediscovering your Creative Self*. Croydon: Souvenir Press.

For a practical exploration of taking ethical decisions, you can also read:

Steare, R. (2009) *Ethicability: How to Decide What's Right and Find the Courage to Do It*. London: Roger Steare Consulting.

# Part II

## Ethical Practice

# 3

# Developing the
# Coaching Relationship

## Chapter aims

- To emphasise the significance of developing the coaching relationship in an ethical manner.
- To analyse the primary ethical issues that are embedded in the development of the coaching relationship.
- To stress the importance of educating the client about the purpose of coaching, setting clear expectations of roles and outcomes.
- To reflect on the influence of the coach's 'use of self' in the development of the coaching relationship.
- To consider ethical issues stemming from working with 'challenging' clients and the termination of the coaching process.

## Chapter overview

In this chapter, we explore some of the ethical issues that are embedded in the development of the coaching relationship. These are primarily confidentiality and trust, contracting, the autonomy of the client, working with 'challenging' clients, and the effective termination of the coaching relationship. Before discussing these in detail, we outline some of the key ingredients of an effective coaching relationship between a coach and a coachee. We also ponder the tension between the personal and the professional and explore how the coach can manage the thoughts, beliefs, reactions and behaviours that are evoked by the client. Our main argument is that, as the coaching relationship is co-created by both parties in the alliance, it is important to educate coachees about the nature, purpose and expectations of the coaching from the very set-up of the coaching relationship.

## Key words

relationship, co-creation, confidentiality, trust, contracting, 'challenging' clients, termination

## Introduction

'Relationship' is a commonly used term in our daily interactions. It is widely defined as 'the way two or more things are connected' (Pelham, 2016: 1). But this definition is barely adequate to encapsulate the complex processes that are at play when a relationship between two or more people develops. Consider, for example, the following questions: Have you ever noticed that you work better with colleagues who understand you, value your point of view, and give you constructive feedback? Do you prefer to spend your spare time with friends who are good-natured and value you for who you are or those who spend the time you share together talking about themselves with no regard for you or what is happening in your life? When do you feel most appreciated by your partner: when they listen attentively to your needs and try to understand your point of view, or when your wishes and needs just don't enter the equation? These simple questions are intended to help you reflect on the complexity of relationships.

A relationship is a product of co-creation between a minimum of two entities. For this co-creation to take place, those involved in it need to be valued and appreciated. Indeed, as social beings, we have an innate need to be around people who understand us, accept us and appreciate us for who we are. The coaching relationship is no different to others. It is generally portrayed as 'a confidential relationship between two people in distinct roles (coach and coachee) who are not otherwise involved with each other, and it is this set-up which makes it safe for the coachee to work on very sensitive issues' (Pelham, 2016: 113). This portrayal of the coaching relationship is reminiscent of the therapeutic relationship. This is not accidental, because coaching is traditionally rooted in the relevant discipline of psychotherapy (O'Connor and Lages, 2007; Wildflower, 2013). In particular, the development of the coaching relationship has been influenced by the humanistic movement of psychotherapy, which was premised on the work of Carl Rogers

(1951, 1961; see also Thomson, 2009). Within this context, the client is conceptualised as an autonomous individual who holds the answer to the questions she or he may have.

The above conceptualisation of the coaching client as an autonomous individual means that, in order to develop the coaching relationship, the coach ought to emotionally 'tune into' the coachee, show interest and confidence in her ability to work towards set goals and create the conditions that will enable her to start sharing her story (Pelham, 2016: 39–40). It follows, then, that the coaching relationship is immersed in an intense tension between the personal and the professional (ibid.: 6). The boundary between these two elements comprises one of the primary ethical issues that are ingrained in the coaching relationship. Before we discuss some of the more prominent ethical issues that may arise in the process of developing the coaching relationship, we would like to briefly discuss what we consider to be the key ingredients for the coaching relationship to flourish.

## Ingredients of the coaching relationship

A growing number of empirical studies have started to reveal the key ingredients of an effective coaching relationship. Machin (2010) saw the coach as a key determinant of a fruitful coaching relationship. Specifically, voicing arguments that evoke Carl Rogers' views on person-centred therapy (PCT) (Rogers, 1951, 1961), Machin claimed that the coach's ability to show empathy, listen attentively, keep a non-judgemental stance and demonstrate congruence and acceptance formed the basis of an effective coaching relationship. Similar studies in the realm of psychotherapy found that it was easier for clients to achieve intended outcomes when they felt that their therapists were consistent, warm, empathic and non-judgemental (Orlinsky et al., 1994; Watson and Greenberg, 1994; Stiles et al., 1998; Asay and Lambert, 2001; Bohart et al., 2002).

Jowett et al. (2012) recently investigated five coach–client dyads using the 3+1 Cs relationship model, which was developed in the sports domain to describe the coach–athlete relationship. The 3+1 Cs model comprises four components: closeness, commitment, complementarity and co-orientation. Their research highlighted the importance of: closeness expressed through trust and respect; commitment, which involved developing a strong, enduring and motivating working alliance; complementarity, which entailed good collaboration with defined roles for each individual; and co-orientation that is premised on open and honest communication. Overall, trust and honesty were deemed highly important by both coaches and coachees for the development of the coaching relationship (ibid.).

Findings from the studies mentioned above indicate that the more clients feel they can confide in a professional who respects them, appreciates them and listens to them with a non-judgemental attitude, the easier it is for them to reap the benefits of a trusting relationship, in order to achieve their coaching goals. Incidentally, Machin (2010) argued that the goal-setting framework of coaching lays the groundwork for an effective relationship, especially when both coach and coachee have a clear understanding of the intended outcomes. This is an important aspect of the process and we will discuss it in detail below. 'Educating' the coachee about the process and purpose of coaching and setting clear expectations of the different roles and potential coaching outcomes is a significant determinant of the development of an effective coaching relationship (Pelham, 2016: 146).

This brings us to the issue of the role and responsibility of the coachee in the coaching relationship. It is not only the coach's attitude that can have an impact on the development of the partnership between coach and coachee: also the coachee's readiness in embracing the coaching process constitutes a determining factor in the quality of the coaching relationship (Machin, 2010). The coachee who is willing to embrace coaching – what Paul Stokes (2007) termed the 'skilled coachee', based on the seminal work by Pearn and Downs (1989) on the skilled learner – displays some distinct characteristic behaviours, such as honesty, openness to change, willingness to invite and accept challenge, ability to overcome unpleasant difficulties, and an overall positive attitude towards the coaching process (Machin, 2010). It follows, then, that the coachee's attitude plays a dynamic part in the coaching relationship.

## From principles to practice: practitioner's reflection

### Paul Stokes, Director of the Coaching and Mentoring Research Unit, Sheffield Hallam University

Typically, the literature and research that has been done on coaching tends to privilege the roles and skills of the coach. Despite commentators placing the coachee at the centre of the coaching relationship, this does not extend to affording the coachee any process skills as part of that relationship. However, that 'map' did not seem to describe the territory of coaching as I was experiencing it. Hence, I decided to conduct a piece of qualitative research, looking at the role of the skilled coachee within the coaching relationship. What I found was that coachees demonstrated two sets of skills: enabling and defensive.

Coachees use a range of conversational devices – engagement with metaphor, being clear about goals, stating what is important – which enable coaching conversations to progress. Through my research, I found that the enabling strategies used by the coachee are: practising difficult conversations, scenario planning, remaining open to different processes, and seeking to challenge their own thinking. The defensive strategies, however, include deflection and diversion. The coachee employs these, often unconsciously, to protect themselves from embarrassment or threat and to avoid engaging too deeply in areas that they do not wish to discuss in depth at that particular time. These devices and strategies are often employed in combination with each other, as the relationship progresses, and they interact with the skills employed by the coach to inform how the coaching relationship plays out.

What was important to recognise in my research was that the defensive skills employed by the coachee could render the skilled coach relatively powerless in terms of progressing the conversation and the relationship, despite having a range of skills, tools and techniques at their disposal. This was because the coachee was able to fend off the coach by moderating their responses, avoiding areas of greater depth and vulnerability, but still seeming to engage in a relatively open dialogue, from the coach's perspective. This has interesting implications for ethical practice within coaching.

Most professional bodies have ethical codes of practice, which often have at their core an emphasis on protecting the client. However, my research suggests that coachees/clients are more adept at protecting themselves and influencing the coaching relationship than the dominant discourse on coaching practice would have us believe. This, amongst other things, suggests a review of what we understand by ethical coaching practice.

## Ethical issues in the coaching relationship

In the following section, we will focus on some ethical issues that are at the forefront of the development of an effective coaching relationship. These are, namely, confidentiality and trust, contracting, client autonomy, working with 'challenging' clients, and ending the coaching relationship. Let's explore these key elements one by one.

### Confidentiality and trust

Confidentiality and trust form the foundation of every healthy relationship. Especially within the realm of the 'helping' professions, trust and confidentiality are the pillars of any effective working relationship (Gyllensten and Palmer, 2007). Confidentiality entails showing respect for the client's right to secrecy, privacy and commitment to not disclosing the client's private information. Indeed, any effective coaching practice is grounded in the premise that whatever is mentioned during the coaching stays in the room. Yet, this is not always as straightforward as it sounds. What would you do, for instance, if your client revealed to you that she is planning to harm herself? Is it ethical for you to intervene and report her or is it not your place to do so? What about if a client revealed to you that he has been engaging in illegal activities? Confidentiality, therefore, has limitations, since there are compelling reasons for disclosure. But who determines the compulsion?

## Pause for reflection

Consider an imaginary scenario where you're the client in a coaching relationship that has been formed within the context of business coaching. The coaching has been commissioned by your line manager, and an internal coach has been assigned for this purpose. In your final coaching session, which took place last week, you confided in your coach that you're not happy with your manager's behaviour towards you, which you feel is rather patronising and, at times, verges on bullying. Two days later, you find out that your coach discussed some of the content of the session with your line manager without your prior consent:

- How would you feel about this?
- What would your reaction be?

How would this development affect: a) your faith in the coaching process; and b) your relationship with your coach?

There is a reason why, in the above scenario, we asked you to put yourself in the coachee's shoes. This is because we wanted you to reflect on the issue of disclosure and, by extension, on the potential of breach of confidentiality. What are ethically acceptable reasons for this to happen? Brock (2006) states that breach of confidentiality is justified if so required by law. This means that there is foreseeable imminent danger of harm to the client or someone else. Whether you ethically agree or disagree with this view, there are ways to anticipate and prevent scenarios like the one we just explored. We will discuss them in detail below. But, before we do this, we think it important to consider exceptions to the coach's duty of confidentiality.

## Exceptions to the duty of confidentiality

While confidentiality is the cornerstone of the coaching relationship, there are exceptions to a general duty to honour it. These can be summed up in three broad categories:

*Informed consent*: This means that the client gives you permission to disclose specific information to specific people or organisations for specific purposes. The best way to overcome any potential ethical pitfalls in this scenario is to seek the client's consent and make a record of it. This record should include the conditions set by the client as to what may be disclosed and to whom. If disclosure has been made, it is ethically (and legally) good practice to keep a record of what was disclosed, to whom and when.

*Moral obligation*: In the helping professions, the practitioner is required 'to balance the public interest between the public good served by preserving confidentiality and the public good served by breaching confidentiality' (Bond, 2015: 174–5). Accordingly, the coach has a moral obligation to protect the client and other members of the public from physical harm. This may lead to breach of confidentiality. There are no rigid criteria that determine when you are morally obliged to override confidentiality but you may want to consider the degree of risk, the seriousness of the harm, the imminence of the harm, and the effectiveness of the breach of confidentiality (Bond and Mitchels, 2015). If you feel morally obliged to disclose confidential information, the disclosure should be made on a strictly confidential basis to a person or organisation capable of preventing the harm, and it should be restricted to that information which will help prevent the harm.

*Legal obligation*: A coach has a legal obligation to disclose confidential information that will help detect and prevent serious crime. According to the *NHS Code of Practice for Confidentiality*, serious crime includes murder, manslaughter, rape, treason, kidnapping, child abuse and any other case where individuals have suffered or may suffer serious harm (Department of Health (DH), 2003: 35).

Except for the above cases, confidentiality is a requirement for an effective coaching practice and it ought to be built on mutual trust. Trust is an essential prerequisite for any relationship to work and it needs to be reciprocal. It takes trust on the part of the coach to work and, at times, to challenge the coachee. And it takes trust on the part of the coachee to put their faith in the coach as a facilitator in the coaching process.

Therefore, a co-creation of trust needs to happen, in order for the coaching relationship to flourish. This is particularly important – if not challenging – when both coach and coachee work in the same organisation, as in the scenario mentioned above. But this is why trust is so critical for the coaching relationship to develop, as trust is the ingredient that enables the relationship to be built on a personal level, rather than a strictly business-related one (Machin, 2010). The pertinent issue of prioritising the professional over the personal (Cavanagh and Grant, 2004) in the realm of business coaching will be discussed in detail in Chapter 8.

The ethical takeaway from this discussion is that confidentiality and trust are the cornerstones of the coaching relationship. These are not black-and-white terms. There will be cases where confidentiality may have to be breached, especially to protect the client or other individuals from harm. Sharing anonymised clients' stories for learning and development purposes in supervision contexts is also justified, if not encouraged (Hay, 2007). To ensure the continuation of trust, it is important to come to a mutual agreement with clients as to the purpose and boundaries of coaching, as well as the limitations of confidentiality. This is where contracting comes in.

## Contracting

Contracting is the part of the coaching relationship that has the potential to minimise several ethical pitfalls you might fall into as a coach, especially as a novice coach. On a basic level, a clear and explicit contract demarcates the way in which coach and coachee will work together and the conditions under which this will be made possible. The contract, therefore, delineates expectations and outlines basic logistical practicalities, such as the duration of the coaching intervention, the time, place, frequency and cost of sessions, as well as the expectations of the intervention. Where there is a third party involved, like a line manager or HR professional who commissions the coaching, the contract should clearly explain the common goals and, importantly, how feedback to the sponsor will be dealt with and delivered, if feedback is expected. Charged with several issues of confidentiality, this particular parameter should be considered from the contracting stage.

Since contracting is that part of the coaching relationship that, if done properly, can help you anticipate and prevent several ethical dilemmas which you might face in your practice, we encourage you to take it seriously and to do it formally, rather than informally. A comprehensive contract provides the solid ground on which the relationship will be built. In it, you pledge to keep matters confidential and you clearly delineate the circumstances in which this confidentiality may be broken, for instance in cases of illegal activity or harm to the client or others. These cases will be determined by your own code of ethics or, if you subscribe to the code of a professional coaching association, you can directly communicate to the client the latter's clauses. The AC, for instance, state in their Code of Ethics that: 'While confidentiality will be an essential aspect of your commitment to Clients, your contract will make clear that if evidence of illegal activity or the potential for harm to the Client or others is disclosed during the engagement, you may have to inform the appropriate authorities' (AC, undated *a*). Regardless of the code of ethics you opt to subscribe to, we invite you to consider the significance of having a clear and mutual agreement with your clients and sponsors about the conditions under which confidentiality will not be honoured.

---

## Activity

This activity will be particularly useful to the novice coach or those coaches who have not produced their own coaching contract yet:

- We invite you to take some time to jot down the key clauses that you wish your coaching contract to include.
- Now choose one or more of the professional coaching bodies' codes of ethics and carefully study them. This will not take too long, as most professional coaching associations have produced concise yet comprehensive ethics documents. Did you get any more ideas as to further clauses that you could include in your contract?
- Having done this, consider drafting your own coaching contract. How can you make it as clear and concise for your clients?

---

Setting up the coaching relationship in practice is not always easy. As coaching is still a relatively new discipline, many people who agree to it have limited understanding of what coaching really is, and an even more narrow grasp of the conditions required for its effectiveness (Pelham, 2016: 31). This lack of firm understanding on the part of the client brings to the fore issues of authority. This is because the coach can be seen as the person in control and, therefore, the one who is in a position of power in the relationship. This is not necessarily a bad thing, as long as the coach exercises his or her 'power' for the well-being of everyone involved in the relationship. This type of authority has been termed 'good authority' (Pitt-Aikens and Thomas Ellis, 1990). A clear contract, therefore, not only provides the solid foundation for the coaching relationship to develop, but also allows both coach and coachee to have a clear understanding of their roles, expectations and entitlements as part of the relationship. In other words, a comprehensive contract can help educate clients on what is involved in coaching, and, in consequence, to manage expectations. But what happens when a client is referred to the coach against their will?

## Autonomy of the client

A leading educationalist claimed that coaching should first and foremost be an authentic partnership between two (or more) people of equal status (Knight, 2011). This equity presupposes respecting the autonomy of the client. Autonomy refers to each person's right to determine their own course of action freely and independently, without any external interference (Gillon, 1985). However, this is not always feasible in practice. While in the realm of counselling, respect for the client's autonomy has been deemed paramount for the counselling relationship to work (Bond, 2015), in other contexts, for instance in organisational settings, the client may be required to participate in coaching sessions against her will. Under such circumstances, the coach–client relationship faces numerous challenges. First, the coachee may not be allowed to decide for herself whether she actually wants coaching. Second, as in the case of organisational counselling (Bond, 2015), the intended outcome and goals of the coaching may have already been decided upon by the organisation and may not be approved by the client. In such cases, we need to consider whether the client's autonomy is undermined, and how we can approach the situation from an ethical perspective. Do we go ahead and push the client to work towards the set institutional goals or do we give them the space they need to explore and set their own agenda?

## Story from practice

Indira has been working for a national law firm for 14 years, where she has enjoyed the reputation of one of the most loyal and hard-working employees. Lately, a senior partner in the firm has noticed that Indira has been making use of consecutive leaves of absence, while her concentration at work has been deteriorating. Not knowing what is causing Indira's lack of concentration, and unwilling to intervene, the senior manager employs an internal coach to help Indira return to her normal patterns of working. Indira willingly attends the first session but later politely informs the coach that she does not wish to proceed with the coaching. In fact, she confides in the coach that she recently embarked on psychotherapy to address some critical and deeply rooted personal issues. Coaching, she fears, will interfere with her therapy and potentially cause more confusion. Indira also tells the coach that she is hoping to address her professional challenges within the context of her psychotherapy. Therefore, she kindly asks the coach to inform the senior partner that the coaching sessions are unnecessary, and requests that the coach does not communicate to him the reason for her rejection.

In this scenario, the coach has to deal with two separate agendas: the client's and the organisation's. Questions to consider:

- Whose agenda will she prioritise?
- How can she respect Indira's autonomy to pursue her own therapy when she has been assigned the role of helping her improve her productivity for the benefit of the firm?
- How is her stance going to affect her relationship with the senior partner, who is most probably her superior? What about her relationship with Indira?
- Can she actually inform the senior partner that she will not be working with Indira without disclosing the real reason for Indira's refusal to continue with the coaching?

This is a challenging ethical dilemma for the coach that can compromise the development of a trusting relationship with her client. At this point, you may be thinking that the coaching relationship has not been properly established yet, as Indira only attended one introductory session and does not intend follow it up. Again, our own personal value system is at work here. Indira may have met with the coach only once, but during that session she trusted the coach, disclosed highly sensitive information about her life, and asked the coach to respect her wish to deal with her personal issues in the way she thinks is best for her, without breaking confidentiality. Has a relationship started to form in this case or not? Is it actually the amount of time we spend in a relationship that renders the relationship valid or is it the quality of the relationship and the values we bring into it that strengthen the bond between the coach and the client? We believe that the relationship starts to form from the very first session, and the autonomy of the client ought to be at the centre of its development.

In the relevant discipline of counselling, the client's autonomy to choose her own counsellor is a determining factor of the intervention's effectiveness (Bond, 2015). This autonomy entails one's liberty to perform a cost–benefit analysis of the options, including freedom to decide on the actual therapist and the commencement of the counselling process. It goes without saying, that coaching should be premised on similar parameters. In this respect, we also need to consider how these guidelines can actually be followed in cases when we are asked to work with clients who have not consented to coaching, such as in the case of an organisation that deploys coaching for remedial purposes. Who is the client in this case? Is it the organisation or the employee? Moreover, what happens if the organisation has a specific agenda about the goals and duration of the coaching that, in your experience, is not realistic? Such issues will be discussed in detail in Chapter 8. For now, we maintain that in order to facilitate the learning of any coachee within or beyond organisational contexts, the coaching relationship should be premised on the autonomy of the client.

## Working with 'challenging' clients

During our coaching career, inevitably, some coaches will come across a few 'challenging' clients. It is not our intention to apply pejorative connotations to the word 'challenging' here. A 'challenging' client is one who has the potential to make us question our ethical boundaries as practitioners. To gain a better insight into what we call a 'challenging' client here, let's consider some practical examples:

1. Amanda received a phone call by a potential client who wishes to start coaching so as to improve the performance of his small private business. During the contracting meeting, the client insists that Amanda reduces her fee substantially, calling upon severe financial difficulties. Amanda understands that her client is in a difficult financial situation but she feels that she cannot reduce her fees to the value proposed by the client. How should Amanda address the issue?
2. Trevor is working with a client who systematically refuses to take responsibility for her circumstances. She uses the coaching as a means to complain about everything that is going wrong in her personal and professional relationships but, when it comes to taking action, she is reluctant to pursue the goals agreed upon during coaching. In essence, the client keeps sabotaging herself by entering a vicious circle of complaints, demotivation, inaction, further demotivation and more complaints. Trevor cannot help but feel frustrated as he sees the coaching becoming stagnant and the relationship deteriorating. Consequently, he gently confronts the client, who, in her turn, accuses Trevor of an inability to help her. How should Trevor react in this situation?
3. Aisha is approached by the parents of an adolescent; they commission her services in an effort to help their son manage the stress stemming from his school and extra-curricular commitments. In practice, they want to see him prioritising and achieving certain goals, as well as becoming more confident and assertive. The teenage boy is really keen to start his coaching

sessions. The parents demand that Aisha informs them of the coaching progress and, in essence, anything significant that is discussed in the sessions. They feel that, since they are paying for the coaching, and since their son is a minor, they have the right to know what he brings into the sessions and what steps are taken to achieve set goals. How should Aisha react in this case? In fact, who is Aisha's client: the coachee or the paying parents?

In all of the above scenarios, each coach is embroiled in a situation where their professional ethics are challenged by clients' demands. In most cases, a clear contract from the set-up of the relationship would have anticipated some – if not all – of these issues. This does not mean that these issues are easy to handle. Yet, they generate thoughts, feelings, reactions and behaviours towards the coachee that, we believe, it is important to welcome and reflect on. This process, which Pelham (2016: 65) termed 'self-experience', has been gaining currency amongst practitioners, with some of them even regarding this 'use of self' as 'the highest order of coaching skills [...] the difference between good and great coaching' (Bluckert, 2006: 84).

## Pause for reflection

Take a few minutes to reflect on how your value system affects your thoughts, beliefs, reactions and behaviours towards the coachee. Now, consider the following questions:

- How do you bring and manage yourself (the personal) in the relationship while staying professional?
- Where is the line between the personal and the professional in the relationship?
- How do you know if you have crossed it? And when is it OK to cross it?

These questions are not easy to answer and, actually, there does not seem to be a right answer; the latter will depend on the coach's professional ethics. Whatever your position on the matter, you can be guided by a keen focus towards the welfare of the coachee and the set agreement about the purpose of coaching. A clear contract from the outset of the relationship, therefore, will enable the establishment of boundaries and, in consequence, the building of the relationship on solid (and ethical) foundations. It goes without saying that, the more experience a coach has with such 'challenging' clients, the more dexterous she can become in anticipating and dealing with them. Bringing such issues to supervision or discussing them in a confidential manner with other colleagues for the purpose of reflection and learning can shift the heavy load of a demanding situation off one's shoulders and help observe the relationship from a more objective standpoint. This may be beneficial for both coach and client.

## Ending the coaching relationship

Coaching is a process with a start and end point. Eventually, the coaching relationship will come to an end. Ideally, this will happen when all the learning objectives have been accomplished and the needs addressed in the sessions have been met (Thorpe and Clifford, 2007). It is important that the end of the coaching relationship is aptly planned, talked through and celebrated, in such a way that the coachee can smoothly integrate the changes that have occurred as a result of the coaching. Elaine Cox (2010: 179) expressed it beautifully by arguing that: 'an ending marks a threshold that must be crossed and the possibility of a new beginning'. Accordingly, a smooth termination of the coaching journey involves having integrated the positive outcomes that have occurred as part of the coaching, and feeling confident and safe to continue one's journey with the coach's assistance.

While the process of naturally terminating the coaching relationship is beyond the scope of this chapter, some ethical implications might arise that we need to consider. What happens, for instance, when the relationship must end abruptly? Indeed, there are cases when this is inevitable: when the coachee feels that the relationship is not working or she sees no progress stemming from the coaching; or when the coach feels he is inadequately prepared to support the coachee and has to refer her to another specialist, for example a psychotherapist (we will discuss this issue further in Chapter 7). There are several reasons why the coaching relationship must terminate earlier than expected. If this is inevitable, the coach ought to help the coachee express any concerns and ensure that all necessary arrangements have been made, should the coachee require further assistance and support, for example through referral to another coach, therapist or counsellor (Cox, 2010). By respecting a coachee's wish to terminate the relationship, or by referring him to another colleague when the coach feels that her expertise is not sufficient to assist him, she shows genuine interest and respect and acts in an ethical manner.

A critical issue to consider before the coaching relationship terminates is what happens next. It may be that you are an internal coach in an organisation but suddenly you are promoted to a different role that requires you to stop acting as a coach. How do you smoothly navigate from one role to the other? You may also encounter a situation where, upon terminating the relationship, your client invites you to dinner to thank you for your valuable service. How do you respond to such a proposition? Do you accept the invitation or do you decline it? Indeed, having clearly delineated boundaries from the outset of the relationship – ideally, set out in the coaching contract – will help you deal with the termination process in an effective manner, either by making a smooth transition from one role to the other or by ending the relationship in a way that benefits the client.

## Conclusion

In this chapter, we focused on the ethical issues that may arise as part of developing the coaching relationship. We explored several ethical dilemmas that coaches might face during the development of the relationship, and proposed ways in which they can be anticipated. Moreover, we discussed the 'use of self' and argued that both coach and coachee need to have a clear understanding of the purpose of the coaching, as well as the roles involved in the coaching relationship. For this to happen, we recommended the use of a well-defined, clear contract at the very start of the coaching relationship, as a crucial strategy to forestall and avoid potential ethical issues that can be anticipated.

It is our view that, in order to develop a fruitful coaching relationship, coaches need to reflect on it constantly. Coaches who work from an ethical perspective do not only rely on their instinct but also keep asking themselves what seems to be working in the relationship and what needs to be addressed further, in order to maintain an effective coaching practice. Additionally, the clients' expectations of the development of the relationship and the coaching process are also of paramount importance to them. Regularly checking in with our clients to ensure that their needs and expectations are met will enable them to feel secure, valued, even fulfilled. Such a stance not only has a positive impact on the coaching relationship but also bolsters client autonomy and contributes to maintaining an ethical coaching practice. We will address ways in which we can develop and maintain an ethical coaching practice in the following chapter.

## Chapter summary

- The coaching relationship is a co-creation between the coach and the coachee and should be orientated towards the welfare of the coachee.
- Clear contracting at the outset of coaching has the potential of anticipating several ethical issues that may arise in the development of the coaching relationship.

- The way in which a client perceives the coaching relationship will have a powerful impact on whether the relationship will actually be successful or not.
- Before the coaching relationship terminates, all necessary steps must be taken to ensure that clients feel that they have achieved their goals or that they have been offered assistance to seek further help and support elsewhere.

---

## Suggestions for further reading

For an engaging discussion on the coaching relationship, we would suggest:
Pelham, G. (2016) *The Coaching Relationship in Practice*. London: Sage Publishing.

See also:
Palmer, S. and McDowall, A. (eds) (2010) *The Coaching Relationship: Putting People First*. London: Routledge.

For a detailed discussion on contracting and the different levels of coaching contracts, we recommend:
Sills, C. (2012) 'The coaching contract: A mutual commitment', in E. de Haan and C. Sills (eds), *Coaching Relationships: The Relational Coaching Fieldbook*. Faringdon: Libri, pp. 93–110.

If you are interested in a thorough and engaging account of the subject of confidentiality, we suggest:
Bond, T. and Mitchels, B. (2015) *Confidentiality and Record Keeping in Counselling and Psychotherapy*, 2nd edn. London: Sage Publishing.

If you wish to read further about the psychological heritage of coaching, consider taking a look at:
Wildflower, L. (2013) *The Hidden History of Coaching*. Maidenhead: Open University Press.

---

# 4

# Maintaining an
# Ethical Coaching Practice

## Chapter aims

- To raise awareness about some of the challenges that face coaching as a discipline and practice.
- To acknowledge the importance of competencies, training and education in coaching.
- To recognise the significance of continuing professional development for maintaining an ethical coaching practice. We pay particular attention to the instrumentality of supervision and knowledge expansion.
- To reiterate the importance of maintaining an ethical coaching practice.

## Chapter overview

In Chapter 3, we looked at a range of factors that determine the development of an ethical coaching relationship from inception to termination. In this chapter, we explore ways to maintain an ethical coaching practice. We start the discussion by looking at some of the challenges that the discipline of coaching is faced with today, due to the absence of professional status. We particularly focus on this issue to show how the lack of professionalisation can have ethical implications for the practice of coaching. We then go on to discuss several ways in which we can develop and maintain an ethical coaching practice. In particular, we discuss the significance of competence, educational background and continuing professional development through supervision and the expansion of one's knowledge base.

## Key words

competencies, training, education, continuing professional development, supervision, knowledge base

## Introduction

In the previous chapter, we explored how we can develop the coaching relationship in an ethical manner. This presupposes educating the coachee as to the function, purpose and expectations of coaching. In this chapter, we focus on the initiatives and actions a coach needs to take in order to develop and maintain an ethical coaching practice. These include: developing competence; reflecting on the instrumentality of the coach's educational and professional background in her coaching practice; and pursuing continuing professional development through supervision and constantly updating and expanding her knowledge base in coaching. We will discuss these pursuits in due course. But before we proceed to this discussion, it is important to understand where coaching stands today in terms of professional status. This is because the latter, as we shall explain, has direct implications on developing and maintaining an ethical coaching practice.

As we already discussed in Chapter 1, coaching is still not recognised as a legitimate, stand-alone profession. The lack of systemised regulation by an independent – or even endogenous – authority has been deemed the key reason for this (Drake, 2008; Brennan and Wildflower, 2014; Lane et al., 2014). The inability of the discipline of coaching to achieve full professional status has significant implications for the coaching practice. Before explaining these implications, it is important to clarify what we mean by 'profession' here. Echoing Soltis (1986: 3), we see a profession as a 'community of practice with a telos, a general purpose that one must be committed to in order to be a professional'. Being part of such a community of practice presupposes subjecting one's professional freedom to its ethical principles and standards (ibid.). The very lack of regulatory imposition of ethical standards in coaching has, therefore, hindered its advancement into a stand-alone profession. Importantly, this regulatory absence has offered fertile ground for the development of independent professional activity and, in consequence, idiosyncratic and self-imposed ethical standards in the coaching practice, which beg the question: what constitutes professional coaching practice?

Against this backdrop, we start this chapter by introducing the challenges arising from the lack of formal professionalisation of coaching, and its impact on our conceptualisation of professional and, in addition, ethical coaching practice. We also invite you to consider how developing and maintaining an ethical practice can be achieved in the absence of an independently imposed set of principles and ethical standards. We then explore some of the ways that can help coaches to develop and maintain an ethical coaching practice. These include: developing key competencies; reflecting on one's educational and professional background; and pursuing continuing professional development. The latter can be achieved through supervision and the expansion of one's knowledge base.

## The professional status of coaching: implications for the coaching practice

In order for any professional service to be recognised as an independent, stand-alone profession, it needs to fulfil a number of criteria. These include recognised (academic) training, licence to practice, a commonly accepted code of ethics, independent (and often governmental) regulation, and development of a common body of knowledge and skills (Spence, 2007: 261). Coaching falls short in several of these benchmarks. In consequence, coaching has still not achieved full professional status and this has implications for its reliability as a professional service (Lane et al., 2014; Stober, 2014). To rectify this issue, several scholars and practitioners have tried to outline the key criteria that coaching needs to fulfil in order to be recognised as a fully fledged, independent profession. For instance, following a thorough literature review Bennett (2006: 241–2) identified the following:

- The acquisition of distinguishable and distinct skills, which are generally accepted as enhancing the performance of skilled coaching.
- Training and education and continuing professional development; competencies which are generally acknowledged as supplementing coaching practice; and measures for evaluating competence.
- Development of a commonly accepted and enforced code of ethics and systems for monitoring and implementing ethical conduct by coaches, which could result in the obligation to cease practising, if this is deemed necessary.
- Practice that is driven by altruistic motives rather than monetary gains.
- Formation of a generally acknowledged organisation that represents the profession and those who practise coaching.
- Evaluation of credentialing and self-regulation.

- Establishment of a practitioner community, which will encourage the development of relationships and exchange of thought related to coaching and the production of coaching-related publications.
- Status or state of recognition associated with membership in the profession.
- General professional recognition from other professions.
- Practice founded on clear theoretical foundation and empirical research.

Although coaching fulfils some of these criteria, there are still significant gaps that hinder its progression to full professional status (Bennett, 2006). This has implications for the coaching practice. At this point, one may ask: what is the link between the inadequacy of the discipline of coaching to fulfil these criteria and the prospect of developing and maintaining an ethical coaching practice? The answer lies in the close examination of these criteria that reveals a strong link between proposed practical guidelines and an effective and therefore ethical coaching practice. Training and education, for instance, are still not a prerequisite for coaching, even though the contemporary coach training market offers a variety of educational options from strictly practical to purely theoretical (Bennett, 2006; Grant et al., 2010).

Instead, coaches enter the service from a variety of educational and professional backgrounds, and premise their coaching practice primarily on their professional expertise as retiring executives, human resource managers, academics and teachers, psychologists, counsellors and psychotherapists, amongst others (Bluckert, 2004; Bachkirova et al., 2014: 2–6). Furthermore, the theoretical and empirical background of coaching is still to a large extent reliant on relevant disciplines while, to this day, there are no recognised distinct skills that coaches are required to possess (Bennett, 2006) – although general recommendations have been welcomed by the practitioner community (see, for instance, Thomson, 2009, 2014; Rogers, 2012; van Nieuwerburgh, 2014). Such guidelines, therefore, are not intended to 'police' coaching but to act as a shield that protects the coach, the client and the coaching service and, in consequence, promotes an ethical coaching practice.

## Pause for reflection

Take a few minutes to consider and reflect on the following questions:

- What guidelines and standards do you adhere to as a coach? Do you subscribe, for instance, to the code of ethics of any professional coaching association?

- If the answer to the above question is yes, are the ethical standards imposed by your preferred coaching association adequate to help you monitor and maintain an ethical coaching practice?
- Aside from established codes of ethics, what other steps do you take to maintain an ethical coaching practice?

These questions are intended to raise your awareness about the way in which you ensure that your coaching practice maintains high ethical standards, in absence of systematic regulation of coaching. While the debate over who, if anyone, ought to regulate coaching is one that still awaits serious consideration, it is beyond the scope of this book. The lack of independent regulation, however, means that anyone can embark on the coaching practice even without relevant competencies, academic and professional credentials, or formal guidelines for ethical behaviour. In consequence, the title of the coach remains unprotected and this can be detrimental for the credibility of the service and its professionals.

The rather bleak picture painted above does not mean that coaches are powerless in their efforts to bolster their professional credibility and enhance their coaching practice. In the following sections of this chapter, we discuss some of the ways in which coaches can boost and safeguard their professional credibility and, by extension, maintain an ethical coaching practice. We particularly focus on issues of competence, education and training, and continuous professional development. Let's start with competence.

## Competence in coaching

'A strong coach, in my view, is one "who knows what he or she doesn't know" and has a strong enough ego to admit it,' maintained, quite appositely, Beverly Brooks (2001: 99). Within the context of coaching, competence encompasses the combination of knowledge, skills, aptitude and behaviour to practise as a coach. As Brooks (ibid.) argues, it entails consciously accepting not only what you know and can do but also what you don't know and cannot do. In other words, competence presupposes knowing your limits. This means acknowledging when your expertise is insufficient to support a client and, therefore, a referral must be considered.

Competence features prominently in the codes of ethics of all major professional coaching bodies. The AC (undated *a*), for instance, states the following:

- You will have qualifications, skills and experience appropriate to the needs of your Client. If not, you should refer your Client to those who do, such as more experienced coaches, coaching supervisors, counselors, psychotherapists or others offering specialist services.

- A Client may need levels of psychological support you are not competent to provide. If so, the Client should be referred to an appropriate source of care, such as the Client's GP, a counsellor, psychotherapist, or another appropriate service or agency.

So far, no specific competence models have been proposed as suitable to coaching (Brotman et al., 1998; Bennett, 2006). Stober produced a list of the most common competency characteristics, as they are prescribed by the major professional coaching bodies. These include:

- Ethical standards which promote 'do no harm' and respect towards the coachee.
- The effective establishment of the coaching relationship based on trust, support and open communication.
- The promotion of growth and change for the coachee through realistic goal setting.
- Continuing professional development on the part of the coach, which is linked to the coach's specific area of practice (for example, life coaching, executive coaching, business coaching). (2014: 424)

As these characteristics have not been empirically tested (ibid.), we encourage you to critically enquire into their applicability. We also invite you to reflect on your key coaching competencies and consider any developmental needs you might have. What steps do you need to take in order to cultivate and develop your coaching competence further? Evaluating your competence in order to address your developmental needs is a major step in the process of developing and maintaining an ethical coaching practice. Similarly, evaluating your knowledge and expertise will allow you to identify any intellectual gaps that may interfere with your practice. It will also enable you to critically reflect on how your educational background underpins and even determines the kind of coaching you practise. This is important for an effective and ethical coaching practice. For this reason, in the next session we engage in a discussion on the significance of the coach's education and training.

## Educational background and training for coaches

Much as the practitioner literature advocating the merits of coaching has grown in size and intensity, to date there is no consensus on mandatory education and training for coaches. As a result, there are no specific guidelines as to what constitutes appropriate coach training and education. In most cases, coaching has been integrated into corporate learning and development agendas as a free-standing training programme for professionals, while there are private institutions that award 'licence to practise' after only a few hours of workshop attendance. Generally, the coach-training market is multifaceted and offers professional qualifications that range from a few days' workshops to full-blown academic courses on a postgraduate level. The unsystematic evaluation of these qualifications can be detrimental to their trustworthiness (Devine et al., 2013), because, in effect, anyone can call themselves a coach, even after attending only a few workshops.

Despite the plethora of coach-specific training and education options, these are not a prerequisite for practice. Instead, coaches enter the profession from a variety of educational and professional backgrounds. These range from management and education to counselling and psychotherapy, to name but a few (Bluckert, 2004; Bachkirova et al., 2014: 2–6). This means that the emerging knowledge base of coaching is influenced and enriched by several disciplines, which, in turn, allow for various approaches, traditions and schools of practice (Bachkirova et al., 2014: 4). As a result, there has been no consensus on what the most suitable bodies of knowledge for coach training and education are, and this has implications for the coaching practice, since all these disciplines view and approach coaching from a different theoretical and professional vantage point (Stober, 2014). In consequence, coaches who are trained in different traditions may disagree profoundly as to the essence, purpose and even the practical application of coaching (Campone and Awal, 2012; Stober, 2014). For example, coaches with a background in clinical psychology have been found to welcome emotional expression when working through work-related issues and are more prone to using emotion-related interventions (Campone and Awal, 2012; Stober, 2014). Would an executive coach with a business-related educational and professional background equally welcome a potential outburst of tears during an executive coaching session?

## Pause for reflection

Take a few minutes to consider your personal approach to coaching:

- What educational and professional background do you bring into your coaching practice?
- Is coaching your primary profession or are you a professional in another discipline (for example, an HR manager) applying coaching skills to your practice?
- Do you recognise any difference in the disciplines you are involved with?
- How does your educational and professional background affect your preferred coaching approaches?
- Finally, what is your view on the significance of coach training and education? Do you think it should be a prerequisite for practice?

This 'hybridity' of educational and professional backgrounds with which coaches enter the coaching practice can cause perplexity and confusion, which we shall discuss in more detail in Chapter 7. This diversity, however, signifies that coaches bring to the discipline a great variety of knowledge and expertise. The ethical issue that arises here is the following: what is the most appropriate knowledge for a discipline that still does not have a distinct body of knowledge? We will discuss this question further in Chapter 5. For now, a key issue we need to consider is whether, as practitioners, we are looking to apply coaching techniques to our primary discipline (for example, coaching skills in management) or whether we are looking to practise coaching as a core profession. If our answer is the latter, then we need to address the question of what constitutes coach training and education and how it can enable us to practise in a more ethical manner.

Elliott (1972) argued that entry to a profession requires robust training in a higher education context. While this is a very broad statement that excludes reliable professions that do not require a university degree as a prerequisite (consider, for example, the professions of the plumber and electrician or those of the nurse or accountant that, until fairly recently, an academic qualification was not a prerequisite to practise), we agree with other colleagues that the route to professionalisation is dependent on the development of a shared body of applied knowledge (Grant and Cavanagh, 2004: 3). Theoretically informed and evidence-based training and education can play a significant role in this process. In this respect, we invite you to consider your educational background. How has it prepared you for your coaching commitments? Is it adequate to help you address the constantly changing needs of the individuals you work with? Or do you find yourself needing continuing professional development in order to support your clients effectively?

## Continuing professional development (CPD)

The Health and Care Professions Council (HCPC) defines CPD as: 'a range of learning activities through which health professionals maintain and develop throughout their career to ensure that they retain their capacity to practise safely, effectively and legally within their evolving scope of practice' (HCPC, undated). Accordingly, in coaching, CPD may involve: reading about the current empirical findings in the field and even applying some to your practice; attending and participating in conferences, workshops, seminars and scientific meetings related to coaching; 'consuming' and conducting coaching-related research; attending peer-coaching or peer-mentoring meetings and networks; pursuing further qualifications and training; and attending supervision sessions. In the pages that follow, we invite you to reflect on how CPD activities can help you develop and maintain an ethical coaching practice. We particularly focus on two integral elements of CPD – supervision and expanding your knowledge base.

## Supervision

Coaching is first and foremost a helping service. This means that a coach needs to have and maintain the competence, effectiveness and resilience to help clients achieve their set goals. While at times this is a fairly straightforward process, occasionally it may become emotionally onerous, both for the coach and the client. As a result, the coach can be placed under considerable demands that can lead to emotional burnout. It is the coach's responsibility to monitor her responses to coaching sessions and to protect her own well-being in the process. Regular supervision will help anticipate and manage any issues that emerge from the coach's practice.

Supervision is defined as a 'type of professional mentoring widely used in the talking therapies to enhance the quality of service provided to clients' (Bond, 2015: 39). Specifically within a coaching context, supervision is 'the process by which a coach with the help of a supervisor can attend to understanding better both the client system and themselves as part of the client–coach system, and, by so doing, transform their work and develop their craft' (Hawkins and Smith, 2006: 12). According to Hawkins and Smith (ibid.), the three distinctive functions of coaching supervision are:

- Developmental: to develop the skills and capabilities of the coach.
- Resourcing: to safeguard the well-being of the coaching.
- Qualitative: to ensure coaching quality and, importantly, adherence to ethical standards.

Much as all these functions are crucial to maintaining an effective – and ethical – coaching practice, supervision is still not mandatory in coaching. This is in stark contrast to other helping professions, such as counselling and psychotherapy. The debate over the need for compulsory supervision (and supervision training) in coaching has been gradually gaining momentum, and several scholars and practitioners have welcomed and engaged with it (Hawkins and Smith, 2006; Bachkirova et al., 2011; Passmore, 2011; de Haan, 2012; Hawkins, 2014). This, indeed, is one of the burning issues facing the discipline of coaching today. Should coaches pursue regular and ongoing supervision? And should supervision be a compulsory element of the coach's practice?

As nearly all professional coaching bodies advocate in their individual codes of ethics, supervision is an important process for the coach's continuing professional development and quality assurance. This is because supervision offers coaches a safe space for ongoing reflection on their coaching practice and on their relationship with clients. Indeed, supervision provides the opportunity to reflect on and evaluate any reactions and behaviours that coaches wish to explore further. Moreover, supervision allows coaches to form a clear understanding of their preferred approach to coaching, their role and responsibilities as a coach, and the values and ethics that underpin their practice. Ultimately, this understanding allows coaches to articulate and communicate these attributes more effectively to clients, sponsors and any relevant stakeholders (Hawkins, 2014).

## Pause for reflection

Take a few minutes to consider the significance of supervision in your practice:

- Do you pursue supervision on a regular basis? If so, what form does it take?
- What are the elements of supervision that you find more beneficial for your continuing professional development as a coach?

The answers to these questions will vary. We agree with other coaching scholars and practitioners who make a strong case for the instrumentality of supervision for the professional development of a coach. Shaw and Linnecar (2007) saw it as a key factor in ensuring high-quality coaching, while Beverly Brooks boldly claimed that it is: 'naïve at best, and dangerous at worst, if the coaching is not supervised by another professional with some psychological expertise' (cited in Thomson, 2014: 65). This claim is valid, considering the complexity of the coach's work, which involves working through individual, interpersonal and organisational issues. In the final analysis, the fundamental case for supervision is that it supports the well-being of the coach which, in consequence, benefits and safeguards the coachee (Pelham, 2016: 124). In this context, supervision becomes a prerequisite of CPD and, by extension, an ethical coaching practice. But it is not the only prerequisite. Expanding one's knowledge base in order to address the constantly evolving complexities of the settings where coaching takes place is also imperative for maintaining an ethical coaching practice.

## Expanding one's knowledge base

Due to the absence of systematic regulation of coaching and, in consequence, well-defined guidelines as to what the theoretical and educational requirements are, the coach's knowledge base can range from limited to extensive. This variability has been detrimental to the professional credibility of the coach and the coaching practice. As we have already argued, critically reflecting on one's existing knowledge base is beneficial to evaluating strengths and limitations. An ethical coaching practice, however, calls for the continuous expansion of one's knowledge base. This can be materialised in a variety of ways. Attending conferences, even presenting your own papers in them, comprises one of the ways. Reading current developments in the field is another avenue for expanding your knowledge base, and you have a pool of resources to draw from. This is because the empirical establishment of coaching, while fairly new and gradual, has been gaining currency amongst scholars and practitioners. A consequence of this is the emergence of several specialist coaching journals, including *Coaching: An International Journal of Theory, Research and Practice*; the *International Journal of Evidence Based Coaching and Mentoring*; and *International Coaching Psychology Review*, amongst others.

Aside from 'consuming' empirical research in coaching you may want to consider contributing to empirical research, even conducting research to enhance and promote the evidence base of coaching. For some coaches this is an exciting prospect, while others may find it daunting. We will devote the following chapter to an exploration of how engaging with evidence-based research and adopting a stance of critical enquiry not only enable the development of our ethical capabilities (Iordanou and Williams, 2016), but also help promote an effective and ethical coaching practice and, in consequence, bolster the professional credibility of the coaching discipline. However, before we proceed to this discussion, we would like to conclude by sharing our conviction that the methodical expansion of the coach's knowledge base, which can take place in a variety of ways, is instrumental in maintaining an ethical coaching practice. This is because it gives us the opportunity to engage with new developments in coaching and in relevant fields, which we can make use of for the benefit of our clients, our service and the coaching community as a whole.

## Conclusion

In this chapter, we looked at some of the key constituents for developing and maintaining an ethical coaching practice. A primary constituent is developing and enhancing coaching competencies. You can achieve this by critically reflecting on your coaching skills and capabilities and, importantly, on the boundaries of these capabilities. Understanding what you are capable of and where your capability stops will allow you to act in a professionally ethical manner. It goes without saying that it is impossible to specialise in everything. This is why it is so important to acknowledge the boundaries and limitations of your professional expertise. Such limitations don't have to be permanent impediments. Capitalising on the professional expertise you bring into the coaching practice is an excellent way of enhancing it. For example, coaches who come from a counselling background will find it quite natural to use some of the core coaching skills of active listening, empathy and positive regard, as they stem from the realm of psychotherapy (Campone and Awal, 2012). We welcome such interdisciplinary approaches as conducive to developing and maintaining an ethical coaching practice.

Understanding what knowledge base you bring into your coaching practice, by reflecting on your educational background, is the second constituent of an ethical coaching practice. You may have formal training qualifications or you may have entered the service through a relevant discipline. You may not even be a professional coach but use coaching skills as part of your professional practice. Regardless of your educational and professional background, you are part of a community of practitioners who have in common their diverse backgrounds. We see this propensity of the discipline of coaching to borrow approaches from other relevant disciplines as positive, even necessary, for the professional establishment of coaching. If anything, this shows that coaching is striving to enhance its knowledge base, which, by extension, can promote an ethical coaching practice. We encourage you, therefore, to consciously reflect on how your education and training have equipped you to pursue an effective and ethical coaching practice and we recommend continuing professional development as a means of addressing the needs of a constantly evolving client base.

Importantly, we see supervision as a fundamental prerequisite for an ethical coaching practice. This is because it provides a safe space for coaches to reflect on their practice and their relationship with their clients and any other stakeholders that are involved in the coaching process. Supervision allows you to identify developmental needs and, in consequence, to seek further training for the constant improvement of your coaching service (Hawkins and Smith, 2006: 12). Much as supervision is not a mandatory prerequisite for the coach, we invite you to consider its fundamental usefulness for maintaining an ethical coaching practice.

The final prerequisite for developing and maintaining an ethical coaching practice is expanding your knowledge base through a variety of CPD activities, such as attending conferences and practitioner meetings, reading about recent developments in the field and pursuing further training and qualifications. There is one specific constituent of expanding one's knowledge base to which we did not refer here. This is developing an evidence-based practice (EBP) by actively engaging with empirical research, either indirectly (reading the latest developments in the field) or even directly (conducting evidence-based research yourself). Several scholars and practitioners have argued that developing an evidence-based practice will boost – if not expedite – the professionalisation of the coaching service (Grant, 2003; Page, 2005; Kauffman, 2005). We will discuss this in the following chapter, where we will explore in detail another key constituent of an ethical coaching practice: embracing the evidence-based approach by means of adopting a stance of critical enquiry.

## Chapter summary

- The lack of distinct professional criteria in coaching has implications for maintaining an ethical coaching practice.
- Coaches bring into the coaching practice a variety of professional and educational backgrounds that can be complementary or conflicting.
- Developing competencies through education and training is a key determinant for an ethical coaching practice.
- Continuous professional development by means of supervision and expanding one's knowledge base can promote an ethical coaching practice.

## Suggestions for further reading

For a comprehensive overview of the diverse knowledge base of coaching, we consider the following book to be extremely thorough and engaging:

Cox, E., Bachkirova, T. and Clutterbuck, D. (eds) (2014) *The Complete Handbook of Coaching*, 2nd edn. London: Sage Publishing.

*(Continued)*

*(Continued)*

For a comprehensive overview of knowledge-based coaching, we eagerly recommend:
Wildflower, L. and Brennan, D. (2011) *The Handbook of Knowledge-Based Coaching: From Theory to Practice.* San Francisco, CA: Jossey-Bass.

For an array of views on the role of supervision in the coaching practice, we recommend:
Passmore, J. (ed.) (2011) *Supervision in Coaching: Supervision, Ethics and Continuous Professional Development.* London: Kogan Page.

# 5

# Developing an Evidence-Based Coaching Practice

## Chapter aims

- To raise awareness of the link between evidence-based and ethical coaching practice.
- To explore ways in which coaches can develop and maintain an evidence-based practice.
- To introduce the *scientist-practitioner model* as a vehicle towards an evidence-based coaching practice.
- To raise awareness of how our values impact on our understanding of knowledge and, in consequence, how we construct knowledge about our coaching practice.
- To reiterate the significance of adopting a stance of critical enquiry for an ethical coaching practice.
- To offer a brief introduction on some paradigms of enquiry.

## Chapter overview

In Chapter 4, we discussed some key ethical issues pertaining to the coach's background knowledge and continuing professional development, in order to promote a knowledge-based coaching practice. We also touched upon the significance of evidence-based research as a vehicle for an ethically informed practice. In this chapter, we cast our focus on the importance of developing and maintaining an evidence-based coaching practice by adopting a stance of critical enquiry. Specifically, we discuss the significance of the coach's involvement with evidence-based research for developing an ethical coaching practice. This involvement can take different forms. It can be indirect, in the case where the coach becomes a 'consumer' of evidence-based research. Or it can be direct, which entails the coach conducting research with the purpose of advancing her practice. As such, we support a stance of critical enquiry and we explore the scientist-practitioner model. In the final part of the chapter, we also engage in a brief discussion of some prominent paradigms of enquiry, especially for those readers who are interested in enhancing their knowledge about actively engaging in evidence-based research. We conclude the chapter by arguing that developing an evidence-based coaching practice, either through reading research findings or by means of conducting research ourselves, enhances our chances of being critical about the values and ethics we bring into our coaching practice; this spawns benefits for our clients, our practice and the coaching profession as a whole.

## Key words

evidence-based practice, stance of enquiry, research, scientist-practitioner model

## Introduction

As we discussed in the previous chapter, the fact that the knowledge base of coaching derives from a variety of disciplines – such as business, management, education, counselling and psychotherapy, amongst others – is beneficial for the service, as long as coaches acknowledge and address their professional development needs (Lane and Corrie, 2006; Bachkirova et al., 2014). Drawing from so many different knowledge pools, however, can be somewhat detrimental for coaching, as it relies on evidence from other disciplines to establish its theoretical background, while its empirical foundation has been lagging behind. This, as we already discussed in the previous chapter, has had serious implications for the advancement of coaching into a distinct, independent profession. Moreover, the lack of empirical foundation has had a negative impact on the professional reliability of coaching.

To address this issue, several scholars and practitioners gradually started to urge for a more empirically grounded coaching practice. Professional membership bodies followed suit, in an effort to increase the reliability of the service as a whole. In consequence, all major professional coaching associations now hold dedicated annual research conferences that attract both coaching practitioners and scholars (Grant, 2003; Biswas-Diener, 2009). Moreover, as we already mentioned in Chapter 4, specialist coaching journals that are dedicated to the study of theory, research and practice of coaching have emerged. Finally, coaching has started to enter the realm of higher education as an evidence-based, academic discipline (Iordanou et al., 2015). All these efforts aim at one specific objective: to develop and maintain an evidence-based coaching practice that will boost the discipline's reliability and, hopefully, open the road to the professionalisation of coaching.

## Evidence-based practice

The term *evidence-based practice* was popularised in the 1990s and refers to any type of treatment or intervention whose effectiveness is assessed through scientific means (Bond, 2015). The evidence-based practice movement began primarily in healthcare in order to justify expenditure of large sums (Rowland and Goss, 2000). More specifically, the approach was developed to ask the question: 'What works for whom' in the most cost-effective way (Fonagy et al., 2005), so that the client's health is safeguarded and any kind of harm is prevented?

In coaching, adopting an evidence-based approach means premising one's practice on empirical research findings. This approach has several benefits. For instance, it enables deeper knowledge of recent advancements in the coaching practice. It also helps exercise more critical thinking in distinguishing between the most appropriate coaching tools and methods for each client's individual needs. Moreover, it renders the coaching practice more scientifically and theoretically informed, which has the potential of boosting the professional reliability of the coach. The challenge lies in deciding what evidence best applies to the coach's work and how the coach can use this evidence in order to maintain and promote a high-quality, ethical coaching practice (Stober, 2014).

In practice, an evidence-based approach to coaching combines three vital components: first, the most recent knowledge (research findings); second, the coach's know-how (the application of research findings in practice); and third, the adaptation of findings on the coachee's needs, according to his or her distinctive characteristics, such as personality traits, strengths and values (ibid.). In other words, evidence-based practice enables coaches to make use of empirical research findings and apply them to their practice for the benefit of their clients and the coaching service in general. But can coaches do this without basic knowledge of research skills? And what is the relevance of research to an ethical coaching practice?

**Pause for reflection**

Following the discussion above, we invite you to reflect on the following questions:

- Does engagement with evidence-based research – by attending conferences, for instance, or reading journal articles – enhance your coaching practice?
- Should basic knowledge of research skills and methods be a prerequisite for coaches?
- How does engagement with research – directly or indirectly – promote an ethical coaching practice?

Stober (2014) claims that – if coaching practitioners have a basic knowledge of research and are able to decide what research evidence can be applied in the context in which they practise – they will be able to deliver more evidence-based (and thus ethical) services. Some scholars even go further to claim that coaches can and should conduct research, and that this can be beneficial to their practice (Grant and Stober, 2006; Campone, 2011). Campone (ibid.) actually argued that conducting research is not as difficult and intimidating as some coaches may perceive it to be; in fact it can be beneficial, indeed enjoyable, for coaches. This is because actively engaging in research gives coaches the opportunity to reflect upon their practice and to evaluate the tools and methods they use, even compare them with the preferred tools of other colleagues. Moreover, it allows them to make decisions based on evidence rather than common practice. Additionally, it enables coaches to understand the theories and models that provide the framework for their practice (ibid.), an issue that we shall return to in Chapter 7. Finally, and quite importantly for our discussion on values and ethics in coaching, conducting research allows coaches to critically enquire into the beliefs, assumptions and principles that underpin their coaching practice and the very nature of knowledge.

Of course, an ethical question raised here is whether a coach who is not an experienced researcher and, therefore, does not possess research skills, should conduct research. According to Stober (2014), coaches who do not possess knowledge on research methods could benefit from seeking training for it; and those who do could enhance an evidence-based coaching practice by using their research skills in coaching related research (ibid.). Stober went even further to argue that the ability to critically evaluate and conduct research is essential for the professional development of the coach and coaching as a service (ibid.: 422). Although opinions on this matter vary, several scholars and practitioners have advocated the scientist-practitioner model, whereby practising coaches initially become informed consumers, and consequently, if possible, skilled producers of research. This gradual process, they believe, will be instrumental in the professional establishment of coaching (Grant and Cavanagh, 2004; Page, 2005; Kauffman, 2005). In the following section, we discuss in detail the scientist-practitioner model.

## The scientist-practitioner model: challenges and benefits

The *scientist-practitioner* concept was born within the realm of clinical psychology and has since spread to all other fields where psychological approaches are prevalent (Lane et al., 2014). The scientist-practitioner model involves practitioners applying research evidence to their practice in order to render it more empirically and theoretically informed and, by extension, reliable. In essence, they become more informed consumers of research (Page, 2005). While, in practice, this sounds simple, it does not come without challenges. This is because it is not always easy to assess what research is more appropriate for each practitioner's needs. Specifically in coaching, evidence-based research is not always readily available and, even when it is, it is usually communicated in a way that is neither comprehensive nor useful to practitioners (Lane and Corrie, 2006; Lane at al., 2014; Iordanou and Hawley, 2015). In consequence, the scientist-practitioner model is not as easy to achieve as initially conceived.

To address this issue, Stober (2014: 422) proposed a scholar-practitioner approach, which focuses on cultivating the coach's ability to critically evaluate available evidence and to use only those findings that are most applicable to her work (Grant and Stober, 2006). In practice, this means that, instead of expecting coaches to become empirical researchers, we could start applying the scholar-practitioner model in our coaching, whereby we start to critically evaluate the various pieces of research we read and apply those parts of it which are most relevant and suitable. To do this, however, we need to have a basic knowledge of research methods and analysis (Stober, 2014). A basic knowledge of research is beneficial for two primary reasons. First, it allows us to adopt a stance of critical enquiry towards the research evidence that we come across. And second, it enables us to evaluate research findings in order to identify those that are most appropriate for our clients' benefit. This is very important.

In attempting to answer these questions, we believe that critical evaluation of research findings, and therefore adequate knowledge of the mechanics of research, will help you approach your practice from a more ethical standpoint. This is because, if you have basic research knowledge and are thus able to adopt a stance of critical enquiry, you can recognise those research findings that are relevant and applicable to your practice and adapt them to your clients' individual needs. In other words, not only will you be able to develop a more evidence-based coaching practice, but also you will fine-tune your capability of adopting scientific advancements to your clients' individual needs. This approach, then, can render you a more empathetic and ethical practitioner.

Consequently, critical evaluation of research findings is important, as it allows practitioners to integrate critical enquiry into their evidence-based practice. To understand the importance of evaluation for evidence-based practice, we first invite you to spend some time reflecting on the factors you think impact the principles that underpin your coaching practice. Since readers of this book will have varying degrees of experience as researchers, the following section serves as an introduction to the process of enquiring into the coaching practice through conducting research. We hope that you find it stimulating and thought provoking. But before we proceed to it, let's consider the following question.

If you spent some time reflecting in the above activity, we anticipate that you will have come up with several factors that may influence your coaching practice. These will most probably depend on the different contexts in which you practise coaching. Understanding how your own values converge or collide with these factors and how you subsequently proceed to taking action is essential for an ethical coaching practice. This is the reason why it is important to welcome and cultivate a stance of critical enquiry.

## The instrumentality of a stance of critical enquiry

As we already observed in Chapter 2, enquiry, that is, the process of asking questions, is integral to the coaching practice. As a process, it offers excellent opportunities for ongoing learning and development. This is because enquiry allows us to explore and challenge assumptions and beliefs we may hold about others and ourselves. Especially within the realm of coaching, where ethical behaviour transcends the mandates of a codified body of rules, algorithms and orthodox beliefs, it is essential to fine-tune our ability to enquire into the way in which we make decisions and proceed to actions. Ultimately, enquiry is a 'journey of discovery in which intelligent human beings ask questions about ordinary practices and arrive at astonishingly new conclusions' (Garvey and Williamson, 2002: 2). It is, therefore, essential that we develop a stance for enquiry towards the variety of contexts that influence our decisions and actions in our coaching practice.

In a collection of essays on perspectives of context, Bate (2014: 3) creates a compelling case that 'context is everything'. How we think about the context in which coaching takes place will determine how we go about enquiring into the complex phenomena that can influence, even skew, the input of our values in the coaching process. Indeed, taking a critical view of these multifaceted phenomena will offer us the opportunity to assess systematically the ethical parameters of our practice and render us more conscientious practitioners. It will also allow us to bridge the spheres of theory and practice and view them as 'a landscape of ideas with boundaries that can be crossed and new territories to explore' (Garvey and Williamson, 2002: 2). For this purpose, we would like to offer you a short introduction to established ways of enquiry within the realm of social sciences, where coaching is generally situated. We hope that the following section will be of interest to those who are unfamiliar with more systemised ways of enquiry, as well as those who embark on formal or informal research for their coaching training and practice. Ultimately, our aim is to show you that, while the principles of coaching can be common, the way we apply them is determined by the contextual parameters of how we (and others) view the world.

## Theoretical perspectives for enquiry

The values and ethics that determine the coaching practice are complex and multifaceted phenomena, influenced by interactions between language, meaning and experience. What often get in the way of people setting and actually achieving a goal are the beliefs that they hold about themselves. During the coaching practice, we may reinforce or dispel these beliefs of our clients through our behaviour as coaches. Such behaviour is reflective of our own beliefs and values. It is therefore significant to pause, explore and reflect on them in a manner that is methodical and systematic. To do so – that is, to systematically explore how the beliefs and values we and others hold can influence our coaching practice – we need to understand what philosophical perspectives are most appropriate for such enquiry. In this section, we offer a brief introduction on a range of theoretical perspectives that can undergird such enquiry into our coaching practice.

According to Guba (1990), perspectives of enquiry – what we more formally call *paradigms* – are characterised through their *ontology* (what is reality?), *epistemology* (how do you know something?) and *methodology* (how do you go about finding out about something?). These characteristics determine how we create knowledge and how we see ourselves in relation to this knowledge. They also dictate the methodological strategies we might employ to discover new knowledge; in our case, to enquire into the values and ethics that underpin our coaching practice and how other external factors can influence them.

There are a plethora of theoretical perspectives: philosophical, sociological and psychological. These determine the methodology of any critical enquiry and can challenge a range of assumptions, including our own and those of others. To navigate this complex landscape with 'consciousness', coaching practitioners and researchers need to be explicit about the problem or phenomenon they wish to explore and the lens through which they view the world (Creswell, 2012). Too often, enquiry focuses more on methodology and method, failing to take account of the theoretical assumptions that sit behind these choices (Slife and Williams, 1995; Gray, 2014). Yet, without theory it is difficult to contextualise practice.

In this chapter, we have chosen to explore three perspectives that we believe might support your current or future enquiry into aspects of values and ethics in coaching. These are interpretivism, critical theories and positivism. The spirit in which we write is not propelled by a search for the truth or being right or wrong. Rather, we are driven by a wish to help you understand the relative merits and limitations of conducting your enquiry from a range of perspectives.

## The contribution of social science: an interpretivist perspective

The interpretivist paradigm emerged as a perspective which looks for 'culturally derived and historically situated interpretations of the social world' (Crotty, 1998: 67), such as the coaching relationship. This approach enables us to understand and explain human and social reality, looking for the uniqueness of individual experiences (ibid.: 6).

From this perspective, a coach may seek to understand, rather than explain, how her values can influence the coaching practice and the relationship that develops within it. It therefore focuses on an individual's subjective experiences. Accordingly, one of the restrictions of interpretive enquiry is that it limits the potential to generalise across contexts. We ask you to consider whether coaching, which is premised on personal experiences, lends itself to general theorisations and applications. The topic of one's own personal and professional values for instance, while worth exploring for some, is not necessarily conducive to generalisations. What the enquirer is primarily interested in is specific subjective experiences, not the general conclusions that could be derived from them. In consequence, the nature of this approach requires the interpretive researcher to carry a sense of co-creation and acceptance so that, given a different set of circumstances, he or she may reveal different findings despite using the same methods.

## The contribution of social science: a critical perspective

The critical perspective for enquiry originates from critical theory and the belief that research is conducted 'for the emancipation of individuals and groups in an egalitarian society' (Cohen et al., 2007: 26). The critical enquirer seeks not only to understand or offer an account of coaching behaviours but also to change behaviour and attitude.

Enquiring into values and ethics in coaching from a critical perspective tends to have an agenda for change: to change people's lives, or the coaching culture, or the organisational structures that support coaching activities. This perspective of enquiry can be useful for influencing issues such as future coaching standards for ethical practice.

The critical perspective emerged from criticism that earlier approaches, such as positivism (which we will discuss below), were too technical and overly concerned with efficiency. Contrary to the interpretivist perspective that focuses on one's subjective experience, the critical paradigm highlights that earlier approaches had perhaps neglected social inequities and issues of power within relationships that, from a coaching perspective, are enmeshed in the coaching practice. Critical approaches, therefore, tend to challenge reproductions of inequalities, for example a growth of coaching in the public sector in response to the government's call for more person-centred care and relationships (Hamersley, 2013).

## The contribution of social science: a positivist perspective

The positivist perspective maintains that the researcher is the observer of objective reality. In essence, the enquirer is interested in observing natural phenomena and the relationship between them. Information derives from the senses and is premised on logic and reason.

A positivist researcher is interested in objective reality, as is represented by facts. Within a coaching context, our positivist enquirer would wish to find out how many coaches discuss ethical issues in their supervision, for instance. Yet, while having hard data on the percentage of coaches who pursue supervision is important, the positive stance disregards the kind of evidence that would help to develop new insights about the coach's subjective experience during the supervision process and how the latter improves or hinders her personal and professional development. Subsequently, although approaches on the positivist paradigm may have a place in coaching enquiry, they are deemed insufficient to explain the dynamics of people's individual experience of the coaching relationship.

Although the positivist perspective is steeped in a rich historical narrative, by the second half of the twentieth century there was increasing criticism of positivist ideas for applying scientific method to human affairs (Hamersley, 2013), such as the issue of values and ethics in coaching. However, despite the passage of time, positivism claims a certain degree of objectivity that can be helpful in such enquiries. It 'seeks to approximate the truth rather than aspiring to grasp it in its totality' (Crotty, 1998: 29). Nevertheless, in relation to exploring values and ethics within the coaching practice, the limitations of this approach must be acknowledged. The positivist ideology of parsimony, advocating that theories should be as simple as possible, does not sit comfortably with our view of the coaching world, where meaning is constructed through interaction.

## Pause for reflection

- Consider the possibility of engaging in some systematic enquiry over your own values and ethics as a coach. Which perspective would suit your enquiry best?

Let us be clear here: no philosophical perspective can represent the objective reality of the complex phenomenon of values and ethics within the coaching practice. It is important, however, to clarify from the outset of the enquiry what kinds of question you wish to ask. Making conscious choices in enquiry can help you ensure that you select the best possible approach that will help to answer your question(s).

As you may have noticed, established ways of enquiring into our coaching practices can be systematic, even complex at times. If you are amongst those who wonder why we need enquiry to critically evaluate our practice, we invite you to reflect on the instrumentality of critical enquiry – which entails empirical research and theory creation – for any discipline. Consider how essential enquiry is for a professional service like coaching which still strives to be accepted as a standard, stand-alone profession. Indeed, to ensure that coaching is given the appropriate recognition as a legitimate professional activity, it must be grounded in enquiry, empirical research and theory generation. For this reason, we invite you to consider the benefits of adopting a systematic stance of enquiry in and on your coaching practice.

## Conclusion

This crescendo in the popularity of coaching has brought about inexorable advancements in the coaching practice. These have inevitably called for the reconceptualisation of established ethical practices that are congruent with changes in society and the contexts in which coaching takes place. This is contingent upon adopting a stance for enquiry towards what shapes our ethical standards in our practice as coaches. The starting point for this process is the conscious understanding of the personal, institutional, social and political factors that can determine the ethical prism through which our decisions are taken. We wish to welcome – and not fear – the conscientious questioning of the drivers behind our decisions and actions in our coaching practice. This can happen by actively listening to the voices of our own consciousness, and those of our clients and our employers.

To conclude, we agree with Williams et al. (2006) that the sustainable self-regulation of coaching necessitates a synergy between applied research and quality skills provision. We contend that the latter needs to be enhanced by the cultivation of a stance of critical enquiry. In consequence, we support Grant and Cavanagh's (2004) assertions on the importance of the scientist-practitioner model, whereby practising coaches are encouraged to be critical consumers and, if possible, even producers of research. In other words, a stance of critical enquiry enhances our perception of our service and enables the intellectual growth of the coach, the coaching practice and the coaching profession as a whole. It thus could provide one of the avenues that lead to the professionalisation of coaching.

While the debate on the professionalisation of coaching is still ongoing, some scholars have started to accept that a unified coaching profession may not even be possible any more (see, for instance, Drake, 2008). Instead, they have shifted their attention to the instrumentality of systematic evidence as the basis for professional practice, marking this new era of evidence-based initiatives as *postprofessional* (Drake and Stober, 2005). Indeed, in this postprofessional era, which has seen enormous evidence-based advances in related disciplines such as medicine and psychotherapy, coaching has started to embrace the use of evidence-based research and practice in its pursuit of establishment as a valid discipline (Drake, 2008). This, of course, is contingent upon more unified and widely accepted ethical standards. In order for the coaching service to respond to this challenge, there needs to be a solid consensus not only on the significance of evidence, but also, as Drake (ibid.: 20) appositely put it, on the discipline's 'desired relationship to evidence and to the EBP paradigm itself'. Ideally, we ought to cast the focus on how we bridge differences of opinion on what constitutes 'evidence' and its contribution to practice. Evidence, however, is more reliable when it is produced and interpreted through reflexivity. This will be our subject of discussion in the following chapter.

## Chapter summary

- Our personal values and ethics affect how we understand our coaching practice.
- A stance of critical enquiry helps us understand the factors that affect our coaching practice.
- Being able to engage with coaching research helps promote an evidence-based and ethical coaching practice.
- The application of the scientist-practitioner model in coaching can foster the development of evidence-based practice.
- Incorporating different paradigms of enquiry into our practice can be beneficial for the coach, the coaching clients and the coaching service as a whole.

---

### Suggestions for further reading

For a simple exploration of ideas around knowledge creation and how we view the world, we would suggest:

Garvey, D. and Williamson, B. (2002) *Beyond Knowledge Management: Dialogue, Creativity and the Corporate Curriculum*. Harlow: Pearson.

For developments in the debate about coaching professionalisation, we suggest:

Drake, D.B. (2008) 'Finding our way home: Coaching's search for identity in a new era', *Coaching*, 1(1): 15–26.

For an interesting discussion on the professional status of coaching, you may wish to read:

Lane, D., Stelter, R. and Stout-Rostron, S. (2014) 'The future of coaching as a profession', in E. Cox, T. Bachkirova and D. Clutterbuck (eds), *The Complete Handbook of Coaching*, 2nd edn. London: Sage Publishing, pp. 418–30.

Finally, if you are interested in a general introduction on how to conduct social science research, we recommend the following two books:

Cresswell, J.W. (2012) *Qualitative Inquiry & Research Design: Choosing Among Five Approaches*, 3rd edn. London: Sage Publishing.

and

Crotty, M. (1998) *The Foundations of Social Research: Meaning and Perspective in the Research Process*. London: Sage Publishing.

# 6

# Practising Reflexively

## Chapter aims

- To define and discuss further the concepts of reflection and reflexivity and the role they play in developing an ethical mindset.
- To consider both the distinctive and complementary aspects of reflective and reflexive practice.
- To explore ways in which coaches can stimulate reflexive thinking and practice.
- To share expert practitioners' reflections on strategies for building reflexivity.
- To engage in activities that enable the development of reflexive coaching practice.

## Chapter overview

This chapter builds on our initial discussion on reflective practice in Chapter 2. Here, we further explore the meanings of reflective and reflexive practice in order to show the connectedness between these two approaches and also their distinctive features. Our focus moves to reflexive practice as a primary strategy for coaching ethically. As we have been doing throughout this book, we encourage you to reflect on your personal experiences and engage in a critical self-dialogue, in order to explore and comprehend further ethical issues in practice. This is because we are committed to the view that coaching with a good understanding of personal and professional values can open up new avenues for supporting clients effectively. Just as in Chapter 2, this chapter constitutes a metaphorical mirror, based on the premise that you are how you coach. In this chapter, however, you are invited to step through the looking glass in order to gain new perspectives for developing an ethical coaching practice.

The activities in this chapter are designed to help you enquire critically into established values and beliefs about coaching and the different contexts in which coaching takes place. We consider how we come to make decisions ethically, highlighting the need to continually bend our thinking back on itself (Webster, 2008). To understand this process further, we invite expert practitioners to share their own reflections on how approaches such as critical thinking and mindfulness can contribute to reflexive practice. These stories aim at shifting the discussion from principles to practice. Ultimately, we move beyond the complexity of definitions to explore how developing reflexivity guides attitude and behaviours in our coaching practice towards an ethical way of being.

## Key words

reflection, reflexivity, critical enquiry, critical thinking, mindfulness

## Introduction: the challenge of definition

This chapter builds on Chapter 2, where we explored a range of approaches to help develop reflection in our practice. Here, we further explore the meanings of reflection and reflexivity in order to show the connectedness between these two approaches but also their distinctive features. These two terms, which are frequently used interchangeably by practitioners and thinkers, are related to each other: reflection is the starting point of critical enquiry into one's coaching practice, while reflexivity, placed on the other end of the spectrum, is a more in-depth process of reviewing and revising ethical ways of being and relating (Cunliffe, 2009). There is a key common denominator between the two – critical enquiry – and this plays a vital role in developing and maintaining an ethical coaching practice. In this chapter, we seek to explore these concepts further in order to show how focusing on reflexivity and, in consequence, reflexive practice can help us enhance our ethical stance in our role as coaches. But let's start by reminding ourselves of what we mean by 'reflection'.

### Reflection

The term 'reflection' derives from the Latin verb *reflectere*, which literally means 'to bend back'. This compound word is made up of the prefix *re*, which means 'back', and the stem *flectere*, which means 'to bend'. This definition was first applied in the context of light itself bending back on reflective surfaces (Dallos and Stedmon, 2009: 1). It is therefore no surprise that, just as others before us, we have been drawn towards the metaphor of 'mirror', reflecting (quite literally) our own image back to us. This metaphor readily springs to mind as a way of exploring ourselves as coaches and the way in which we practise. Consider for a moment the hunter Narcissus who, according to Greek mythology, fell in love with his own reflection. Is this self-indulgence, as it may initially seem?

We agree with Gillie Bolton (2014) that we need to cast this view to one side. This is because reflection is purposeful, as it opens up 'explorative and expressive' avenues for critically evaluating ourselves within specific contexts (ibid.: 16–17). By extension, reflecting on our practice as coaches is 'not narcissistic because rather than falling in love with our own beauty, we bravely face the discomfort and uncertainty of attempting to perceive how things are' (ibid.: 17). Facing this kind of discomfort in our practice plays an important role in our journey towards ethical maturity. Thus, 'far from trapping us in a state of self-adulation, the discipline of engaging in reflective practice activities enables us to be self-critical, nurturing us in our professional development' (Dallos and Stedmon, 2009: 1). As coaches, we can use reflection within our daily practice to help us see ourselves more completely and to explore the ethical dilemmas we face from different perspectives, as through another person's eyes.

## Activity

Contemplating, daydreaming, guessing, intuiting, criticising, learning: all these states of mind (and more) might be evoked when we ask ourselves what we are doing in reflective moments (Dallos and Stedmon, 2009: 1).

- What are the first words that spring to your mind when you think of the phrase 'reflective moments'? Write a short list.
- Now think about how you understand the terms 'reflection' and 'reflective practice'.
- Write down a brief definition of both terms.

Reflection is a deeply subjective process that can have different meanings for different people. Ethical coaching requires you to stimulate your thinking about the meaning and process of reflection. In Chapter 2, we defined reflection as the in-depth consideration of events, situations, words and actions in order to achieve a deeper and clearer understanding of them and how you view yourself through them. The defining features of reflection are:

- Reflection can occur both 'in' action and 'on' action.
- Reflection can be enacted as both a lone activity, for example through reflective thought or writing, or with others, for example in supervision.
- Reflection in supervision creates a safe space in which the meanings associated with ethical moments can be encouraged and explored in order to open new perspectives.
- Reflection helps us to develop our self-awareness, because it enables us to explore our personal and professional values, ethical issues and the context in which we coach.
- Reflection helps us maintain an element of control of how we think about ethical issues.

## Reflexivity

The term 'reflexivity' is a more slippery concept than reflection. Different scholars, thinkers and practitioners appear to conjure it up in different ways. Michael Lynch (cited in Webster, 2008: 65) goes some way towards illustrating the array of definitions that exist. He identifies six categories of reflexivity: mechanical reflexivity, substantive reflexivity, methodological reflexivity, meta-theoretical reflexivity, interpretative reflexivity and ethno-methodological reflexivity. While explaining these terms is beyond the scope of this chapter, we are drawn to Webster's (2008) concept of confessional reflexivity, which is built on Lynch's definitions and supporting theories. We will discuss the concept of confessional reflexivity and its contribution to developing an ethical coaching practice later on in this chapter.

Despite variations of the term 'reflexivity', most definitions share a common theme, referring to a kind of conceptual 'bending back' of thought 'upon itself' (ibid.: 65). It is the emphasis on 'shifting our thinking about thinking', which differentiates reflexivity from reflection. While reflection involves in-depth consideration of situations and events, reflexivity focuses on in-depth reflection upon one's perspective, assumptions, beliefs and values (Bolton, 2014: xxiii). Reflexivity, therefore, is the process of reflecting upon the way in which we interpret events, situations, words and actions. In other words, reflexivity is reflection on the product of our reflection. On a similar note, Bolton (ibid.: 7) defined reflexivity as the act of 'finding strategies to question our own attitudes, theories-in-use, values, assumptions, prejudices and habitual actions; to understand our complex roles in relation to others'.

In a coaching context, the role of reflexivity is to problematise the 'self' and our identity, socially, politically and professionally. What do we mean by 'problematise the self' here? Basically, through reflexivity, we ask the question: who is the *me* who interprets this situation in this way and why? Let's explain this further. Imagine a nurse who is also a coach. What professional expertise will prevail when she is faced with ethical dilemmas or ethical moments of choice: that of the nurse or that of the coach? Furthermore, how do social, cultural, political, professional and other factors influence our thinking, choices and practice as coaches? Consider, for example, whether your political views or religious beliefs influence in any way your coaching practice. Upon reflection, you may think that your practice is unblemished and impartial when it comes to such norms. But how does this impartiality impact your work with coachees whose strong religious beliefs or notions of, say, honour and duty take precedence over self-actualisation and individual choice? If you have come across such clients, you may have experienced that the diverse *me* you bring into the relationship will determine the way you understand and deal with issues (Pelham, 2016: 99–101). In consequence, being reflexive in how we think about our coaching practice helps us to construct and sustain our professional identity as coaches, an issue that we will discuss further in Chapter 7, when we focus on coaching across professional contexts and boundaries. Reflexivity, therefore, allows us to consider not only who we are as coaches, but also who we are not. Bolton sums up this process beautifully by explaining reflexivity as:

> the near impossible adventure of making aspects of the self strange: attempting to stand back from belief and value systems and observe habitual ways of thinking and relating to others, structures of understanding ourselves, our relationship to the world, and the way that we are experienced and perceived and their assumptions about the way the world impinges on them. (2014: 8)

The defining features of reflexivity are:

- Reflexivity is a conscious and cognitive process.
- Reflexivity uses a combination of knowledge, theory and questioning on those ethical issues we encounter, in order to discover new or hidden perspectives and meanings.
- Reflexivity encourages us to question who we are in the coaching relationship, our approach to ethical issues, and our overall coaching practice.
- Reflexivity helps us to challenge and let go of deeply rooted assumptions, encouraging changes in attitude and behaviour.

**Pause for reflection**

Think of an experience in your coaching practice, training or supervision, where you were prompted to reflect on a moment of earlier reflection:

● How did you attempt to deconstruct the situation?
● What approaches were most enabling for you?

## The continuum between reflection and reflexivity

Having explained how we perceive reflection and reflexivity, it is fair to say that we see both these approaches as parts of a spectrum. As depicted in Figure 6.1, reflection is situated on one side of the spectrum and reflexivity on the other. Think of a continuum, or rather a chain of interconnectivity. This process begins by introducing reflection into our day-to-day practice. Reflection can be viewed as the in-depth consideration of events, situations, words and actions. This, we suggest, is a starting point for ethical coaching, which unfolds into reflexivity, a point when we become more adept at continually bending our thinking back on itself – and thus reflecting on it – as we navigate ethical moments in our practice.

Establishing a commitment to reflection enables us to critically assess our reaction to situations, words and actions. In consequence, this allows us to gain a richer understanding of our personal and professional values. When we start to reflect back critically on our reactions

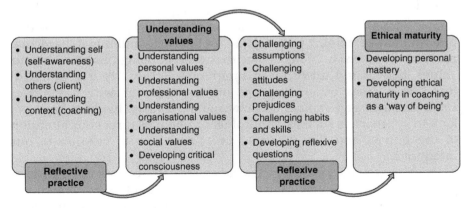

**Figure 6.1**   The reflexivity chain for ethical coaching

in the coaching relationship – rather than simply consciously acknowledging such reaction – we reach a tipping point. This is where the process of reflexivity begins. This is not a linear process; rather, it is the act of reflective and reflexive practice ebbing and flowing. The challenge lies in learning to recognise the difference between the two processes, both of which have the potential of helping us to enhance our ethical maturity. Take a few minutes to consider whether you employ any or both approaches in your coaching practice.

## Reflexivity in coaching

Reflection and reflexivity are each considered 'moral and principled practices based upon ethical values' (Bolton, 2014: 21). Together, they form the foundations for ethical practice. Hence, they are congruent with ethical coaching. The terms 'reflective practice', which entails reflection, and 'reflexive practice', which is premised on reflexivity, are often used interchangeably in the literature, as well as in practice, to describe the act of critically considering one's actions as a practitioner. In this section, we argue that reflexive practice, which encourages in-depth reflection on one's perspectives, assumptions, values and beliefs, can be more effective in facilitating an ethical coaching practice. To be sure, reflective practice, which denotes a mere critical stance towards events, situations, words and actions, is an integral part of an ethical coaching practice. But, as we have seen, reflexive practice can offer richer perspectives for developing and maintaining ethical coaching in practice.

As well as the development of our own reflexivity, we cannot ignore one of the fundamental roles of the coach, which is to facilitate reflexive agency in others, in order to help coachees to make conscious choices in every interaction. Schön (1984: 60) suggests that practitioners in helping professions can too easily fall into a 'parochial narrowness of vision'. This means that we risk being blinkered by our values, beliefs and unwitting assumptions. Reflexivity is a powerful tool that enables us to challenge our assumptions with a sense of self-awareness and critical consciousness. Against this backdrop, we look to approaches such as mindfulness to help us direct our attention to the impact and the outcomes of our actions in relation to our intentions.

Despite growing evidence that advocates the benefits of reflexive practice (see, for instance, Wright, 2012; Bolton, 2014), some arguments against it still prevail. Such arguments are, in our view, less compelling. For example, Copeland et al. (1993) point to lack of time as a barrier to reflexivity. We live in an era of exponential change and complexity that demands the ability to adapt to ongoing change. In consequence, we tend to spend less and less time reflecting on our practise, replacing reflexivity with ethical idealism, that is, taking for granted that we practise ethically because our intentions are ethical. Paradoxically, the issue of lack of time increases the urgency for reflective and reflexive thinking and practice, both for the coach and the coachee. In the sections that follow we seek to demonstrate that reflexive thinking and practice are essential components of ethical coaching. This is because, far from trapping us in self-adulation, reflective and reflexive practices help us to harness the potential to be self-critical and, ultimately, more ethical in every coaching interaction. To illuminate this, we invite the reflections of coaches who share their stories of how they built their reflexive practice.

## From principles to practice: strategies for building reflexive practice

In this section, we move beyond definition and theoretical perspectives to explore some key strategies and principles for building reflexivity in our coaching practice. We begin with the notion that ethical coaching is about having ethical conversations. In Chapter 2, we explored the tool of questions. Bolton (2014: 4) reminds us that Einstein was successful partly because he constantly asked questions with seemingly obvious answers – why? what? how? Good questions enable reflexivity. Spending time with other coaches, for instance, in a supervisory context, creates a safe space in which to raise questions about ethical moments at a distance and to explore these within the coaching relationship and the context in which the coaching takes place. The bracketing of judgements and new meaning-making that ensues from such practice enables coaches to see their own idiosyncratic interpretations as just another perspective (Cox, 2013). In this way the nature of truth becomes perspectival, too.

There is plentiful guidance on how to formulate and ask good questions, some of which we discussed in Chapter 2. In this chapter, we make particular use of reflexive questions, which seek to take apart assumptions and enable us to rethink previously accepted structures and relationships. In essence, reflexive questioning can offer insights into the thoughts and motives of people and organisations (Bolton, 2014: 24). Against this backdrop, we are drawn to Webster's concept of 'confessional reflexivity': 'the act of continually bending one's own conceptual practice back upon itself, by employing the "virtuous" mechanisms of introspection and avowal to produce the truth of certain claims, all within a discursive field saturated by specific power relations' (2008: 71). This kind of reflexivity is premised on the use of reflexive questions. In order to illuminate the value of confessional reflexivity, expert coaching practitioners share their reflections on building reflexivity in their coaching practice. Their tales take the format of confessional reflexivity. Each tale is told through a lens of coaching that they feel is significant in supporting reflexive coaching practice, forming foundations for bridging theory and practice.

## Critical thinking

We introduced principles of critical thinking in Chapter 2. Critical thinking is often mentioned in the literature as a fundamental activity for reflexive practice (Wright, 2012; Cox, 2013: 90; Bolton, 2014). Few authors mention reflexive practice and critical thinking as separate activities (Price, 2004; Jones-Devitt and Smith, 2007). Concurring with Brockbank and McGill (2006), we have also found that when we become critical thinkers we develop greater awareness of the assumptions under which we think and act. Critically, as coaches we become more attentive to the context in which the ideas that inform our practice were generated, as well as the influence of our values and beliefs on these ideas. Fundamentally, just like coaching, critical thinking is a learning process, as Stella Jones-Devitt appositely shows below.

## From principles to practice: practitioner's reflection

### Stella Jones-Devitt, Head of Research, Evaluation and Student Engagement, Sheffield Hallam University

When I worked in public health as a health promotion specialist, I came across 'Ann', who is presented in the following story. After reading it, see if you can determine why I responded in the ways I did, and how and why I reconsidered my approach, using a critical thinking process (Paul and Elder, 2005) to engage more reflexively.

Ann is a drug rehabilitation worker in the voluntary sector working with vulnerable people. She officially works 30 hours per week, yet really enjoys her job and does 50–60 hours on a regular basis. Until recently, Ann thrived on being busy, priding herself on her capacity for hard work. Yet, she began to experience intermittent chest pain and tiredness, for which she sought the GP's advice. At the time, Ann lived with her daughter, Vicky, who was about to leave home for university. Because of her very busy working life, Ann did not have many other friends outside of work, so she confided to her GP that she felt a bit isolated at times. The GP referred Ann to me to help her with her lifestyle problems, in light of finding no obvious physical issues.

In the initial meeting I used coaching principles to explore what I considered to be the underpinning issues; namely social isolation and fear of being more alone when her daughter had gone. I felt that the meeting went really well, as we drew up an action plan with attendant goals that appeared to meet Ann's needs. One of them was that she would join the gym, as a way to meet more people. We agreed to meet one month later to assess progress. I felt it was a job well done!

Ann turned up on time at the follow-up meeting and told me that she was enjoying the gym but her chest pains were still prevalent along with breathlessness. I proceeded to question Ann to ascertain if she was receiving the right level of supervision in the gym, as I assumed that she was possibly working too hard and could be experiencing exercise-induced asthma or even angina. Without warning, Ann burst into tears and confessed that her real problem was her guilt over not being able to help one of her clients to the best of her abilities owing to organisational imperatives. This had been continuing for some time and Ann was at a loss to know what to do next: she felt powerless. As a result, she was experiencing acute anxiety symptoms. I had got it completely wrong.

I retraced my approach by applying the *Critical Thinking Competency Standards* devised by Paul and Elder (2005). This highlighted some of the key issues regarding the nature of assumptions and presuppositions or inferences, that is, taken-for-granted beliefs. They suggest that all thinking can only be judged as sound, or otherwise, dependent on the initial assumptions underpinning the original thoughts. I found this very helpful. I had assumed that Ann was lonely and that this was the underpinning cause, especially as her daughter was leaving home. Given this spurious starting point, I had then gone on to infer the wrong actions that I thought would 'fix' the problem. Loneliness was not Ann's problem as my first assumption suggested. If I had allowed her the time and space to examine her own context – without my need to rush to find over-simplified solutions in a judgemental manner, she might have been able to explore her work-related anxiety at an earlier point.

I had taken up the assumed professional stereotypes of my role without ever really fully exploring the wider context of Ann's life. As a key learning point from this example, I now ask myself the following questions in order to avoid making similar mistakes:

- What stereotyping surrounds my professional assumptions, if any?
- Where do these views come from?
- Are they helpful in understanding the context of others and in supporting them to find possible solutions?

When we become accomplished critical thinkers, we develop an enhanced awareness of the assumptions that enter the coaching relationship with us, and that influence who we are as a coach and the way we act in ethical moments of choice. Becoming more mindful of these assumptions will help us mobilise our critical thinking mechanism, in an effort to become more ethical practitioners.

## Mindfulness

Holding its roots in Buddhist teaching, mindfulness is an invaluable approach to developing ethical practice. In one of the most widely used quotations, Jon Kabat-Zinn (1994: 4) defines mindfulness as: 'paying attention in a particular way: on purpose, in the present moment, and non-judgementally'. Within the context of coaching, we perceive mindfulness as simply focusing in the present moment, noticing, and being consciously aware of what is taking place and what is not taking place; what is said and what is not said; what is felt and what is not felt. Mindfulness, therefore, 'reflects a particular state of consciousness, typified by relaxed, non-judgemental awareness of moment-by-moment experience' (Spence, 2015: 20). Below, Christian van Nieuwerburgh shares his experience of how he has incorporated mindfulness in his coaching practice.

### From principles to practice: practitioner's reflection

Christian van Nieuwerburgh, Associate Professor of Coaching, Henley Business School

I enjoy coaching. It's become an important part of what I do and who I am. I have developed as a professional and a person through being coached, coaching others and reflecting on my own practice.

For me, reflexivity starts from noticing. Often, I used to miss things. Sometimes I would not notice something very important. And on a few occasions, I would notice something and pretend to myself I hadn't.

With experience I have become better at not missing things. I trained myself to notice more within coaching conversations. I built in time for reflection before and after my coaching sessions: just quiet time – before the session, to allow my mind to settle; and after the session, to allow my mind to reflect. This helps me to notice more, because I would be alert during the sessions. In that quiet reflection after the session, I ask myself three questions: What did I notice during that session? What did I notice about my coachee? And what did I notice about myself?

If I look at some of my notes from recent coaching conversations, I see the following scribbles in relation to the session: 'Noticed that the session was over quickly' … 'Noticed that the session felt very formal – as if I was sitting in on an interview'. In relation to the coachee, over the last year, I've jotted these things down: 'Noticed that she smiled sarcastically when I asked her what she'd like to get out of the coaching session' … 'Noticed that **** looked down a lot' … 'Noticed that he was demanding things of me' … 'Noticed that she wanted my approval'. Finally, in relation to myself – I'd rather not share what's in my journal. It's very personal. So this is how I try to make sure that I notice important things that occur during coaching conversations. As you can see, I write down my reflections. Often these generate the topics that I take to coaching supervision.

And you may have spotted that I have left 'noticing something and pretending I hadn't' till last. Often our minds try to un-notice discordant thoughts. So I always try to stay alert to fleeting thoughts or insights. I try to attend to feelings of discomfort or guilt. These little nudges feel like myself trying to raise my own awareness about something. I'm simply trying to notice what I'm saying to myself. I listen harder than I used to.

Beyond coaching, mindfulness-based approaches to medicine, psychology, neuroscience, healthcare, education, business leadership and other disciplines have become increasingly common (Williams and Kabat-Zinn, 2013). The space that mindfulness affords for noticing is conducive to reflection on ethical issues in our coaching practice. In this respect, we agree with Spence (2015: 20), who points out that: 'an important consequence of cultivating this wakeful, open stated mind is that one becomes more sensitive to important aspects of self (e.g. values, interest, institutions), which represent a form of intrapersonal attunement'. We would encourage you, therefore, to consider the possibility of incorporating mindfulness in your practice.

## Pause for reflection

- How relevant do you think mindfulness is to how you approach ethical moments in coaching?
- How do (or will) you use mindfulness to enhance your reflexivity?

## Harvesting emotional intelligence

Both practices of critical thinking and mindfulness contribute towards harvesting emotional intelligence in coaching. Emotional intelligence (EI) is increasingly viewed as a key ingredient for developing effective relationships in helping professions such as coaching, and more widely in leadership and management. Since Daniel Goleman (1995, 2001) popularised the concept of emotional intelligence in the 1990s, it has become increasingly accepted as part of the language used within the context of relational concepts such as coaching. It thus holds relevance for building reflexivity in our practice. Although a deeper exploration of emotional intelligence is beyond the scope of this book, we could not resist but show the significance of its connection with reflexive practice.

The relevance of emotional intelligence reaches beyond the coaching interaction itself, to the wider coaching contexts that we go on to explore further in Part III. Like reflexivity, the underlying assumption of emotional intelligence is that the individual is always in the process of 'becoming', rather than having a fixed and determined level of emotional intelligence (Stokes, 2014). Thus, both reflexivity and emotional intelligence share the assumption that the coach and coachee are always in the process of 'becoming', learning and developing through reflection on experiences, beliefs, values and principles. According to van Nieuwerburgh (2014), being consciously aware of and reflecting on your principles and values will enable you to recognise and approach ethical issues as they arise with confidence and competence, enhancing emotional intelligence.

## Conclusion

It is important to have a moral compass to guide us in how we make choices and take decisions in our coaching practice (Law et al., 2007: 196). Our values, alongside technical knowledge and expertise, can take the role of such a compass. These, however, are rarely challenged and questioned (Bolton, 2014: 22). Senge (2006) theorised the inevitable gap between our vision for coaching (that is, our espoused values) and our practice (the reality of everyday practice) as holding creative tensions that are always pulling towards the other. Have you experienced any such tensions?

David Clutterbuck (2013) argues that 'unethical and illegal behaviour in organisations rarely happens because people, as individuals or a group of people, set out to do wrong. Rather it starts with small breeches and gradually grows in scope and scale.' This is why we see reflexivity as an integral part of an ethical coaching practice. To be truly reflexive, it is first necessary for us to step outside of our self. We need to be prepared to share our experiences with others, and to challenge our assumptions and beliefs. Together, reflective and reflexive practices enable us to understand our values, our beliefs and ethical issues that emerge in our coaching practice. In this way, ethical moments become landmarks on our coaching journey. Just like so many famous landmarks across the world – such as Nelson's Column in London, the Arc de Triomphe in Paris, or the Statue of Liberty in New York – we may revisit them over time and discover new meaning and connections.

Coaching, which takes place in increasingly complex and changing contexts, is dependent on this kind of reflexive practice. Through reflexivity, we develop the kind of self-awareness and understanding that Senge (2006: 7) so beautifully articulates as our 'personal mastery'. He suggests that 'people with a high level of personal mastery are able to constantly realize the results that matter most deeply to them'. In effect, this means approaching our practice, as coaches, just as an artist would approach a work of art. Thinking about our thinking, then, becomes the way we do coaching. We hope that you will find the process of embedding reflexivity in your practice as enjoyable as we do. The more you build it into your practice, the more natural it becomes. Importantly, becoming reflexive in your thinking is central to becoming an ethical coaching practitioner. This is a complex artistry to master but one that is worth the effort.

## Chapter summary

- Reflection and reflexivity are essential components of an ethical practice.
- Despite variations, most definitions of reflexivity share a common theme, referring to a kind of conceptual 'bending back' of thought 'upon itself' (Webster, 2008: 65).
- Exposure to ethical issues in practice, combined with conscious reflection on our response to them, builds reflexivity.
- There is no single framework for ethical coaching, due to competing values and contexts.
- To be truly reflexive we need first to step outside our self, share our experiences with others, and be prepared to challenge our assumptions and beliefs.

## Suggestions for further reading

For a practical application of developing reflective and reflective coaching practice and research, we recommend:
Bolton, G. (2014) *Reflective Practice: Writing and Professional Development.* 4th edn. London: Sage Publishing.

And the classic text:
Schön, D.A. (1984) *The Reflective Practitioner: How Professionals Think in Action.* New York: Basic Books.

For a deeper exploration on how we think about thinking, we recommend:
Webster, J. (2008) 'Establishing the "truth" of the matter: Confessional reflexivity as introspection and avowal', *Psychology and Society*, 1(1): 65–76.

If you wish to read an engaging, thought-provoking and humorous text on how the mindful brain 'exercises', and which bridges science and practical guidance to show how mindfulness can benefit us all, consider the following:
Wax, R. (2006) *A Mindfulness Guide for the Frazzled.* London: Penguin.

For a deeper exploration of how mindfulness can build reflexivity in coaching, we suggest:
Hall, L. (2013) *Mindful Coaching: How Mindfulness Can Transform Coaching Practice.* London: Kogan Page.

# 7

# Coaching across Professional Boundaries and Contexts

## Chapter aims

- To unravel key ethical issues for coaching across professional contexts.
- To explore the nuances of different professional contexts by asking three important questions that carry ethical connotations: *Who* are we in the coaching relationship? *Where* are we when we coach? And *how* do we coach?
- To suggest ways in which coaches can learn individually and collectively from coaching across professional contexts and their boundaries, while being able to distinguish the context-specific ethical issues that may emerge in the coaching practice.

## Chapter overview

Coaching is a complex and multifaceted phenomenon that, with the passage of time, has been applied across increasingly diverse professional contexts. In this chapter, we underline the importance of understanding the context in which we coach, as a key factor for an ethical coaching practice. We discuss ethical implications that are significant for coaching in different professional contexts, from a range of professional and theoretical perspectives. Throughout the chapter, we encourage you to engage in a critical self-dialogue, as we address the following questions: *Who* are you when you coach? *Where* are you when you coach?

*How* do you coach? The *who* question seeks to explore the context of your professional background and the implications of this. The *where* question addresses the institutional or organisational context in which you coach. And the *how* question refers to the conceptual and theoretical background of your preferred style of coaching. We illuminate some key ethical issues that are context-specific and discuss some underpinning principles that can be applied to coaching across professional contexts, in order to enhance an ethical coaching practice. Our aim is to show that the practice of ethical coaching entails having conscious understanding of the boundaries between the professional contexts where coaching takes place. This chapter forms the backdrop to Part III of the book, where we explore in greater depth specific coaching contexts and the primary ethical issues that may arise in them.

## Key words

professional background, professional contexts, genres, models, approaches

## Introduction: coaching – one word, two syllables, many contexts

Coaches offer their services in a variety of distinct contexts. A life coach, for example, might also work in a business context, helping employees to enhance their performance. As such, the very nature of coaching across diverse professional contexts is complex. This complexity carries ethical implications. Imagine for a moment the variations in settings such as business, sports, education and health, to name just a few. Before we embark on an exploration of ethical issues that arise when we coach across professional contexts, we first need to consider the importance of definition. As we discussed earlier in the book, a plethora of definitions exist to describe coaching. Some of these are in agreement, while others differ substantially (Brockbank and McGill, 2006: 1). Garvey (2004: 6–8) expresses the thought-provoking view that, while the term we use to denote coaching matters, it is the meaning we place on the term that matters more. This is important in our discussion because, in order to understand and deal with ethical issues that emerge in coaching, we must be clear regarding the meaning we apply to coaching in the different contexts it takes place.

So, what do we mean by 'context' here? We use the term 'context' to refer primarily to the professional settings in which coaching takes place. These include the corporate world, healthcare, education, and sports, amongst others. We also include in this category what in Cox et al. (2014) is referred to as *applied* contexts or *genres*. These are particular styles of coaching that can be used in a variety of professional settings, such as performance coaching, career coaching, life coaching, etc. Regardless of the historical narrative of coaching, the context in which we coach will determine our perception(s) of the coaching practice, the values and beliefs we bring into it, and the ethical issues that may arise in it. In consequence, in order to understand values and ethics in coaching, we must first seek to appreciate the context in which we coach. We argue that understanding context is crucial for ethical coaching, as adopting a 'one-size-fits-all' approach does not achieve the best results, nor does it guarantee high ethical standards.

To help you reflect on the significance of having a clear understanding of the diverse coaching contexts in which you might operate, in the following sections we will ask you three important questions that carry ethical implications: Who are you when you coach? Where are you when you coach? And how do you coach? Our hope is to show that, while coaches often practise coaching in different roles and settings, it is important to be aware of the distinct nuances of these roles and settings in order to promote an ethical coaching practice. In other words, it is significant to be able to discern the boundaries between different roles and contexts where coaching is used as an approach. Understanding these boundaries makes us more adept at identifying and dealing with the range of ethical issues that arise in our day-to-day practice. As we go on to explore the ethical questions of who, where and how, we would like you to keep in mind that: 'you are not putting together a puzzle whose picture you already know. You are constructing a picture that takes shape as you collect and examine the parts' (Bogdan and Biklen, 2006: 6). So, let's start with the first question.

---

**Pause for reflection:**
**who are you when you coach?**

Take a few minutes to consider the following questions:

- What is your professional background?
- How do you see yourself as a coach?
- How do you define your professional identity as a coach?

---

## Who are you when you coach?

As we already discussed in Chapters 2 and 4, consciously reflecting on the professional background you bring into your coaching, in order to understand who you are as a coach, is the golden thread that runs through an ethical coaching practice. Reflecting on the above question may lead to the realisation that your professional identity is not fixed. Rather, you continually shape and develop it, consciously and unconsciously, according to your understanding of your *self* and your *context* (Proctor, 2014). Understanding, therefore, who you are as a coach will help you address a follow-up question: Who are you in the coaching relationship? This is also a significant question to ask, as the answer to it will influence *where* and *how* you coach, which we will discuss in the following sections. But, let's go back to the 'who' question. Who are you in the coaching relationship: a professional coach? a manager who coaches? a psychotherapist who coaches? Fundamentally, understanding your professional *self*, and thus who you are in the coaching relationship, determines the quality of the coaching you offer but also its boundaries. The professional background you bring into coaching, or, rather, your professional identity, will have implications on how you view and practise coaching.

In his wonderful book entitled *Coaching across Cultures*, Rosinski (2003: 105) posed a powerful question that is pertinent in our discussion: 'How do you define your identity and what is your purpose in life?' Rosinsky identified some distinct types of professional identity – namely, Being, Doing, Individualistic and Collectivistic – that are culturally dependent. Developing an appreciation of distinct professional identities in coaching can enrich our understanding of our own identity as a coach, as well as our preferences, strengths, limitations and boundaries in our practice. The professional background we bring into our coaching, therefore, shapes our professional identity as a coach. To illuminate this observation with an example, we reflect on our own professional backgrounds. As the three authors of this book, we began the collective process of writing it from three unique professional backgrounds: Ioanna as an academic in a business school, Rachel with a clinical background in nursing, and Christiana as a psychologist. Each of our professional backgrounds influences our views on coaching and, by extension, how we approached the views expressed in this book, in ways that we cannot ignore.

So, how might you consider the ethical issues that arise as a result of your professional background and identity? Importantly, how might you deal with potential boundaries and limitations in your practice? If, for example, you are a practising coach with a background in counselling or nursing, are these roles competing or complementary? Are there any ethical issues that may arise from practising coaching with a distinct professional background? To explore these questions further, we offer a comparison between two related disciplines – coaching and psychotherapy. Despite clear distinctions, coaching and psychotherapy share remarkable similarities. We use Biswas-Diener's (2009) seminal article to summarise the key differences and similarities between the two disciplines, as shown below.

---

Differences between coaching and psychotherapy:

- Coaching is future-orientated, unlike psychotherapy, which tends to cast its gaze backwards.
- A coach assumes the role of the facilitator who assists clients to achieve desirable changes that are self-initiated, while a therapist is expected to have a thorough understanding of the client's psychological state.
- Coaching attracts clients who wish to focus on improving performance in specific areas of life. Conversely, therapy is primarily concerned with the aetiology (cause) and then improvement of a person's psychopathology.
- Coaching does not address mental health issues whereas therapy starts from the point that something is not going well in the life of the client and it needs to be addressed and worked through in order for the client to experience relief.

Similarities between coaching and psychotherapy:

- Both place emphasis on the formation of a partnership whose main goal is change, by means of client growth and development.
- Both aim to help the client address and overcome potential challenges that may have a negative impact on her quality of life.
- Both make use of psychotherapeutic approaches, such as cognitive, behavioural and solution-focused techniques.

---

It becomes apparent that the practices of coaching and psychotherapy have a great deal in common, especially in relation to style and approaches used (de Haan, 2008). The primary difference lies in the intention of the intervention: while coaching is future-orientated and the coachee's emotions matter in so far as they restrict or enable the achievement of specific goals, therapy centres on the internal world of the client, with a particular focus on changing some aspects in it that may be problematic for the individual (Pelham, 2016). This key distinction in intention constitutes the boundary between the professional contexts of coaching and psychotherapy. Crossing it, as a coach, 'would be exploring the coachee's internal world further than is necessary to achieve their coaching goal' (ibid.: 39). Is this ethical?

## Story from practice

Raj is a coach with a background in psychotherapy, who works with young adults. He recently started to coach Nita, who is not happy in her current job but is unsure of what she wishes to do in the future, professionally. During the first few sessions, Raj begins to sense that Nita is showing signs of depression and anxiety. While at first he attributes those to Nita's unhappiness at work, Raj begins to realise that some deeply rooted personal issues are interfering with Nita's progress in coaching. Eventually, Nita reveals to Raj that, in order to cope with the work pressure and other personal issues, she has begun to consume excessive quantities of alcohol, even during work hours. It is obvious that Nita is showing signs of a mental condition that, as an issue, is beyond Raj's professional remit as a coach.

Questions to consider:

- How should Raj continue working with Nita?
- Should he continue working with Nita?
- What can Raj do to ensure Nita's needs are met?
- How might Raj avoid such ethical pitfalls in the future?

The surfacing of mental health problems in coaching is not uncommon. The coach's task is to support the development of the client. Yet, it is important to understand the fine line between coaching and therapy. While Raj has a background in psychotherapy, he needs to be consciously aware of the remit and boundaries of coaching, which is not intended to address mental health problems – or, indeed, the issue of potential alcohol dependence. As such, even with a background in psychotherapy, Raj needs to explicitly delineate the boundaries of coaching, and refer Nita to an appropriate mental health professional for the personal issues that she is facing. This does not mean that Raj ought to terminate the coaching process. Raj and Nita might agree that while the latter will seek a therapist to explore her personal life issues, she can continue working with Raj on career-related concerns (Thomson, 2014: 49, 64). Overall, just like any coaching professional, a coach with professional expertise in other disciplines can anticipate such ethical dilemmas by clearly explicating at the outset of the coaching relationship the professional boundaries of her role as a coach. The contracting stage offers the ideal opportunity to do this.

This story from practice shows how important professional boundary management is for an ethical coaching practice. As such, it brings us back to the significance of understanding *who* you are when you coach. Irrespective of whether you are a professional coach or a coach with a background in therapy or in any other helping profession, we encourage you to consciously reflect on the boundaries between professional backgrounds and professional identities when you practise coaching. To facilitate this process of reflection, we invite you to consider the question: how does the professional context in which you coach influence your coaching practice? To answer this question, you need to consider the context, that is, *where* you coach.

## Where are you when you coach?
## Coaching across professional contexts

In this section we consider the ways in which the professional contexts in which we coach can influence how we practise coaching. By 'professional contexts' we mean the setting in which coaching takes place, such as a corporate setting or the public sector. We also mean the type or genre of coaching that we practise. You may, for instance, be a career coach in a university or a life coach running your own business. These different settings and genres are indicative of the variety of professional contexts in which you may practise coaching. While the aims of coaching may be similar, the practical application of it will differ according to the context (Bachkirova et al., 2014: 1), and this engenders several ethical issues.

---

**Pause for reflection:**
**where are you when you coach?**

Take a few minutes to consider the following questions:

- What are the professional contexts in which you practise coaching?
- What genres of coaching do you practise?
- What factors influence your choice of professional contexts and genres?

---

As we have seen, while there might be coaches who only practise in a particular context – for example, in business – others may find themselves navigating from one context to another. This has ethical implications, as different professional contexts are complex systems that impose their own institutional imperatives, which can interfere with our professional values. Having conscious understanding of the subtleties of these diverse contexts will enable you to anticipate and deal with several context-specific issues that may arise. To clarify, we are not arguing against coaching across professional contexts. But building and sustaining an ethical coaching practice, as we move from context to context, requires us to challenge context-specific assumptions – our own and those of others. For example, should executive coaching or performance coaching deal with personal life issues? What if, in consequence of business coaching, the coachee realises that she is in the wrong job and decides to leave the organisation? Should the business coach assist her in this decision?

These context-specific ethical issues that may arise in coaching show that we cannot treat the individual as anything else but as a whole – a complex system with capabilities and limitations that are interconnected. Coaching across professional contexts confers the opportunity to keep reflecting on this issue in order to offer the most ethical coaching possible. It also means, however, that, in order to treat the individual as a whole, we must be able to discern the nuances of professional contexts and genres. The tools we use and the models we employ when working with coachees across professional contexts has a role to play in this. Let's explore this further.

## How do you coach? Coaching theories and models in context

A study by the Work Foundation and School of Coaching drew attention to an alarming lack of knowledge on what theoretical perspectives and models we base our coaching practice on (Dembkowski and Eldridge, 2004). Specifically, the findings revealed that around 33 per cent of coaches did not know which model they were using; 34 per cent used the well-established GROW model, while the remaining 33 per cent of coaches used a variety of models and theoretical approaches, although it is not certain whether they could actually identify and name all of them. We invite you to consider the ethical implications of these findings. What is your immediate response? Do you know which approaches and models you use in your coaching practice? Do you prefer a specific one or do you opt for a mixture? How might a combination of models and approaches enhance or hamper your coaching practice?

### Pause for reflection: how do you coach?

Take a few minutes to reflect on the following questions:

- How did you come to coach how you coach?
- In what ways does the organisational culture in which you practise influence how you choose to coach?

The writing of this chapter stimulated our own reflections on these questions. Like several other coaches, our initial introduction to the coaching practice was through the GROW model, which was popularised by John Whitmore (2002). The GROW model is a simple yet powerful framework that facilitates a simple structure of coaching sessions. Still, it is not sufficient to enable us to deal with the variety of complex issues that we encounter in coaching. Indeed, today, coaches are trained in an elaborate range of theoretical approaches and coaching models (see, for instance, Cox et al., 2014). The more we understand and know how to use them, the more flexibility we will have in our coaching practice. Used well, these models offer the necessary structure from which to build the relationship.

Opening our senses to several coaching approaches and models allows us to develop a connectivity between our earlier experiences of who we are when we coach and the professional contexts in which we may coach. For example, the gestalt approach to coaching (Latner, 2000) emphasises the need for the coach's awareness in the moment and thus makes a powerful contribution to developing the kind of self-awareness and critical-consciousness that supports the development of the coach (and the coachee). Learning from different coaching models and theoretical approaches facilitates the process of navigating ethical issues across the complex contexts in which coaching takes place. There is no single model that has all the answers to the ethical challenges you may face, as a coach. Yet each one, at some time, in some way, may have a role to play. By developing an understanding of each model's commonalities and distinct features, you can make conscious decisions about the most effective approach for your coaching, according to the context in which you coach and the ethical dilemmas that might emerge in your practice.

## Boundaries between professional contexts: from blurriness to clarity

As outlined earlier, one of the purposes of this chapter is to explore the landscape for coaching across professional boundaries and contexts. We argued that, when we are clear about the nuances of who, where and how, we become more dexterous in anticipating and dealing with ethical issues that arise in specific professional contexts. We hope that this resonates with some of the unique aspects that you may have observed or experienced about coaching in particular professional contexts, just as you may have reflected on some similarities. It is important to be able to understand the distinct features of specific professional contexts where coaching takes place, in order to determine what the best approach is for the coach. Van Nieuwerburgh's (2015: 253–4) recent investigation on this matter illuminates some of the key distinct features and similarities between professional contexts, as shown below.

---

Unique features about coaching in specific professional contexts:

- Organisations and contexts have different hierarchical structures.
- Some key concerns seem to be more prevalent in some organisations than others.
- The extent to which return on investment is measured varies.
- Career paths can be more complex in some organisations than in others.
- The relative priority given to the well-being of staff can be variable.
- Some contexts give more importance to coaching supervision.
- The extent to which coaching is used to support performance management varies between contexts.
- In some professional contexts, there seems to be more pressure to adopt more directive approaches to coaching.

At the same time, some themes emerge as relatively consistent across contexts:

- Broadly speaking, senior leaders seem to prefer being coached by external executive coaches.
- Generally, middle managers and other staff are coached by internal coaches.
- External coaches have a role in supporting internal coaches.
- Despite the argument that coaches need not be experts in the topic of the coaching conversations, professionals, on the whole, see coaches with relevant industry experience as more credible.
- A strong theme is recognition of the importance of evaluation and assessment of the efficiency of the coaching interventions.
- There seems to be broad agreement on the need for high-level, quality-assured training of coaches.
- It emerges that many people recognise that there is no 'one-size-fits-all' solution when it comes to coaching.
- It is agreed that coaching is about the conversation, and not only that, it is about the quality of the conversation.
- There seems to be consistent interest in 'coaching cultures', with the view that coaching interventions can lead to such cultures.

---

As we become more seasoned in our coaching practice, it is as though we develop a toolbox that, over time, fills with theories, knowledge, models and, of course, learning from lived experiences. Dealing with ethical issues effectively involves using the best combination of tools according to the coaching context. When we ask ourselves who we are when we coach, where we are when we coach, and how we coach, we eliminate the blurriness of the boundaries between professional backgrounds and contexts. Instead, we become more akin to holding a kaleidoscope, where boundaries are clearly demarcated with distinct, vivid colours.

We suggest that critically reflecting on these three questions – *who* we are when we coach (what is our professional background?), *where* we are when we coach (what is the setting or genre of coaching?), and *how* we coach (what models and approaches do we use?) – means that we become more able to anticipate and deal with ethical issues across professional contexts with competence and confidence. As we become more able to align these three dimensions of ethical practice, we can see the values and ethics in our coaching more clearly.

## Coaching ethically across professional boundaries and contexts

In this chapter, we argued that an ethical coaching practice is contingent upon our ability to understand the nuanced boundaries between professional backgrounds and contexts. Understanding and critically reflecting on our professional identity, the settings in which we practise, and the theoretical approaches and models that we use to practise enables us to deal with ethical issues that arise as part of these nuances more effectively. Importantly, being able to distinguish between these nuances allows us to form a clear picture of all the distinct parts that make up the coaching practice. To elaborate on this view, we make use of a fable 'often referred to, seldom known' that Mintzberg et al. (2008: 2) remind us of. This is 'The Blind Men and the Elephant' by John Godfrey Saxe (1816–87), from which we draw on the following lines:

> It was six men from Indostan
>
> To learning much inclined,
>
> Who went to see the Elephant
>
> (Though each of them was blind),
>
> That each by observation
>
> Might satisfy his mind.

Those blind men investigated a different part of the elephant each and, as a result, they disagreed about the nature of the beast – just as we may disagree about the nature of coaching and the ethical issues that arise in it.

Understanding the nature of the different professional coaching contexts and the ethical issues that arise in them can be a bit like that. The challenge is to integrate ethical thinking in meaningful ways in coaching practice, education and research. To do so, we must be consciously mindful of the diverse coaching backgrounds, contexts, genres, models and theories. Each has a role to play in developing and maintaining an ethical coaching practice:

And so these men from Indostan

Disputed loud and long,

Each in his own opinion

Exceeding stiff and strong,

Though each was partly in the right,

And all were in the wrong!

Ethical coaching is somewhat like this; ethical issues that arise are perspectival. It is important to take a close-up view of every part of our coaching practice, in order to ensure high ethical standards. Having done this, we then need to stand back and observe the coaching context as a whole. This is because ethical coaching is not simply a mixture of skills and competencies that are applicable in distinct settings; rather, it is a set of attributes which emerge from commitment to understanding our values and ethics in context. It is the synthesis of all of these views that brings the best results for coaching across boundaries and contexts. While this can be a complex landscape, stepping back to explore coaching in this way provides clarity and helps to build an ethical coaching practice. In short, it allows us to see clearly the whole elephant, just as we discovered through the poem above.

> ## Pause for reflection
>
> - How do you feel when you read this chapter? What resonates with you?
> - How do you feel about coaching across boundaries and contexts?
> - To what extent do your personal and professional values help or hinder your choices for how you coach in different contexts?
> - How is your view of how you coach challenged or enriched by what you read?

## Conclusion

It is important to explore ethical issues in the context of who we are as coaches, where we practise as coaches and how we practise. Mintzberg et al.'s

(2008) book *Strategy Safari* reminds us of the importance of ensuring that multiple perspectives are interwoven into coaching. The real point is that no individual perspective is wrong. We simply need to stand back and see the whole. As Daloz (1999: 42) appositely put it, 'it is the people not the stages, the moving picture not the snapshots, that should command our attention'. This is particularly important for considering coaching across professional boundaries and contexts. Exploring the idea of values and ethics, in relation to *who* we are in the coaching relationship, *where* we are when we coach, and *how* we coach, highlights the importance of contextualising meaning for coaching across contexts and their boundaries. In Part III of the book, we will discuss some of the most common ethical issues that may arise in specific professional contexts in which coaching takes place.

## Chapter summary

- Coaching is practised in diverse professional contexts. Understanding their distinct characteristics is important for developing an ethical coaching practice.
- A coach's professional background influences where and how coaching takes place.
- Coaching ethically across professional boundaries and contexts draws on many fields of knowledge, which are reflected in different models – these provide a rich pool from which coaches can draw according to the coaching context.
- It is important to be able to understand what coaching theories and models we use in our coaching practice.
- Ethical coaching involves being able to step back and see the whole picture of the coaching context in which we practise.

## Suggestions for further reading

For inspiring reflections on coaching across cultural contexts and cultures, we recommend:

Lennard, D. (2010) *Coaching Models: A Cultural Perspective: A Guide to Model Development for Practitioners and Students of Coaching.* New York: Routledge.

See also:

Rosinski, P. (2003) *Coaching across Cultures: New Tools for Leveraging National, Corporate and Professional Differences.* London: Nicholas Brealey.

*(Continued)*

*(Continued)*

For a practical exploration of coaching genres and their theoretical perspectives, we suggest:

Cox, E., Bachkirova T. and Clutterbuck, D. (eds) (2014) *The Complete Handbook of Coaching*, 2nd edn. London: Sage Publishing.

For a recent review of coaching in several professional contexts, consider taking a look at:

van Nieuwerburgh, C. (ed.) (2015) *Coaching in Professional Contexts*. London: Sage Publishing.

Finally, if you are interested in further reading on coaching and mental health, we most certainly recommend:

Buckley, A. and Buckley, C. (2006) *A Guide to Coaching and Mental Health: The Recognition and Management of Psychological Issues*. London: Routledge.

# Part III

## Ethical Issues in Coaching Contexts

# 8

# Ethical Issues
# in Business Coaching

## Chapter aims

- To explore the variety of terms that are used to describe coaching in the business world.
- To analyse the primary ethical issues that arise in business coaching.
- To consider the question: who is the client in business coaching?
- To emphasise the significance of clear contracting from the outset of the process.
- To delineate the boundaries of the business coach's role.
- To reiterate the significance of embracing ethical issues as opportunities for learning and development.

## Chapter overview

In this chapter, we discuss the meaning and essence of business coaching. We look at the several terms that are used to describe coaching in the corporate sphere, such as executive and leadership coaching, and we explore the distinct case of the manager-as-coach model. We then delve into some of the primary ethical issues facing business coaches, such as contracting, confidentiality, the manager-as-coach approach, boundary management and self-management. We take a stance in favour of a thorough and comprehensive contract as one of the most useful tools in the business coach's toolbox. This is because of the complex ethical issues that arise as an outcome of the tripartite relationship between the coach, the coachee and the sponsoring organisation. We pay particular attention to the question of who the client of the business coach is: is it the coachee or the sponsoring organisation? Finally, we reiterate that coaching is first and foremost a learning process and that the coach can use ethical issues as tools for learning and development.

## Key words

business coaching, executive coaching, managerial coaching, contracting, confidentiality, boundary management, self-management, client, sponsor

## Introduction

As we have already seen, coaching is currently one of the fastest-growing industries globally, having seen a ferocious crescendo over the past two decades. In an article graphically entitled 'Executive Coaching: Corporate Therapy', *The Economist* (2003) predicted that the rise of the global turnover of business coaching would be meteoric. Indeed, coaching managed to weather the storm of the recession of 2008 and within a decade, it became a $2 billion-a-year industry, with a global workforce of 47,500 professionals (Scoular, 2011: 1–2; PwC, 2012). In a survey conducted in 2012, the Chartered Institute of Personnel and Development (CIPD, 2012) found that coaching is amongst the most effective talent management activities with the potential to drive organisational change. Other reports in both North America and Europe have also claimed the effectiveness of coaching for improved performance and motivation within corporate settings (AMA, 2008; EFMD, 2009).

Given this proliferation, it is not a coincidence that coaching is becoming increasingly popular within the learning and development programmes of several organisations. Its integration in these settings is happening in a variety of ways. The most widely used are: executive coaching, which aims to enhance the professional development of leaders and managers (Stokes and Jolly, 2014); team coaching for the purpose of collectively coordinated task achievement (Hackman and Wageman, 2005; Clutterbuck, 2007); or even managerial coaching, for example the 'manager-as-coach' model (Ellinger et al., 2014). All of these different ways of coaching in a business setting engender a variety of ethical issues that coaches (and clients) need to be consciously aware of in order to benefit from business coaching.

## What is business coaching?

'Business coaching', 'organisational coaching', 'executive coaching', 'leadership coaching': these are only some of the terms used to describe coaching in the corporate sphere. Even though there may be nuanced distinctions between them, more often than not these terms are used interchangeably to denote any form of training or professional development activity carried out between a coach and an individual holding a middle or senior management position in an organisation (Stokes and Jolly, 2014: 244). Indeed, historically, coaching in the corporate world has been associated with the instruction of subordinates (Kraut et al., 1989), the training and professional development of employees, mainly managers (Morse and Wagner, 1978; Yukl, 1994), and the improvement of poor performance. In this chapter, we use Kilburg's definition of executive coaching, which seems to reflect the current commonly accepted perception of coaching in the business world. According to Kilburg, coaching is:

> a helping relationship formed between a client who has managerial authority and responsibility in an organisation, and a consultant who uses a wide variety of behavioural techniques and methods to help the client achieve a mutually identified set of goals to improve his or her professional performance and personal satisfaction and, consequently, to improve the effectiveness of the client's organisation within a formally defined coaching agreement. (2002: 142)

In this respect, and for clarification purposes, by business coaching we do not mean systematic training in a workshop format, but coaching as a process that enables the coachee to take ownership of his or her learning and development in the organisation (Redshaw, 2000). In this context, the primary objective of coaching is learning and development, and improved performance is only the by-product of the intervention (Mink et al., 1993).

## Ethical issues in business coaching

Contrary to other helping professions, where professionals' work is premised on principles of ethics of care, the world of business revolves around competitive advantage. In consequence, the culture of business is of an inherently proprietary nature, where the primary goal is to advance the organisation's strategy for greater profits. While we are not insinuating that the intentions of organisations are devious or immoral, this emphasis on profit can engender several ethical issues for the coach who works within such contexts.

## Pause for reflection

Consider the following scenario. You are one of the organisation's most valued external executive coaches and have just started a new cycle of coaching sessions with several of the organisation's executives. The human resource development (HRD) manager who commissioned your contract has just invited you to a social event organised by the company and asked you to assess your clients' social skills in the process:

- Do you attend?
- If so, do you conduct the assessment?

As we have already discussed, coaching is primarily focused on the learning and development of an individual for his or her personal and professional advancement. Within organisational contexts, however, there might be different objectives for commissioning coaching, which are not always clearly communicated to the coach or the coachee. This may have implications for the standards of professional conduct a coach is expected to uphold. Being able to anticipate, therefore, some of the most common ethical issues that may occur within the sphere of business coaching can help the coach be better prepared to address the needs of the client and the sponsoring organisation. In the following section, we shall explore some of the key ethical issues that may arise in business coaching, namely who is the client, contracting, confidentiality and boundary management, dual relationships and self-management. Let's start with the first and rather obvious one.

## Who is the client in business coaching?

An obvious ethical question that arises in business coaching is: who is the client? Within business contexts, the coaching relationship usually involves a triad – the coach, the employee to be coached, and the organisation or individual that commissions and sponsors the coaching. For instance, an organisation may commission executive coaching for one or more of its executives; or a line manager or HR manager might set up internal coaching for an employee. In these cases, the coaching process involves three parties. If the coaching is paid for by the organisation, this begs the question: who is the coach's client: the coachee or the paying organisation?

Opinions on this matter vary. Bob Thomson (2014: 51–2) insists that the client is the coachee and that it is essential to clearly delineate the boundaries between the coach, the client and the sponsoring organisation. Similarly, van Nieuwerburgh (2015: 4, emphasis in original) maintains that the role of the executive coach is: 'to support the client [i.e., the coachee] to achieve more of their potential and maintain or enhance their well-being *within* their organisational context'. Other voices, however, especially from the sphere of counselling and psychotherapy, claim that the paying organisation is the client because the contract is between the organisation and the coach (Peltier, 2010; Scoular, 2011). While there is no definitive answer to this question, the European Mentoring and Coaching Council (EMCC) has addressed this issue through the use of distinct terminology. In its Code of Ethics, the commissioning organisation is labelled *sponsor*, while the person to be coached is termed *client*. We adopt the EMCC's terms in this chapter.

Geoff Pelham (2016: 106) has suggested another reason why, in practice rather than in principle, it is difficult to come up with a decisive answer to this question. This is because an organisation is not a 'distinct definable entity', as we usually perceive it, but a 'messy' concept, where a variety of people have a different understanding of what coaching is and, in consequence, diverse motivations for being coached. These dissimilarities make it even more important to consider and anticipate several ethical questions that may arise in business coaching. Let us consider some examples:

- Do you agree to supply the sponsor with coaching reports without the client's prior knowledge or consent?
- Would you provide the sponsor with feedback on the progress of coaching?
- If you use psychometric testing for the coaching, would you supply the sponsor with the results?

For some coaches, the answer to these questions will be obvious; for others it will be puzzling. We believe that practising ethically means that, as coaches, we ensure that all of the parties who are involved in the tripartite relationship – the coach, the client and the sponsor – have a mutual and clear understanding of the expectations of coaching and the responsibilities of each party within this process. If the sponsor has a specific agenda for the coaching, for instance, it may be helpful that you, as the coach, request that this is communicated explicitly to the client by the former. In this respect, there is clarity and transparency as to what the purpose and the objectives of the coaching should be. But can this always happen in practice?

> ## Pause for reflection
>
> - In your own coaching practice, who is your client? Is it the person you are coaching or the organisation that is paying your fees?
> - Whose agenda does the coaching serve? Is it the client's agenda or the sponsoring organisation's?

In order to explore and address these basic ethical questions in business coaching, we need to consider key aspects of the coaching practice that are heavily influenced by several ethical parameters. These are contracting, confidentiality and boundary management, dual relationships and self-regulation.

## Contracting

As we keep reiterating in this book, contracting is that part of the coaching relationship that has the potential of minimising several ethical pitfalls you might find yourself in as a coach. We already discussed the significance of a clear and comprehensive contract as the foundation of an effective coaching relationship in Chapter 3. In this chapter, we are returning to the theme of contracting in order to address some specific contracting issues that are pertinent in the realm of business coaching, where it is more likely to encounter the tripartite relationship of the coach, the client and the sponsor. In this context, a clear and comprehensive contract should not only outline the basic logistical practicalities, such as the duration of the coaching intervention, and the time, place, frequency and cost of sessions; it should also delineate the expected outcomes of coaching and the responsibilities of each party involved in it. Importantly, the contract should clearly state how feedback to the sponsor will be dealt with and delivered, if feedback is expected.

Another important component of the coaching contract should be remuneration. The financial terms of the partnership should be – and we expect that they usually are – clearly disclosed and agreed upon in the contract. This is especially important in cases where the coach requests advance payment for the coaching service to be provided (Brennan and Wildflower, 2014: 435). In some parts of the world, it is common business practice for the coach to receive extra revenue for referral to other services or products (ibid.: 435). If this is the case, then it is only ethical that such propositions are mutually agreed upon in the contracting stage. Doing so will safeguard the coach from any accusation of attempting to exploit the client or the sponsoring organisation.

An aspect of contracting that can be ignored in the realm of business coaching is the termination of the coaching relationship. When does it actually end? The Code of Conduct of the Association for Coaching, for instance, clearly acknowledges 'the Client's right to terminate the coaching at any point during the coaching process' (Thomson, 2014: 62). Yet, what happens, for instance, if the client does not display the intended results within the designated time period that the coaching is supposed to last? How should a coach wrap up the relationship if goals have not been met or the sponsoring funds run out? Is the coach expected to continue the coaching relationship if a client leaves the organisation before the coaching programme is completed? Should the coach offer to continue the coaching, even for a reduced fee that will be paid out of the client's pocket? We find ourselves in agreement with Peltier (2010: 367), that every contracting process should include a clear discussion of when and how the coaching will end. Moreover, we invite you to consider some of the questions we raised above as potential clauses in your coaching contract. Producing and utilising a contract that is underpinned by the principles of openness, honesty and transparency will enable you to anticipate several of the ethical issues you might encounter in your coaching practice within and beyond organisational contexts.

## Confidentiality and boundary management

In Chapter 3, we discussed the instrumentality and complexity of confidentiality in coaching, paying particular attention to those instances where confidentiality may have to be broken. Within the context of business coaching, confidentiality becomes even more complex, as several ethical issues stem from the tripartite relationship.

Business or executive coaches are often required by the sponsoring organisation to report on the coaching process, especially at the initial stages of coaching. Indeed, in a recent study on executive coaching, Kauffman and Coutu (2009: 3) found that 70 per cent of executive coaches kept the client's manager informed of the subordinate's headway, while 55 per cent reported to the organisation's HR department on the progress of their work. This brings us back to the issue of contracting and the necessity for a clear agreement that explicitly delineates the reporting process at the outset of the intervention. Brennan and Wildflower (2014: 435–6) argued that, in order to avoid any unintentional breach of confidentiality, 'the coach should not be in a position to prepare or present a report on the client's progress', as the client is better placed to communicate such information. Peltier (2010: 363), on the other hand, maintained that such progress reports, especially delivered on a regular basis, can enhance the coaching, if done in collaboration with the client. Specifically, he claimed that such reports can actually protect confidentiality because both coach and client can refer anyone enquiring about progress to the written report that will be imminently produced (ibid.: 363).

An important aspect of confidentiality is boundary management. In Chapter 7, we addressed the subject of boundary management, especially in relation to mental health issues that may interfere with the coaching. This is not an infrequent scenario in business coaching, where the need for referral to a specialist, like a counsellor or psychotherapist, might arise. While the potential of referral might have been covered in the initial contracting stage, 'it may feel very different to both client and coach in the immediate reality of their encounter with one another' (Thomson, 2014: 49). Yet, a growing body of emerging research is showing that the distinction between clinical and non-clinical is problematic, and that the boundary between them is blurry and fluid (Cavanagh and Buckley, 2014: 405). This is particularly relevant to professionals and managers – the typical users of business coaching – who have been found to exhibit higher levels of stress, anxiety and depression than semi-skilled and unskilled individuals (Eaton et al., 1990; Cavanagh and Buckley, 2014).

While coaches are usually not trained to offer diagnostic advice on mental health issues and therefore should not seek to do so, it is not always easy, in practical terms, to determine where normal human functioning stops and psychopathology begins. Cavanagh and Buckley (2014: 406) communicated this concern very effectively by posing the following question: when is the worry an executive feels over delivering a key presentation just the normal butterflies associated with public speaking and when is it a symptom of a more pervasive case of social phobia? This is a familiar scenario in the sphere of business coaching. If you have experienced it, it means that you have worked with clients who, in the process of sharing their story, experience and express intense emotions such as fear, shame, guilt and remorse. These feelings and reactions may come to surface unintentionally and render coachees more vulnerable, as they reveal aspects of themselves that may not be directly related to the purpose of coaching. It goes without saying that the welfare of the coachee is at the forefront of the coaching practice. But what happens when institutional deadlines and other organisational parameters strictly delineate the direction that coaching should take? In other words how should the coach, who has been hired to strictly work through business-related issues, respond if other personal issues come to the surface? Can a coach distinguish between the personal and the professional (Cavanagh and Grant, 2004)? Some further ethical questions ought to be considered here:

(a) How might the coach approach any institutional directive towards the purpose of the coaching or, more specifically, towards the side-tracking of the purpose of the coaching?
(b) Should the coach suggest to the client from the set-up of the relation-ship that – irrespective of the nature of coaching – certain psychologically related issues may or may not come to surface during the coaching process and that this is OK?

---

## Pause for reflection

Think of your own practice as a business or executive coach:

- Do you prefer to isolate the coaching within the context it takes place and only focus on specific (even institutional) goals?
- Or do you embrace the individual as a whole, even when the coaching is offered in a concise programme of a few sessions?
- If you prefer the latter approach, how do you communicate it to the sponsoring organisation?

---

Whatever approach you take to the way you work with professionals in organisational contexts, we believe that, for purposes of transparency, it is important to mutually agree with the coachee and the sponsoring organisation on: the purpose of the coaching, its potential limits, and what the options are, if the need for further assistance arises. This is even more crucial if you are an internal coach who works across teams and departments. In this case, an atmosphere of openness and trust presupposes that your position or acquaintances in the organisation will influence your practice. But how feasible is this when you are a manager who is asked to coach an employee you directly line-manage?

## Dual relationships: the coach-manager

Dual relationships are premised on more than one interest between two or more individuals. Can you be the business coach of a good friend, for instance? Importantly, within an organisation, can you be the coach of a person you directly line-manage? This is a key ethical issue in business coaching contexts. If you are a line manager who is asked to coach those directly reporting to you, there are several parameters that you need to take into consideration. For instance, what is the purpose of the coaching? What is your responsibility to the coachee and the organisation? Whom do you report to regarding the coaching process? What is the boundary between being a manager and being a coach? Who is there to support you as a coach if this boundary is trespassed?

Managerial coaching, or the 'manager-as-coach' model, is defined as 'a manager or supervisor serving as a coach or facilitator for learning in the workplace setting, in which he or she enacts specific behaviours that enable his or her employee (coachee) to learn and develop' (Ellinger et al., 2014: 257). Managerial coaching in the workplace has been steadily gaining momentum, as human resource development has fallen within the line manager's responsibilities (Evered and Selman, 1989). Indeed, managerial coaching has been gaining currency amongst coaching exponents who have even gone to the lengths of arguing that coaching is at the very core of managerial practice and effectiveness (Hamlin et al., 2006).

But, how ethical is managerial coaching? Ellinger et al. (2014: 258) delineate the remit and objectives of a manager acting as a coach. Primary in these is the improvement of an employee's performance through learning. This learning, they explain, involves the employee's conscious awareness of their strengths and weaknesses, as well as the enhancement of self-awareness that can improve work-based behaviours and relationships. In essence, therefore, instead of giving orders or micro-managing, a manager can deploy coaching in order to facilitate the employee's own reflection of how they can improve their performance. So far, so good. But what happens when deeper personal or even professional issues affect an employee's performance?

## Story from practice

Shaun has just been promoted to a new role that requires delivering frequent presentations to the senior management team of the organisation. Lizzy, his line manager, has realised that, while Shaun is a diligent and likeable employee, his presentation performance is very poor. One of the firm's senior managers agrees with this and speaks to Lizzy privately about her concerns. Lizzy concurs that Shaun is in need of professional support in order to improve his presentation skills. For this purpose, she arranges training for Shaun. To support him even further with his new role, she also agrees to assume the role of the coach. The objectives of coaching are to help him increase his assertiveness and, in consequence, improve his performance.

What Lizzy does not know is that Shaun has been suffering from anxiety since his teens. This is the main reason why his performance is poor when all eyes and ears are on him during a presentation. As this is a deeply personal mental health issue, Shaun has tried to conceal it from his colleagues. He most certainly does not feel comfortable disclosing it to his line manager and, as a result, he is apprehensive about the coaching. Lizzy, who is oblivious to Shaun's issue, sees no reason for concern. This builds up tension. As a result, Shaun becomes increasingly more anxious at work.

Questions to consider:

- Should Shaun disclose his mental health issue to his line manager?
- Should Lizzy become Shaun's coach? If so, what should the remit and purpose of the coaching be?
- What is Lizzy's responsibility to Shaun? To the organisation?

Ultimately, is it possible for a line manager to be a coach when a manager's role is to 'both coach and evaluate direct reports' (Hunt and Winetraub, 2002b: 16)? How can this be a partnership of equals based on openness and mutual trust, when the line manager has more authority and may, at times, be privy to organisational information that she cannot share with the coachee? These complex issues constitute the reasons why a recent report by the Chartered Institute of Personnel and Development (CIPD) concluded that:

> There appeared to be a consensus within HR teams setting up development opportunities for line managers that the psychological boundary issues for line managers formally 'coaching' their own staff are very difficult to manage. Even if organisations begin with the intention of having 'coaching' as a separate activity for line managers with their teams, we haven't yet found any organisations that have done it successfully. This supports the conventional wisdom and professional standards which say that the roles and responsibilities of line management make formally 'coaching' your own staff very difficult. (Knights, 2008: 7)

Ultimately, it depends on the individuals who makeup part of this rather complex web of roles to determine whether managerial coaching will work or not. If you decide to embark on this process, we encourage you to consider potential impediments, including the manager's lack of training, skills, willingness and time (Goleman, 2000; Hunt and Winetraub, 2002a; Heslin et al., 2006; Gilley et al., 2010). Moreover, employees may not feel comfortable being coached by their line managers, and this is a factor worth taking into consideration. This is why several scholars and practitioners have advocated a 'coaching mindset' as part of a manager's role (Hunt and Winetraub, 2011), rather than a manager becoming a coach for his or her subordinates.

Managing with a coaching approach means that a manager acknowledges that employees are open to learning and development. It allows managers to help their subordinates develop without trying to micro-manage or control the process. A coaching approach also entails the ability to empathise with others while being able to reflect on one's own managerial practice, as well as being open to feedback from others (Hunt and Winetraub, 2002b, 2011). Ultimately, coaching scholars and practitioners have drawn a clear distinction between management, which is perceived as 'telling, judging, controlling and directing', and a coaching mindset, which involves 'empowering, helping, developing, supporting and removing obstacles' (Ellinger et al., 2014: 258). If you are a manager who has to alternate between these two roles, you may want to ask yourself where you set boundaries for your coaching and what your actual responsibility is to your employee. Indeed, it is important to have a clear understanding of your responsibilities and the boundaries between the different roles you may have in relation to your coachee.

Ultimately, only you can know whether taking on the role of a coach for an individual you directly line-manage is ethical and appropriate. We would encourage you, however, to consider the value of consciously reflecting on your coaching (and managerial) practice, in order to ensure that you do not cross any boundaries that should not be crossed. As Mumford (1993) claimed, any managerial activity has the potential for learning, and this is true both for the manager and the person being managed. This is why conscious reflection on your distinct responsibilities, as a manager and as a coach, is beneficial. You may also want to consider the possibility of finding a supervisor for your coaching role. Finally, if you do end up acting as the coach to people whom you line-manage, it is important that you clearly disclose any potential conflict of interest that may arise from the dual relationships and all related parties. This can be done at the initial contracting stage, which should not be ignored in manager-as-coach situations.

## Self-management

This brings us to another crucial ethical issue that coaches in the business world need to be attuned to: self-management. Brennan and Wildflower (2014: 437) define self-management as: 'recognising bias, preconceived ideas, initial impressions, opinions or stereotypes that can influence the ability to be fully focused and present with the client'. The world of business is premised on extensive networking and, by proxy, growing connections that can help expand one's professional outreach. Coaching is not an exception. Many business coaches consider it vital to expand their network of corporate connections in order to increase their business. In consequence, when they are called to coach within an organisation, it is not improbable that they have prior knowledge of the individual they are asked to coach, either by the individual's reputation or through the individual's colleagues, who the coach may have coached in the past. This is even more likely if the coach is internal to the organisation. Since forming personal opinions is an inherent part of human nature, the coach needs to be aware of potential bias or prejudice that may arise and potentially interfere with the coaching process (Brennan and Wildflower, 2014: 438). If you recognise any instances of bias in your business coaching practice, we encourage you to consider how you can manage yourself in the process. If you feel that you cannot achieve the appropriate level of self-management in order to support the client in an impartial way, then you may need to consider extricating yourself from the engagement and supporting the client in the process of finding another coach.

Finally, it is important for the business coach to understand the limits of coaching. In essence, business coaching aims to help an individual find answers for themselves, rather than being told what the best course of action is. It is not mentoring or consulting. In this respect, the coach has an ethical responsibility to the client to be clear, from the very outset of the relationship, as to what his or her remit is. Although it is expected that the coach may make a suggestion to a client regarding an issue being discussed, ultimately the coach needs to manage her inclination to give advice in order to facilitate the client's learning. If the coach feels tempted to offer advice in order to add value to the service offered to the client or the organisation, then she may need to re-evaluate what services she offers and in what capacity she embarks on the working relationship (ibid.: 438).

## Story from practice

Janet is an expert executive coach who has been working in Fortune 500 organisations for over a decade. She has currently started a new partnership with a large global organisation that dominates the book trade industry. As part of her role, she is asked to coach Linda, a talented executive who has just been promoted to a senior leadership role in the corporation's marketing department. The contracting meeting and the first coaching sessions have gone very well and both coach and client are happy with how the

*(Continued)*

*(Continued)*

coaching is taking shape and form. Starting from the second session, however, it is obvious that Linda wants to angle the coaching towards a very specific objective: to leave the company in order to work for its principal competitor, who has been courting her for over a year. What is more, Linda asks Janet for guidance regarding her ethical dilemma of revealing 'trade secrets' of her current employer to her new employer.
    Questions to consider:

- How should Janet work with Linda?
- What should Janet report to the human resource development manager who commissioned the coaching, when he asks for a progress report?
- Should career progression to another organisation be part of business coaching when it is paid for by the client's current employer?

These are, indeed, difficult ethical questions to consider. If Janet has produced a thorough and comprehensive contract at the contracting stage, then addressing these issues will not be as challenging as it seems. On this occasion, for instance, Janet could alert Linda to the fact that the coaching seems to move away from the agreed objectives. Moreover, she can invite Linda to consider whether she thinks it's OK to focus on something that is not related to the organisation's best interests, since the latter is funding the coaching. Ultimately, coaching is first and foremost a learning process and the coach can use ethical issues as tools for learning and development, for both the coach and the client.

## Conclusion

A clear contract is a key tool in the coach's toolbox that helps avoid ethical pitfalls. Well-defined contractual arrangements can anticipate issues around conflict of interest, boundary management and confidentiality from the outset of the coaching relationship. To be sure, not every circumstance can be foreseen but a clear contract that informs both the sponsor and the client of what the coaching will be about and what avenues of report will be pursued will facilitate a smooth and ethical coaching relationship. Openness from the outset is, therefore, a key safeguard for an ethical coaching practice in the corporate arena.
    Another tool, recommended by Bruce Peltier (2010: 364), is the systematic sharing of expertise by seasoned coaches in the form of written guidelines. Indeed, coaches should consider making their experience and recommendations public for the benefit of the profession and other colleagues in the field. In a service that is striving to become a fully fledged,

independent profession, it would be beneficial to share instances of good practice, in order to establish common consensus, where possible. The learning that may ensue form such pursuits has the potential to support ethical practice.

On this note, we strongly support the view that ethical dilemmas in the coaching practice should be systematically incorporated in formal coach training programmes. If instructed through the consideration of case studies, coaching trainees will have a great opportunity to reflect on and discuss such instances with their peers, with great benefits for the enhancement of their ethical awareness and their coaching practice. Ultimately, ethical issues offer a fantastic opportunity for critical self-reflection, and the coach should embrace the learning opportunity they provide. We will discuss this last issue in the following chapter, where we focus on ethical issues facing those who design and those who deliver coach training and education.

## Chapter summary

- Business coaching is an enabling relationship that provides the coachee with adequate guidance and support to facilitate his or her learning and development in the organisation.
- Contracting is a very important part of the coaching, as it is the stage in which you can clearly set guidelines and expectations and, as a result, anticipate – and minimise the likelihood of – several ethical pitfalls.
- It is important that you have mutual understanding with the client and the sponsor as to the expectations of the coaching and the clear roles and responsibilities of each party involved.
- If you are an internal coach within the organisation, you should be cautious about allowing your position or organisational acquaintances to influence your practice.
- Coaching is first and foremost a learning process and the coach can use ethical issues as tools for learning and development.

---

### Suggestions for further reading

For a succinct overview of the key ethical issues that can emerge in the coaching practice, we recommend:

Brennan, D. and Wildflower L. (2014) 'Ethics in Coaching', in E. Cox, T. Bachkirova and D. Clutterbuck (eds), *The Complete Handbook of Coaching*, 2nd edn. London: Sage Publishing, pp. 430–44.

*(Continued)*

*(Continued)*

For an engaging account of how psychological theories and processes can be effectively translated into the practice of executive coaching, we suggest:
Peltier, B. (2010) *The Psychology of Executive Coaching: Theory and Application*, 2nd edn. New York: Routledge; especially chapter 17, 'Ethics in Coaching'.

For coaching as a developmental tool for managers, you can also read:
Hunt, J.M. and Weintraub, J.R. (2010) *The Coaching Manager: Developing Top Talent in Business*, 2nd edn. Thousand Oaks, CA: Sage Publishing.

9

# Ethical Issues in Coach Education and Training

## Chapter aims

- To explore some of the most pertinent ethical issues in the design and delivery of coach education and training.
- To pose the significant question of whether formal coach education should be compulsory for coaches.
- To explore whether a homogenous code of ethics that underpins coach education and training is beneficial to the field of coaching.
- To show the significance of co-created learning for coach education, where instructors and learners help each other develop ethical consciousness in a safe and supportive environment.

## Chapter overview

In this chapter, we explore some of the most pertinent issues facing those who design and deliver coach education and training. In particular, we debate the primacy of practical skills over academic rigour in coach education and training. We also look at ethical issues of knowledge and power, as well as the boundaries of confidentiality for learning purposes. We discuss a code of ethics for coach training providers and take a stance against a unified, homogenous code of ethics that underpins coach education. Ultimately, we show how we view coach training as a co-creation of learning between instructor and learners, and we argue in favour of developing ethical consciousness and incorporating it in the design and delivery of coach education and training.

## Introduction

So far in this book, we have argued that values are socially constructed. In consequence, it would be impractical to talk about a universal and uniform set of values and ethics that underpins behaviours and actions in the coaching practice. This, however, does not preclude the existence of a universally accepted moral principle, that of being concerned and looking out for the 'other'. This, indeed, is the underlying principle of all morally good actions and it is particularly relevant in the domain of education and training (Jarvis, 1997). In this chapter, we enter the realm of coach education to explore some of the most pertinent ethical issues that may interfere with the work of those who design and those who deliver coach training.

As we have already discussed in Chapter 1, a growing number of professional bodies have initiated attempts to formally professionalise coaching through accreditation processes. This development is in response to a growing anxiety of both coaches and coaching buyers over the professional standards of the coaching practitioner. Indeed, during the last few decades, which have seen a crescendo in the practice of coaching, coaches have been entering the field from a variety of backgrounds such as business, human resource management, education, psychology, counselling and psychotherapy (Bluckert, 2004; Bachkirova et al., 2014: 2–6). The lack of systemised regulation means that there are still no formal or standardised qualifications that coaches ought to obtain in order to practise coaching (Bennett, 2006). In consequence, coaching has been criticised for not being ring-fenced from self-proclaimed coaches whose lack of credentials and professional expertise could jeopardise the service's reputation and legitimacy (Williams et al., 2006).

In response to this issue, the realm of business has been particularly proactive in issuing guidelines and standards of selecting suitable coaches (Jarvis, 2006). The same cannot be argued for the average buyers of coaching, however, who are still left to their own devices in order to choose an appropriate practitioner, as no professional coaching body has managed to gain authority in alleviating this anxiety (Lane, 2011). As a result of this, there has been a gradual proliferation of professional and academic coach training programmes that offer and certify coaching credentials. Yet, scholars and practitioners have not caught up with exploring and evaluating their effectiveness. It is exactly at this point that the first ethical questions emerge: Can we actually teach people how to coach? And if so, what is the best approach? *Is* there a best approach?

Providing a clear answer to these questions is challenging. The challenge lies in the lack of a standardised way of training coaches, which, by extension, has implications for ethical understanding and behaviour (Ives and Cox, 2014: 138). In this chapter, we explore some of the most pertinent issues facing those who design and deliver coach education and training. We start with debating the primacy of practical skills over academic rigour in coach education. We then move on to look at the issue of power and authority in terms of who the 'custodian' of knowledge is – the instructor or the learners. Finally, we discuss the boundaries of confidentiality for the purposes of learning. By exploring these ethical issues, we uncover the idiosyncrasy of the educational needs of the coach. As such, we argue that a homogenous code of ethics is inadequate to support the complexities of coach education and training. We therefore prioritise the development of ethical consciousness and its incorporation in the design and delivery of coach education and training, as significant constituents in this process.

## Coaching in education

As we have already seen, coaching is a relatively new field that has benefited from the knowledge base of several disciplines, such as management, education, philosophy and psychology (Bachkirova et al., 2014: 4). This diversity has been nourishing the ongoing debates on its 'conceptual foundation' (Nelson and Hogan, 2009). Yet, especially over the last decade, professional and academic courses in coaching have seen a proliferation that is commensurate with the exponential growth of the service. In the Anglosphere – and more recently, beyond it – professional coach training programmes have seen such a prolific growth, that the major professional coaching bodies have started to put in place accreditation mechanisms. The latter aim to ensure that courses meet the standards 'for comprehensive coach training, encompassing the application of coaching competencies, working within ethical guidelines, and providing practical experience' (AC, undated *b*).

The entrance of coaching in the realm of higher education has been more sluggish. It started gradually with the incorporation of coaching elements within relevant courses such as management and organisation studies, particularly on a postgraduate level (Williams et al., 2006; Grant et al., 2010; Iordanou et al., 2015). More recently, several academic institutions have started to offer stand-alone coaching qualifications. The number of these institutions is constantly on the rise. In the UK, for example, the University Forum for Human Resource Development (UFHRD) lists at least ten universities that offer fully developed coaching programmes and nearly a hundred universities that incorporate coaching in their Human Resource Development and Management courses (see UFHRD, 2015).

So profuse has the proliferation of individual coach training providers been that, at the beginning of the twenty-first century, representatives from a handful of coach training institutions based in the US founded the Association of Coach Training Organizations (ACTO). Originally intended for knowledge exchange, discussing ethical coach training, and training collaboration, this non-profit organisation soon assumed the responsibility of upholding the standards of coach training and education in North America (for more information, see ACTO, undated). To date, ACTO enumerates over 60 member coach training organisations.

Espousing the ICF's ethical principles, ACTO's work is grounded in five core values: integrity, respect, cooperation, cultural awareness and engaged relationships. Grounded in the values of the ICF, ACTO have created their own code of ethics that entails the following primary principles:

1. Embody and fully live the ACTO core values in all behaviours and activities of the organisation's individual schools.
2. Use ACTO members' teaching and coaching expertise to realise ACTO's mission while respecting the individual nature of each member.
3. Do not solicit members for personal purposes and do not use the contact information provided on the website and at events to send mass mailing without the written permission of the ACTO president.
4. Conduct all of ACTO member teaching, coaching, and education which align with the ACTO values, encouraging and fostering high ethical standards as an example to other ACTO members and students.
5. Promote recognition and respect for all member schools that benefit the world coach education community.
6. Offer best practices to provide information for member schools to engage in continuous improvement for the sake of all.
7. Honour the trust that member schools have with one another and do not do anything that will bring disfavour or reflect adversely on other schools.
8. Do not seek privilege or advantage from other member schools to advance ACTO member schools. Members will offer full attribution for any and all Intellectual Property that is used from other schools.

9. Teach Coaching and Ethics in all coach education curricula in a manner that allows students to know what to do in the event of ethical challenges.

10. Abide by the International Coach Federation Code of Ethics and Ethics Pledge.

In essence, ACTO's guidelines comprise a code of ethics for training providers, specifically those operating in the USA. While well-intentioned, these guidelines are broad and generic. The term 'best practice', for instance, can be interpreted differently by different institutions. As such, codes of ethics like these bring us back to an issue we discussed in the beginning of the book: are codes of ethics adequate to support an ethical practice, in this case, the ethical design and delivery of coach education and training? It is not easy to provide an answer to this question unless we identify some of the primary ethical issues that are involved in the process of designing and delivering it. Hence, in the following section, we embark on a discussion of some of the key ethical issues that arise in coach education and training.

## Ethical issues in coach education and training

The prolific emergence and development of a variety of coach education and training programmes in both public and private spheres comes with a great degree of responsibility and a certain degree of notoriety. This is because the lack of systematic evaluation of such programmes (Devine et al., 2013) has wider implications for the quality assurance of courses on offer. While we acknowledge that accreditation mechanisms that have been put in place by some professional coaching bodies can offer a first level of quality assurance, they are not always adequate to protect the training designer and provider from the variety of ethical issues that may arise in the design and delivery of coach training and education. In this section, we will attempt to address some of these issues. These are, namely: the balance between academic rigour and practical application; the power of the instructor as the 'custodian' of knowledge; and the boundaries of confidentiality for learning purposes. Let's start with the first one.

### Academic rigour versus practical skills

In Chapter 4, we discussed the issue of the educational background of the coach. Specifically, we saw how coaches enter the coaching practice from a variety of educational backgrounds, since formal coach training and education are still not a prerequisite for the coaching practice

(Bennett, 2006). In this chapter, we look at the nature of coach training and education programmes in order to raise some pertinent questions with an ethical undertone. Should coaching programmes promote theoretical knowledge or practical application? Should there be a balance between academic rigour and professional skills development in coach training and education? More specifically, should higher education be focusing on professional practice and should professional training be enriched with academic theories?

Let's explore these questions further. Consider a Postgraduate Certificate in Coaching offered by a higher education institution. Aiming at high attainment of academic rigour, the programme prioritises critical engagement with scholarly theories and research over practical application. Yet, the qualification is perceived as a licence to practise by the learner, her potential clients, and even the awarding and accrediting institutions. Is it ethical to award such a qualification if the practical application of theories has only been a small fraction of the programme? Conversely, is it ethical to offer a coaching qualification that is only premised on practical training but does not engage with relevant theories that can provide the conceptual frameworks for understanding the principles underpinning the coaching practice?

These are all significant issues to consider when designing and delivering coach education and training. In agreement with Williams et al. (2006), we endorse the synergy between theory, applied research and quality skills provision as paramount for the professional development of the coach. To this end, we also support Grant and Cavanagh's (2004) assertions on the importance of the scientist-practitioner model that we discussed in Chapter 5. The scientist-practitioner model supports the view that practising coaches will benefit from engaging with evidence-based and theoretically informed research. Due to the complexity of the coaching practice, where coaches are faced with several complicated issues that emerge in the individual, interpersonal and organisational contexts in which they work, we see the scientist-practitioner model as a particularly suitable approach to learning in the realm of coach education. This is because it enables learners to develop their practical skills through critical reflection on established academic theories and, if possible, active engagement with empirical research. In this respect, coaching learners can combine their practical application of coaching skills with theoretical and empirical knowledge. The combination of these can sharpen their critical thinking abilities that, as we argued in Chapters 2 and 6, contribute to the development of an ethical coaching practice. Ultimately, we believe that an ethical approach to the design of coach training programmes promotes a balanced combination of theoretical knowledge, practice, reflection on practice, and critical reflection or reflexivity. But who determines what kind of knowledge will be taught in these programmes and how it will be taught? We discuss this ethical issue in the following section.

## Power and the role of the trainer: who is the 'custodian' of knowledge?

In his *Meditationes Sacrae* (1597) Francis Bacon argued that *'ipsa scientia potestas est'*, which means that knowledge itself is power. Thomas Hobbes, a disciple of Bacon's, allegedly reverberated the latter's ruminations by claiming that *'scientia potestas est'*. Put simply, Hobbes exclaimed that knowledge is power. While the disputed pedigree of this Latin aphorism is beyond the scope of this chapter, it would not be misguiding to argue that the phrase *knowledge is power* has held resonance in our cultural understanding of the value of knowledge (Scheg, 2014). Indeed, educators and trainers have traditionally been perceived as the gatekeepers of knowledge, the source we must tap into in order to expand our own intellectual horizons. What are the ethical implications of this generally accepted tenet?

As we already discussed in Chapter 1, *ethics of power and structure* advocate that dominant discourses in a society can determine and shape the prevailing ideologies in that society. These discourses are usually proposed by those who wield power and exert influence. In consequence, the norms of behaviour and action seem to favour the most powerful within a social system. To borrow an example from Jarvis (1997: 16), the 'politicians' desire to "leave it to the market" is actually an action in favour of those who control business and commerce'. The realm of education, with the normative conceptualisation of the educator as the 'custodian' of knowledge, can be seen as one of those social systems that favour, if not induce, this type of ethics.

The notion of knowledge as a source of power has particularly been explored in the realm of adult education (see, for instance, Jarvis, 1997), where coaching is predominantly situated (Iordanou et al., 2015). Indeed, in normative educational settings the tutors might use their position to influence the teaching and learning process. In doing so, they might impose their own predilections on the learners, using teaching 'as an opportunity of self-aggrandisement, while the students are forced to be the recipients of the tutors' performance, eloquence, wit, etc.' (Jarvis, 1997: 31). This teacher-centred approach to education has been characterised by Bourdieu and Passeron (1977: 5) as the pedagogic expression of 'objectively symbolic power insofar as it is the imposition of a cultural arbitrary by an arbitrary power'. Within this context, the teacher's self-interests may be prioritised over the students' learning needs and preferences. But does coach education and training reflect this educational context?

---

## Pause for reflection

Take a few minutes to reflect on your coach training, either as a trainer or as a trainee:

- Who really holds the knowledge? Whose knowledge and experiences do you use to build your knowledge on?
- If you have played the role of both a trainer and a trainee, we encourage you to consider these questions from both perspectives.

---

The issue of power in coaching still remains largely underexplored (Welman and Bachkirova, 2010). If you have taken some time to reflect on the questions above, you may have realised that it is not easy to detect the 'gatekeeper' of knowledge and power in coach training and education. This is because, in most coach training programmes, learners are expected to practise their coaching skills and, as such, use their reflection on such experiences as learning components. Moreover, students are encouraged to use and reflect on their professional experience as part of their learning. It is not, therefore, easy to discern who holds the power in such settings. The coaching literature is silent on the matter, as coaching scholars and practitioners have not yet systematically addressed these questions. Still, the issue of who holds the knowledge and, therefore, power in coaching carries important ethical implications. In consequence, we consider it worthwhile to delve into it further.

Since there is no substantial evidence in the sphere of coach training to help us in this process, we seek analogies and practical similarities in the domain of coach supervision. This is because supervision is an alternative form of professional development for coaches, where the supervisor is deemed to be the source of knowledge and expertise, regardless of how this seniority in experience is used. Coach supervision, therefore, just like coach training, involves similar power dynamics (Hawkins and Shohet, 2006). Drawing from the work of social psychologists French and Raven (1959), Hawkins and Shohet (2006: 112) highlighted the *legitimate* power that is inherent in the role of the supervisor, whose superiority lies in the accumulated expertise compared to the more junior professional status of the supervisee. He also noted the *coercive* and *reward* power that the supervisor can wield in order to exert influence on the supervisee. This can be manifested in the form of offering or withholding rewards, a practice that is anything but unfamiliar to educators. Finally, Hawkins emphasised the power of *resources*, which entails the capacity of the supervisor to offer or remove resources. Overall, as the supervisor is expected to be more experienced, he or she can exercise *expert* power.

Similarly, in the sphere of coach training and education, educators are expected to have solid awareness of key theoretical concepts. As such, they can be seen as the holders of expertise and knowledge and, therefore, the ones wielding *legitimate* power in delivering training and, by extension, certification. But as far as the reflection on practical application is concerned, are educators the main custodians of knowledge? Could effective coach training take place without the trainee's reflection on practice? Opinions on this matter vary. We espouse an academic tradition that sees learning – especially learning about coaching – as a co-creation of knowledge between the instructor-as-facilitator and the learners. The authority of the educator lies in his or her ability to use knowledge as the impetus for reflection and to facilitate debate. In this manner, the educator's power is used not abused (Hawkins and Shohet, 2006: 112; Kadushin, 2002). Viewed from this perspective, the various aspects of power that operate in the teacher–learner relationship can be utilised as a tool for ethical reflection by both teachers and learners in the process of co-creating knowledge. But what happens when such reflections involve sensitive information from individuals who are part of this co-creation process? We shall attempt to explore this ethical issue in the following section.

## The boundaries of confidentiality in the learning process

Most coach training and education programmes encourage the practice of coaching skills, in one way or another. In practice, coaching learners and trainees are often tasked with practising coaching, either with each other in class or with 'practice clients'. These are individuals who volunteer as coachees to facilitate the training and development of coaches. In such circumstances, confidentiality is a primary ethical issue that needs to be embedded and emphasised in the process. However, when coaching is carried out for training purposes, and reflection on the coaching practice is a vital component of learning, can the shared reflection on the particulars of the coaching experience risk trespassing the boundaries of confidentiality?

Confidentiality is not merely a process of concealing and protecting information. It extends to not using and not referring to such information even in indirect ways. A primary ethical issue arises when learners are asked to practise coaching and, consequently, to reflect on their practical experience. Such discussions can inexorably lead to restricted territories of sensitive information, even if the credentials of the coachee are not disclosed. This becomes more problematic if the coachee happens to be a fellow member of the learning group. In a more paradoxical manner, the same educational system that dictates rigid confidentiality strictures also compels learners to share potentially confidential information as part of their written assignments, where, in most cases, they are asked to reflect on their coaching practice. Therefore, confidentiality cannot be maintained in its entirety and this raises another ethical issue for the coach educator. What are the boundaries of confidentiality in the learning process?

## Story from practice

Marta is currently pursuing her MA in Coaching and Mentoring at a reputable university. As part of her education, she is required to participate in trio coaching sessions. In essence, these entail a coach, a coachee and an observer, who alternate in assuming the different roles and offer feedback to each other. The sessions adhere to strict confidentiality rules and Marta, just like her colleagues, finds them highly beneficial for learning. However, the last coaching session Marta participated in proved to be an overwhelming experience. This is because her colleague, who assumed the role of the coachee, was reduced to tears owing to her reflections on a deeply emotional issue. Marta was shaken by the experience, which left her feeling uncomfortable. This is a topic she wishes to explore in her assessed assignment but she is afraid that she might be trespassing confidentiality boundaries. Questions to consider:

- If you were Marta's instructor, how would you advise her to approach the issue?
- Would Marta be breaching confidentiality if she wrote about it?
- What might coach educators learn from Marta's case?

Well-defined guidelines that clearly delineate confidentiality boundaries would help anticipate such issues and the anxiety that could ensue from them. Confidentiality is by no means a privileged commodity for the trainee coach, and coaching instructors need to explicitly communicate this to learners and trainees. However, just like in the context of coach supervision, confidential information may be used for the purpose of reflection and learning, as long as it is treated with utmost discretion to protect anonymity. In the case of coach education and training, informed consent is one tool that can be used by the learners, and instructors can introduce such tools to students from the outset of the course. Marta, therefore, might seek her colleague's permission to share part of their mutual experience in an anonymous manner. She might even pass on her draft assignment to her colleague prior to submission for approval. In fact, such cases provide an excellent opportunity for reflection on matters of ethical practice, in safe environments that have been created strictly for learning purposes.

Ultimately, this story from practice shows the significance of clearly demarcating the boundaries of confidentiality. While discussing such cases over coffee during a break from classes is a major ethical misdemeanour, reflecting on the issue in safe, ring-fenced learning environments, like a supervision session or a written assignment, can only help raise and enhance ethical awareness. In this respect, we encourage coach trainers to reflect on the various ethical issues that arise in their professional practice and consider the value of integrating clear ethical guidelines for the coach learner even from the design stage of coach education and training.

## Designing ethical coach education and training

The process of acting ethically is complex and ambiguous (Caroll, 1996). So is the process of learning. In order for learning to have sustained impact, it needs to be situated in a context of critical reflection and reflexivity (Reynolds, 1998). In a similar vein, the most important aspect of creating training that is premised on ethical foundations is to critically reflect on both its design and its delivery. Although there is neither a formula nor a panacea for this process, a way forward may be to integrate some ethical decision-making specifications from the outset of training design. We have found Hawkins and Shohet's checklist (on making ethical decisions in the field of coach supervision) suitable and apt for our purposes. The key parameters that are fit for coach education and training are (2006: 55, 146):

1.  Creating ethical sensitivity:

    -   Create one's own list of moral principles.
    -   Read ethical codes and related literature.
    -   Use case vignettes on ethical and transcultural issues.
    -   Share critical incidents from members' own experience.

2.  Formulating a moral course of action:

    -   Identify the ethical problem or dilemma.
    -   Identify the potential issues involved.

- Review the relevant ethical guidelines.
- Ascertain who else should be consulted.
- Consider possible and probable sources of action.
- Enumerate the consequences of the various options.
- Decide on the best course of action.

3.  Implementing an ethical decision:

- Anticipate the potential difficulties in implementing decisions.
- Explore the internal fears and challenges of taking action.
- Set up the necessary support and strategies for dealing with potential difficulties and challenges.

4.  Living with the ambiguities of an ethical decision:

- Live with the anxiety and fears attending the decision.
- Confronting one's internal and anticipated external critical judgements.
- Accepting the limitations involved.
- Formulating the learning from the experience.

A key argument that we keep reiterating in this book is that making ethical decisions is not always an easy process. If you are a coach instructor, we hope that you agree that, as educators, we have a moral obligation to consider the ethical parameters of the training we offer, in order to ensure high-quality training. Being receptive to the ethical issues entrenched in coach education, openly discussing them, and critically reflecting on them will allow us to enhance our ethical mindfulness. Moreover, it will offer our students the opportunity to become actively involved in the exploration of ethical decisions in their learning and their coaching practice. We therefore would like to suggest some guidelines for the coach educator that stem from our discussions in this chapter. These are the following:

1.  Contemplate on which aspect of coaching you place emphasis in your teaching – practical, theoretical, empirical – and for what reason.
2.  Critically reflect on the issue of power and knowledge and explore how you can utilise your expertise and authority in a manner that is ethical and impactful.
3.  Consider evaluating your teaching practice through peer observation and reflection.
4.  Consider incorporating 'ethics in coaching' as a formal section in all training modules. Case studies are wonderfully conducive to this kind of learning.

## Conclusion

As we keep maintaining in this book, two of the primary objectives of coaching are to enable the process of setting and achieving goals and, by extension, to support the development of a person or a team (Segers and Vloeberghs, 2009; Segers et al., 2011). It is important to emphasise that formal academic credentials do not necessarily guarantee optimal professional standards, let alone an ethical coaching practice. This is because the challenges facing the coaching profession and, by extension, the challenges of coach education and training 'require rapid, cross-disciplinary responses' in a way that no 'monopoly of knowledge' can face them in their entirety (Lane, 2011: 93). In fact, in the current age of digitisation, can we even refer to the educators' monopoly of knowledge? Most probably not, granted that the Internet has played a pivotal role in revolutionising and even democratising knowledge.

On the contrary, we see communities of learning that are premised on the co-creation of knowledge between instructors and learners as more appropriate settings for coach training and education. Such communities have the potential of becoming powerhouses of ethical thinking and behaviour. This is because they provide a safe space for reflection and are, therefore, conducive to the critical thinking that is a prerequisite for ethical practice. For the above reasons, we don't see a universal code of ethics for coach training as the solution for ethical coach education. Such a prospect would engender the risk of subordinating individual beliefs and values in favour of those of others. It would also reduce the opportunities to exercise critical reasoning and underestimate a sense of personal responsibility. Instead, through opportunities for reflection on co-created learning, instructors and learners can help each other develop ethical consciousness in a safe and supportive environment. This is undoubtedly a much more worthwhile learning objective.

## Chapter summary

- Several ethical issues are entrenched in coach education training. These include: academic rigour vs practical application; knowledge as power; and the boundaries of confidentiality in the learning process.
- Formal academic credentials do not necessarily guarantee optimal professional standards, let alone an ethical coaching practice.
- Coach education that is premised on a balanced mixture of academic theory, practical application and critical reflection is beneficial for the development of the coach and the professionalising of coaching.

- Communities of practice that favour the co-creation of knowledge amongst participants offer a more appropriate educational setting for coach training and education.
- A universal code of ethics that underscores and determines the nuances of designing and delivering coach training does not guarantee ethical coach education.
- Coach training and education should afford opportunities for ethical reflections on the part of both the educator and the trainee.

## Suggestions for further reading

For an overview of the state of play of coaching in the realm of education, consider reading:
van Nieuwerburgh, C. (ed.) (2012) *Coaching in Education: Getting Better Results for Students, Educators and Parents*. London: Karnac.

For further analysis of the power dynamics in coach supervision, we suggest:
Hawkins, P. and Shohet, R. (2006) *Supervision in the Helping Professions*, 3rd edn. Maidenhead: Open University Press.

# 10

# Ethical Issues in Sports Coaching

## Chapter aims

- To consider the qualities of an effective sports coach.
- To raise awareness about the various ethical issues a sports coach may encounter when working with athletes.
- To recognise the importance of the coach–athlete relationship in coaching.
- To acknowledge why an ethical approach to coaching in the sports domain is beneficial to all stakeholders involved in sport.

## Chapter overview

This chapter discusses some of the ethical issues relating to the role coaches adopt in the sphere of sports, from recreational to professional competitive sport. We place particular emphasis on professional sports, where the role of the coach is pivotal. This allows us to explore and understand more clearly the ethical issues that may affect the coach–athlete relationship, which, as we shall see, is really important for effective coaching to take place. The chapter starts by delineating the differences between a sports coach of a team or club and that of a coach in other professional contexts, such as the sphere of business. Such clarification will enable us to delve into a discussion on why it is imperative that sports coaches possess deep knowledge of both the sporting discipline they represent, and the mental processes that impact athletes' performance. The ethical implications of dealing with athletes whose physical and psychological well-being is at risk are also considered. Ultimately, this chapter discusses some of the moral values that sports coaches need to cultivate within themselves, as well as instilling in athletes, in order to promote a more ethically based sport participation.

## Key words

sports coach, sports domain, elite sports, respect, ethics

## Introduction

Sports play an important role in our everyday life. By the term 'sports' we refer not only to professional and elite sports, but also to recreational sports, physical activity for physical and mental well-being, youth sport participation, and disability sports, to name a few. To give an example of the different kinds of sports participation, players of prominent football teams such as Manchester United and FC Bayern Munich engage in sports on a professional level. Their sport is their profession: they get paid to do it, and, in consequence, they need to train hard for it on a daily basis. On the other hand, a secondary school student may play netball for her local youth team as a hobby. She does so because she enjoys the thrill she feels when she scores a goal; and she cherishes the opportunity to spend time with her teammates and friends. Yet, she may aspire to becoming a professional player one day. The differences between these kinds of sport participation do not lie only on the levels and motives of participation but, also, on the role the coach plays in each of them. For example, we would most probably agree that the coach of Manchester United or FC Bayern Munich carries much more responsibility towards his players' performance than the school netball coach towards her youth athletes. But is this conjecture practically and ethically accurate? In this chapter, we aim to engage in a fruitful discussion about the importance of ethics in the sports domain.

## The significance of ethics in sport

Generally, sport is associated with improved physical and mental health; promoting teamwork; instilling discipline and instructing other vital life skills; and bringing people together by giving a purpose and meaning in life. If you don't believe this last parameter, consider walking into a pub on the night of the World Cup Final. Sport is also related to the development of several moral values, such as respect, sportsmanship, fair play, facing one's fears, and humility, especially in defeat (Austin, 2013). Austin proposes an Aristotelian approach to coaching. Aristotle believed that each society needs moral individuals to serve as role models. Based on this maxim, Austin (ibid.) views sport as a moral practice whose value lies in implanting virtues that are related to a more ethical and intellectual way of being and behaving. He argues that coaches are in a position to play that role and should strive to be role models and moral agents for all those involved in sport (ibid.).

This implies that, in order to thrive and reach a state of optimum performance, the cultivation of sports skills is not enough. Ethics and moral values, such as the ones mentioned above, need to be brought in. Accordingly, we need to view sports as a way of shaping not only physical but ethical development, as well. If sport is a moral practice, it is not difficult to understand the responsibility of the coach in creating an ethical sports setting (Hardman et al., 2010). In consequence, we could infer that all stakeholders involved with sports, such as athletes, coaches, sponsors and parents, ought to embrace the opportunities it offers to promote a more virtuous way of life. In this chapter, we will explore these reflections further. But first we need to understand how the qualities of an effective coach can promote an ethical approach to coaching in the sphere of sports.

## The sports coach and the coaching professional

For all of us who work as coaches in contexts such as business organisations and public sector institutions, to name just a couple, the definition we have of the coaching professional is somewhat different to that of the *sports coach*. According to Bresser and Wilson (2010: 10), coaching refers to: 'empowering people by facilitating self-directed learning, personal growth, and improved performance'. Van Nieuwerburgh (2014) states that coaching is a process that involves a conversation between a coach and a coachee. This process is based on specific conversational techniques and skills, such as listening and encouraging thinking, summarising and paraphrasing the coachee's statements, asking powerful questions, and giving and receiving feedback, in order to enable the coachee to set and achieve goals (see, ibid.: 8).

These key skills in the coach's toolbox seem to differ from the primary attributes of a sports coach. According to sports coach UK (undated), the national sports coaching body, the skills and qualities required to become a sports coach are the following:

- The ability to effectively communicate with athletes/performers in order to evaluate their needs and ambitions and give constructive feedback.
- Planning and organising sessions and specific programmes in order to help performers develop and meet their needs.
- Analysing and evaluating athletes and their performance in order to determine and guide their progress.
- Creating a safe environment that promotes the performers' well-being.
- Willingness to continually evaluate coaching skills and abilities and to constantly strive to improve them.

We can thus infer that a sports coach is responsible for planning and organising the athletes' training programme, supporting them to develop the skills necessary to perform well, and safeguarding their well-being, along with developing their own role and responsibilities as a coach. On the other hand, coaching, as we know it, is a process that involves basic psychological knowledge and practices.

## Pause for reflection

Take a few moments to consider the roles of a sports coach, as defined above, and a coach working in another professional environment (for example, in business):

- What are the differences between these two roles?
- What are the similarities?

We invite you to write down your answers.

Reflecting on the questions above, we come to the realisation that these two distinct roles are not mutually exclusive. In his acclaimed book *The Inner Game of Tennis*, W. Timothy Gallwey (2015 [1974]) argued that aside from external circumstances, our inner mental state plays a pivotal role in achieving set goals, especially in sports. Indeed, limiting beliefs and self-concepts may interfere with our ability to function optimally in a given situation. In consequence, in order to achieve peak performance in sports, one not only has to be physically and technically ready (outer game); one also needs to have mastered – even silenced – self-imposed negative beliefs (inner game), which can negatively affect performance. Gallwey (ibid.) proposed a more athlete-centred approach to coaching, whereby athletes are given the space to learn from experience what really works for them and what doesn't. This process, he claimed, is bound to help athletes improve and optimise their performance. Gallwey's views were revolutionary for their time, and have affected the way coaching is performed today in various professional contexts. In the sports domain particularly, such a stance implies that the coach takes into account the athlete's emotional well-being. Moreover, it requires the relationship between the coach and the athlete to be grounded in mutual trust and respect.

## The coach–athlete relationship

The coach–athlete relationship forms the foundation of coaching, and involves both coach and athlete appreciating and respecting one another as individuals (Jowett, 2005). This relationship is dynamic and shapes the way athletes and coaches express and fulfil their needs (Jowett and Cockerill, 2002). Moreover, it provides the ground on which qualities such as confidence, leadership skills, self-sufficiency and self-determination can grow (Jowett, 2005). The importance of the coach–athlete relationship has been recognised by a variety of sports organisations. For example, the Department for Culture, Media & Sport (DCMS, 2000) acknowledged this relationship, along with the mentoring and supporting attributes of the coach, as imperative in coaching education. This shows that sports coaching is concerned not only with the development of physical and technical skills, but also with the formation and sustainability of a partnership between a coach and an athlete, which can further enhance the latter's development of physical and psychosocial skills (Jowett, 2005). However, this relationship cannot reach its full potential if coaches are unable to appreciate athletes' emotions and inner goals (Ibid.).

It follows that, in domains such as professional sport, where the competition is fierce, a successful coach ought to have a deep understanding of the intrinsic attributes that help athletes reach their peak performance. In such cases, a basic knowledge of psychology and/or learning and development theories are required to achieve maximum results. Thus, the effective sports coach is expected to possess coaching skills, such as the ones used by coaches in other professional fields, to help athletes to set goals, overcome mental blocks, and achieve optimal performance.

## From principles to practice: practitioner's reflection

Pat McCarry, Executive Coach and Management Consultant, former Director of Coaching at UK Elite Soccer

As a youth soccer coach of high-level teams, I constantly feel the tension caused by the apparent dichotomy of winning and the development of healthy, balanced and rounded human beings. This is an embodied tension, which can manifest as extreme stress, particularly on game day. This pressure to win comes from absorbing the will to win of all those stakeholders at our club, including parents, officials, players and, indeed, myself. I know ways of edging us to victory which bend, if not break, the rules of the sport, and the pressure to do so is strong. I also know areas where I can be more ruthless with my own players in order to get short-term results but this conflicts with the fact that I care very much for these athletes. They know I do.

At times, I feel an urge to follow the darker path. It's visceral. However, this clashes violently with a stronger urge and commitment to a wider and loftier picture which is to help develop human beings who enjoy a healthy sense of self and will benefit society. Sport is a great vehicle in which to do this. In fact, my own sense of self and well-being is inherently connected to the path that I choose. The pressure on me, of course, is incomparable to the crushing pressure that the coaches at the highest level have to work with. At times, they are pawns in a larger game of greed and big business.

In my role, I am given time and know that with time I can develop a strong culture of healthy values, attitudes and purpose. I can nurture an environment which feels safe, inclusive and very much oriented to the well-being of my players. It is a strong and in some ways uncompromising environment because well-being is the unquestioned priority. All parties must be on the same page or it won't work. The incredible thing is that with this unshakable foundation, and a carefully crafted training programme, the results start to come. The apparent dichotomy referenced above dissolves, and we have a happy, successful team that behaves impeccably.

Pat McCarry's reflection demonstrates beautifully the need to combine focus on both physical performance and emotional well-being in sports coaching. Yet, there are cases in which the sports coach is not sufficiently equipped to help athletes address issues that relate to their emotional well-being. Although this book examines ethical coaching in various professional contexts, we view athletes not merely as professionals, whose goal is to improve their physical and mental performance. As we shall see later on in this chapter, athletes may be faced with different kinds of difficulties that may hinder them from achieving their best performance, and even threaten their physical and emotional health. The question that we need to ask in this case is the following: when the coach's expertise is inadequate to support an athlete's physical and mental well-being, what ought a coach to do, from an ethical perspective?

## An example from the Olympic Games

In order to understand the significant role that psychological processes play in sports, we are going to use an example from the Olympic Games, arguably the most competitive sporting event worldwide (Wang and Zhang, 2015). Olympic-level athletes spend endless hours trying to improve their physical, technical and psychological performance. It is not uncommon, however, that even when an athlete feels technically and physically at their peak, their psychological disposition – which can be affected by a variety of factors – can negatively influence their performance (see, for instance, Gallwey, 2015 [1974]). Consider, for example, the most technically gifted footballer in the world, physically in peak condition, about to take a penalty in the World Cup Final. He has practised penalties on countless occasions, but in that moment, with the eyes of the world on him, is his technical and physical preparation enough? Probably not. Mastering psychological control, therefore, is crucial, in order to ensure the best outcome during each competition (Wang and Zhang, 2015).

To return to the context of the Olympic Games, the Chinese freestyle skiing aerial jump teams employed two sports psychology consultants to mentally support the athletes for their participation in the Winter Olympic Games (ibid.). Broadly speaking, a sports psychology consultant is a person who has extensive training, expertise and work experience in the field of sport and exercise psychology. These are professionals who are trained in the psychological processes and practices that can help an athlete accomplish great results in their sport. Their role, although not the same as that of the business or executive coach, is closer to the latter, compared to that of the sports coach.

In the above example the athletes achieved highly successful performance, which was deemed to be the result of the joint efforts of a variety of stakeholders, including sports coaches, athletes, team leaders and the sports psychologists (ibid.). Specifically, the sports psychology team worked closely with the athletes, assessing each individual's needs and designing specific mental training methods and techniques to assist them to reach their full potential. In this process, they also worked in close collaboration with the sports coaches, helping them to recognise the impact of their own behaviours on athletes' performance and teaching them how to identify such behaviours in advance. Common behaviours of this sort include exerting pressure on the athletes before the competition; arguing with or shouting at the athlete when losing their temper; giving too many instructions before or during the competition; and over-emphasising the opponents' abilities, amongst others (ibid.).

In the aforementioned scenario, the sports psychology team involved professionals who were highly experienced in the psychological factors that may interfere with the athletes' physical performance in this particular sport. An ethical consideration, here, is whether a sports coach who works with an elite athlete or team is as qualified as a sports psychologist to assess their individual needs, and offer sound guidance on how to achieve set goals. This is one of the key ethical issues engrained in sports coaching.

## Stories from practice

Take some time to read and reflect on the following scenarios:

- Michael is a professional diver preparing to compete in the Olympic Games. He has improved his routines and technique substantially, yet when he competes in a full stadium he experiences severe anxiety, which affects his performance. He informs his coach that every time he is expected to compete in front of a crowd, thoughts such as 'I'll fail' and 'I'll make a fool of myself' start running through his mind, shifting his concentration off his routine.
- Kelly's basketball team has made it through to the finals and is competing for the regional title. Kelly, who is admittedly one of the best players in the team, finds it difficult to concentrate during the game. The reason is that, two days before the final, she broke up with her boyfriend. During the game, her sports coach, who is unaware of Kelly's emotional turmoil, notices that she is distracted. In consequence, he keeps yelling at her. The sports coach's reaction makes Kelly nervous, which leads to her making even more careless mistakes.
- Chloe is an adolescent and a professional-level gymnast who is preparing for the forthcoming World Gymnastics Championship. She spends many hours training daily and, when she is not training, she dedicates most of her time studying for school. Lately, her sports coach has noticed that Chloe seems distracted, doesn't follow through with her routine, and is constantly moody and ill-tempered. As they have an excellent relationship, she approaches Chloe to find out what might be wrong. Chloe confides in her sports coach that she is extremely pressured by the school and training workload, to the point that she cannot sleep at night. Moreover, she is worried that she is not skinny enough for the upcoming tournament. In order to deal with the stress and her poor body image, she resorts to binge eating and purging, by means of vomiting.

Questions to consider:

- Can the sports coach use conventional coaching skills to help these athletes overcome their emotional difficulties and reach their full potential?
- Is it possible to adopt such techniques during the final game, as in Kelly's case, when the atmosphere is charged?

- Would the sports coach be able to help Michael and Kelly deal with their difficulties and reach their peak performance?
- Is it ethical for the sports coach to address Chloe's mental health symptoms without appropriate training?
- Is it ethical for the sports coach to address any of the above issues if she doesn't have sufficient (or any) training on how to deal with such serious psychological matters?

These are important questions that underpin the quality of the coach–athlete relationship. We need to bear in mind that athletes bring into the game not only their physical strength but also their thoughts, emotions and mental health. A qualified sports psychology consultant would be able to deal with issues such as those in the above scenarios. However, from an ethical standpoint, we need to consider whether a sports coach has the expertise and experience to work through such poignant issues. If, for example, the sports coach is not adequately equipped to deal with such matters and concentrates solely on the athletes' physical performance, they could overlook a very important aspect of their athletes' identity and well-being.

In sum, the ethical issue that arises here is whether the sports coach is qualified to deal with matters of such grave importance. If she is not qualified enough to do so, what needs to be done so that the athlete's well-being is safeguarded? We believe that a sports coach who works from an ethical standpoint is aware of the boundaries of her knowledge and expertise, and therefore knows when to refer the athlete to a more appropriate professional, such as a psychologist. In consequence, a coach who values her athletes may choose to raise her concerns with them and either refer them to another professional who is more qualified to help them work through their difficulties, or support them to seek further help themselves. The coach's actions in this case will certainly depend on her professional code of ethics, which will allow her to act in a morally sound manner, for her benefit as well as that of the athletes. But what happens if the benefit of the athlete contradicts that of the team or club? In other words, whom does the coach work for – who is the client?

## Who is the client in sports coaching?

As we already explored in Chapter 8, the question of who is the client is an important one that will define the coaching relationship. It therefore needs to be asked and answered prior to embarking on the coaching process. What happens when the sponsor of a team hires a coach to work with the athletes for the sole purpose of victory at all costs? Who is the client in this case – the sponsor or the athletes?

Let's consider the following scenario. An experienced coach has just been employed by the owner of a mid-level professional sports team to help boost their performance. In particular, he is asked to help the team win games. At the very outset of the coaching process, the coach realises that some of the athletes need to address other deeply rooted issues that are preventing them from maximising performance and achieving set targets. In particular, one athlete has been dealing with a long-term injury, which affects not only his physical performance but also his psychological disposition towards the way he plays; he is reluctant to perform at his best, for fear that his injury might get worse. Another player's performance is adversely affected by constant negative self-talk. In addition, two of the players have not been on good terms lately, and this has had a negative impact on the dynamics of the team during practice. The coach realises that these issues need to be thoroughly addressed so that each player can achieve optimum performance. However, time is limited and the sponsor, who pays his fees, pushes for desirable results. What might the coach do?

A coach who works from an ethical standpoint will first need to consider whether all stakeholders (coach, athletes and sponsor) have a mutual understanding of the purpose of coaching. If their goals and aspiration are not mutual, is it ethical to embark upon this alliance? How will such collaboration affect the team? These are important ethical questions that need to be carefully thought through and agreed upon, ideally during the contracting phase. The coach will then need to address each of the issues the players are dealing with, and work with each one of them individually to make sure that both their physical and mental well-being are safeguarded, which can ultimately have a positive impact on the team's overall performance. Tapping into her value system and assessing her professional values will allow the coach to embark on the relationship with honesty and clarity for the benefit of all stakeholders. It is, therefore, paramount that the sport coach clarifies the ethical parameters in which she works and clearly communicates her work ethic to her employers. A well-defined contract from the outset of the coaching relationship will allow all parties involved to have mutual understanding of the purpose of coaching, and will promote honest and positive communication.

## An ethical approach to coaching in sports

Honest and positive communication between all parties involved in sport is crucial for the unity of the team and the optimum performance of the players (Jowett, 2005). Communication allows for mutual understanding and formation of attributes such as goals, beliefs and values, and promotes the development of the coach–athlete relationship. More specifically, coaches who show an interest in their athletes' daily routines and allow for discussion and self-disclosure are more likely to create truthful and honest relationships with them (ibid.).

This is very important, especially in youth sports, as children and adolescents are in a developmental stage, during which interaction with professionals who consciously strive for an ethical practice can promote the emulation of ethical behaviour. According to Austin (2013), all those involved in sports, particularly youth sports, should strive for sporting excellence, and not mere victory for the sake of it. We know for a fact that sport victory can be the outcome of a variety of factors apart from hard training and technical skills. Such factors include luck, officials' mistakes, injuries and the athlete's mental state. This means that victory is not the only factor that determines athletic excellence. Winning is important and is certainly self-fulfilling but other parameters that are related to winning, such as team spirit, group work, fair play and good communication between coach and players, to name but a few, should also be sought and reflected upon.

Sports coaches ought to be aware that their role and actions influence the athletes they work with. Hardman et al. (2010) view the sports coach as a moral agent who should regard each game as means to exhibit good character and promote fair play, rather than concentrate on winning or losing. It is our belief that a sports coach who works from an ethical standpoint values each athlete not only for their technical and tactical performance, but also as individuals who participate in sports in order to cultivate respect and fairness towards themselves, their team players, their opponents and the sport itself.

To better work with their athletes, sports coaches are urged to cultivate self-awareness. Hardman et al. (ibid.) suggest that sports coaches need to be consciously self-aware before trying to understand their athletes. First, they need to have a good understanding of their own sporting history, which will help them assess how various physical stimuli either hindered or worked in their favour throughout their lives. They then need to assess how their inner states, which include their thoughts, aspirations, emotions and mental well-being, have shaped who they are and how they interact with the world. In the long run, being consciously self-aware can help sport coaches understand that they are individuals with moral responsibility and that their actions influence a great number of people, particularly their athletes (ibid.). Thus, an ethical approach to coaching presupposes that coaches are aware of their own ethical and moral standards before engaging with a sports team or individual.

## Respecting the athlete as an individual

A coach who works from an ethical standpoint will prioritise respect towards the athlete and the opponent. As several scandals making newspaper headlines have recently shown, unethical behaviour is more than uncommon in the realm of sports (Austin, 2013): athletes making use of illegal substances to enhance their performance; becoming violent against opponents and referees; pursuing victory at any cost, regardless of the means; or prioritising personal advancement over effective teamwork – these are some examples of potential breach of 'fair play', aside from several fraud claims involving highly positioned sports officials. Of course, such behaviours are not only evident in the domain of professional sports. In youth sport, for example, there are many instances when parents: force their children to participate for the sake of victory and not for fun; challenge the decisions or authority of sports officials or the coach; and foster a highly competitive environment that is not conducive to enjoyment and effective participation (Austin, 2013). Amidst all this, it is not uncommon that athletes lose sight of the essence of respect for themselves, their team-players, and, importantly, their opponents. Coaches who exhibit genuine concern for their sport and actively show their concern through their own actions and behaviours are more likely to act as role models who inspire young athletes to act in similarly virtuous ways (Jones, 2009; Hardman et al., 2010).

Grounding the coaching relationship on an ethical behaviour will enable the coach to understand the individual needs of any athlete. The ethical standpoint, here, involves accepting that each athlete is unique. By paying attention to each one's individuality, the coach can gain insight into who the athlete really is and what coaching techniques they can benefit more from. Indeed, each athlete possesses not only technical abilities but also a variety of other attributes such as strengths and weaknesses, fears and aspirations, and coping mechanisms and endurances that impact on his or her performance (Hardman et al., 2010). It is only when coaches view athletes as whole persons, and not simply sports professionals, that they can help them set and achieve goals.

## Respecting justice and fair play in sport

Taking this notion a step further, sports coaches have a moral obligation to respect the nature of the sport they serve, in relation to fair play. Hardman et al. (2010) argue that the practice of coaches could be greatly enriched by virtue ethics, which can help understand both the nature of coaching and the attitude of stakeholders related to the sport. Subsequently, performing in the most technically precise, well-executed manner is not enough, if the athlete does not possess specific values such as perseverance, patience, generosity when winning, and accepting defeat with grace.

Can sports coaches help the athlete in these situations? They certainly can. Coaches can set an example for their athletes by taking responsibility for their roles and respecting the rules of their sport. In doing so, they can actively teach their athletes humility, generosity and taking responsibility for one's own actions. This is particularly important in elite sports. When sports coaches take responsibility for their own values and ethics, they set an example for the athletes they work with to approach their sport with dignity, humility and honesty (ibid.). In other words, coaches who work in an ethical manner strive for justice in sports and instil the same desire in their athletes. Such justice is apparent when team players collaborate with each other for the benefit of the whole team, when everyone involved in sports treats each other with respect and values their uniqueness, and when teams compete for a higher purpose (for example, to raise money for charity).

Ultimately, when sports coaches adhere to the values of justice and fair play and when they respect each athlete's individuality, they set a powerful example to emulate. In this manner, coaches act as role models who inspire athletes to respect themselves, their teammates and their opponents. The more respect and integrity that coaches bring into the relationship they form with athletes, the more respect there will be for athletes to exhibit and bring out in sports, which can inevitably lead to a more righteous and venerable sporting world.

## Conclusion

This chapter concentrated mainly on the role of the coach in elite sports, where coaches are increasingly asked to offer their expertise. We invite you to consider the value of the role of the sports coach in professional and recreational sports, and how coaching from an ethical standpoint can benefit them. Given how important sport is in various cultures, we also encourage you to consider whether you think a coach can inspire those involved directly or indirectly with sports (for example, athletes, sponsors, parents and sports fans) to adopt a more ethical stance which is grounded in values such as sportsmanship, teamwork and fair play, to name a few.

As we have already observed, the coach–athlete relationship is the foundation of coaching (Jowett, 2005) and should not only concentrate on performance, achievements and competitive success; it is primarily a moral process with distinct ethical dimensions. It is our belief that in the realm of sports a sports coach with strong ethics is needed to help athletes reach their peak performance. This is particularly pertinent in professional and elite sports, where competition is fierce, performance is the be-all-end-all, and the athletes' physical and psychological skills affect the outcome. An ethical sports coach will have a clear understanding of her abilities and limits: if her expertise is not enough to safeguard the welfare of her athletes, she will not shy away from seeking that guidance from other professionals for the benefit of the athletes. Ultimately, combining her expertise with that of other colleagues will help to promote sports involvement in a way that is ethical and respectful to the athletes themselves and the sport in general.

## Chapter summary

- An effective sports coach enables athletes to achieve peak performance while caring for both their physical and mental well-being.
- A well-defined contract will help delineate the purpose of sports coaching for all relevant stakeholders.
- Awareness of the boundaries of coaching is a major ethical issue in the context of sports coaching.
- When coaches promote values and ethics in sports coaching, they act as role models who inspire athletes to help create a more virtuous world of sports.

---

### Suggestions for further reading

For an overview of how various coaching and psychological principles can be successfully implemented in the sports domain, we recommend:
Gallwey, W.T. (2015 [1974]) *The Inner Game of Tennis: The Ultimate Guide to the Mental Side of Peak Performance*. London: Pan Books.

For a comprehensive anthology on various ethical and philosophical issues facing sports nowadays, we would suggest:
Boxill, J. (ed.) (2003) *Sport Ethics: An Anthology*. Oxford: Blackwell.

If you're interested in an outline of an Aristotelian approach to ethics and values, consider the following:
Crisp, R. (ed.) (2014) *Aristotle: Nicomachean Ethics*, revd edn. Cambridge: Cambridge University Press.

# 11

# Ethical Issues for
# Coaching in Healthcare

## Chapter aims

- To engage in a critical dialogue with the dominant discourses of coaching in health.
- To unravel the ethical issues that surround of coaching in a health context.
- To provide insights from practice.
- To introduce an approach for developing ethical coaching in healthcare: 'making every conversation count'.

## Chapter overview

This final chapter of the book seeks to stimulate thought around the nuances of ethics for coaching in a health context. In recent years, health policy in the UK has cast increasing emphasis on inclusivity. As a result, more equal partnerships between professionals and the public are now considered crucial to improving health service quality. This marks a shift away from traditional approaches of 'doing to' people, towards more collaborative approaches of 'doing with' people. This shift in policy and perspective has implications for the kinds of coaching that take place in healthcare and the ethical issues that emerge as a result of it. Indeed, the context of healthcare creates a rich tapestry of ethical issues that are interwoven between the coaching relationship and the nature of ethics in healthcare more widely. In consequence, coaching in this context is perhaps not as straightforward as in other professional contexts. In this chapter, we attempt to provide a general overview of coaching in healthcare and the ethical issues that arise.

We begin by taking a look at the changing landscape of UK healthcare, in order to contextualise the kind of coaching that takes place within this context. Even though we use the National Health Service (NHS) as the focal point in this chapter, the discussion of ethical issues emerging in this context is more widely applicable beyond UK healthcare. We then examine some of the key ethical challenges for coaching in this context. We particularly focus on an emerging type of coaching in healthcare – health coaching (coaching patients) – and the implications this holds for an ethical coaching practice as a whole. The chapter concludes by offering some overarching principles for guiding ethical practice for coaching in this context. These are represented in the concept of 'making every conversation count' (Hawley, 2012, 2015), a philosophy that underpins this chapter.

## Key words

relationship, power, hierarchy, informal coaching, conversation, coaching patients

## The changing landscape of healthcare in the UK

The landscape of healthcare in the UK is continually changing. Over the last decade, healthcare policies have striven for inclusivity, focusing on more equal partnerships between professionals, patients and the public. Such partnerships are now considered crucial to improving public services (Boyle and Harris, 2009; Boyle et al., 2010; DH, 2010, 2013). As such, with the passage of time, there has been a significant move away from earlier approaches of 'doing to' patients, towards more collaborative approaches of 'doing with' patients.

The dialogue between healthcare professionals and people who use healthcare services is one of the fundamental pillars of the National Health Service (NHS). The increasing call for collaboration between health professionals and patients in UK healthcare reflects the core principles of coaching within this context. As such, coaching has an important role to play against this backdrop. Figure 11.1 shows how healthcare has been evolving since the inception of the NHS, and how too the paradigm for coaching has been changing and developing, reflecting this progression.

The changes that we describe above have led to a growing uptake of coaching in healthcare organisations. This apparent congruence between the evolution of UK healthcare and coaching conceals some key contradictions. For example, until recently, health leaders have

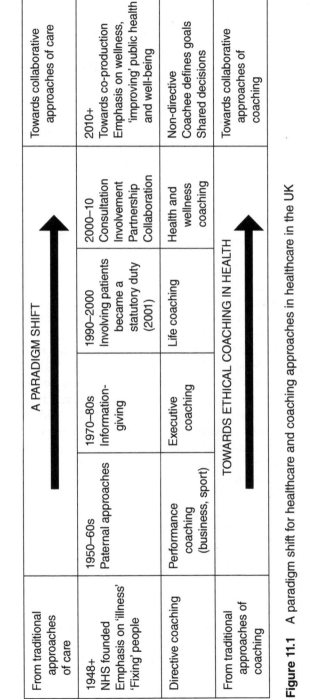

**Figure 11.1** A paradigm shift for healthcare and coaching approaches in healthcare in the UK

tended to favour top-down styles which have focused more on the delivery of targets, than the engagement of the public and staff (Rowling, 2012). Research findings now indicate that such top-down approaches have failed to influence cultural change for greater inclusivity and quality in the desired ways (Coulter, 2012; Coulter et al., 2013). This engenders several ethical issues in healthcare that have implications for coaching in this context. In fact, there seems to be an interrelation between ethical issues in healthcare and the ethical issues that arise for coaching in this context. This interrelation between ethical issues forms the background of this chapter. In this respect, before we move on to examine some of the key ethical issues for coaching in healthcare, it is important to understand what coaching in this context looks like today.

## Where does coaching take place in healthcare?

As we have seen, the landscape of healthcare in the UK (and beyond) is changing. The changes we describe have implications for how we think about the ways in which coaching takes place for healthcare staff, but also for those who use healthcare services. Coaching is not new in this context. On the contrary, it has been evolving over time, taking various shapes and forms, and it is applied in diverse settings across the healthcare sector (MacKensie, 2007; Carter et al., 2015). Here we outline some types of coaching that take place in this context.

Figure 11.2 shows examples of coaching that exist in healthcare. The iceberg visually represents the evident and the less evident coaching that a variety of individuals receive. On the surface, we can only see a proportion of the coaching: the structured type that we know, which primarily senior leaders receive. This does not reflect the whole picture. Beneath the surface, there are a plethora of coaching varieties targeted at the wider NHS workforce. These varieties of coaching permeate the whole healthcare system spanning formal and more informal coaching (and mentoring) relationships. We cannot ignore this vast spectrum, because it carries significant implications for coaching ethically in this context. So, let's take a brief look at the different types of coaching that take place in the healthcare sector.

In such a complex setting as the NHS, which requires decisions that directly or indirectly affect every one of us, it is not unsurprising that coaching has been offered to senior leaders and managers for many years. Coaching at this level is similar to the coaching that is generally offered in other organisational contexts, such as business and education; it can include executive coaching, leadership coaching

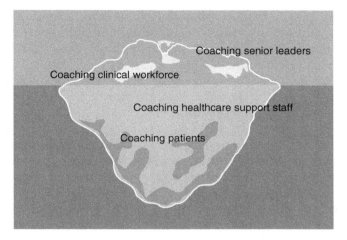

**Figure 11.2** Perspectives of coaching in healthcare: the current view

or performance coaching, for example. As such, coaching supports continuing professional development through one-to-one conversations or group coaching (see, for instance, Ponte et al., 2006).

Thus aside from the evident coaching we see on the surface, coaching permeates the wider healthcare sector. People who receive coaching in this context include for example clinicians (such as doctors, nurses and other allied health professionals), and support staff (such as healthcare assistants and porters), to name just a few (see, for instance, Williamson, 2009; Woodhead, 2011). The landscape here is more blurred. In essence, coaching can be formal, although it often happens informally and is embedded in different learning and development interventions, such as clinical supervision, personal development planning and reviews, and mentoring. The remit of coaching can be developmental and performance related, and employees experience it either on a one-to-one basis or in teams. In this blurry landscape, coaching may not even be called 'coaching' and it is, at times, difficult to recognise.

To complicate matters even more, clinical staff who operate on this level may be both receiving coaching and using coaching approaches in their practice. As such, they assume the dual role of the professional practitioner (be it a manager, clinician or healthcare support staff, amongst others) and the internal coach. The internal coach then, within the healthcare context, is an NHS professional who either coaches consciously in formal ways, or is expected to use coaching skills and conversations in their work with others, in ways that are informal and less conscious. As such, the internal coach may be acting as a coach to peers, or may be using coaching skills with underlings, reflecting the manager-as-coach model (Ellinger et al., 2014) that we discussed in Chapter 8. Increasingly, over the past few years, the internal coach has had a new remit or responsibility – coaching patients.

Coaching patients is a more recently developed type of coaching in healthcare (Moore and Jackson, 2014: 313–28; Hawley, 2015). It involves clinicians and other groups within the NHS who are trained (or even not trained but encouraged) to use coaching skills and coaching conversations in order to encourage patients to take ownership of their condition and health. Coaching patients is an innovative approach that supports patients to become more active participants in their own health. One widely cited definition of this type of coaching describes it as an approach for 'helping people gain the knowledge, skills, tools and confidence to become active participants in their own care so that they can reach their self-identified health goals' (Bennett et al., 2010: 24). Some other terms used to refer to this kind of coaching are 'health coaching', 'wellness coaching' or 'self-management coaching' (Hawley, 2015: 117).

Coaching patients is particularly relevant to the shift towards patient inclusion in healthcare that we discussed above (Coulter et al., 2013; Hibbard and Gilburt, 2014). This is because it enables the conversations that support patient recovery and self-management of long-term conditions. It also reflects the changing emphasis from 'illness' to 'wellness', by supporting lifestyle and behaviour change for improving public health and well-being. Such changes, for example, involve the promotion of physical exercise and smoking cessation (American College of Preventive Medicine, 2009).

The types of coaching described above represent the breadth and depth of coaching that takes place in contemporary healthcare. In particular, the emergence of patient coaching is gradually influencing the way that coaching is adopted in healthcare more widely. In consequence, the shift in healthcare policy towards greater collaboration between health professionals and patients has implications not only for the type of coaching that takes place within healthcare, but also for the ethical issues that arise in it. These, as we shall see, are inextricably intertwined with some of the most pertinent ethical issues facing contemporary healthcare.

## Ethical issues for coaching in healthcare

Against the changing landscape of healthcare, here we seek to highlight some of the key ethical issues for coaching in healthcare. We begin with a discussion on the key ethical issues facing internal coaches in this context, especially those who are asked to coach patients. We then open up the discussion to consider why these issues also affect external coaches and the wider coaching community. Our main argument is that ethical coaching in healthcare needs to be a shared endeavour: both internal and external coaches have a role to play in cultivating and disseminating an ethical coaching mindset.

In the introduction of this chapter, we alluded to the increasing prioritisation of coaching approaches over the habitual preferences of clinicians, who have been trained in more directive approaches to communication with patients. This is one of the core ethical issues facing internal coaches in the NHS. To be more specific, conversations in healthcare take many different forms, ranging from the traditional direct instruction of the expert clinician, to the more contemporary facilitative approach of the coach. The former involves offering direct advice with a focus on solutions, which can result in dependency and fear. The latter entails helping patients take ownership and responsibility of their condition and health. In a way, we see a clash between directive and non-directive approaches. This, in itself, changes the dynamic of the relationship and presents both ethical challenges and opportunities.

Fundamentally, coaching conversations in healthcare start from where the person is. Thus, the coach holds a more facilitative role (Moore and Jackson, 2014). No matter who the coach is (internal or external), 'coaching presumes a collaborative paradigm (asking patients what changes they are willing to make) rather than a directive paradigm (telling patients what to do)' (Bodenheimer et al., 2002, cited in Bennett et al., 2010: 25). In an article pertinently entitled 'Does Your Practice "Give Patient's a Fish" or "Teach Patients to Fish"?', Bennett et al. (2010: 25) argue that 'a good health coach [...] grasps the shift from rescuing to coaching'. These views are reminiscent of the familiar adage: 'Give a man a fish, and he eats for a day; teach a man to fish and he eats for a life-time'; this appositely reflects the difference between traditional approaches in healthcare, which focus on rescuing patients by identifying problems and offering solutions (solution-focused), compared to emerging coaching approaches, which are more facilitative in nature (outcome-focused). In essence, there is an incongruity – even clash – between the expert approach of the clinician and the facilitative approach of the coach, which is summarised in Table 11.1.

The literature is beginning to show that coaching patients, which encourages people to take more ownership of managing their health, can help reduce healthcare cost for issues such as the management of long-term conditions and improving public health and well-being (Wolever et al., 2013). If this is the premise from which we begin, then a

**Table 11.1**  The expert versus coach approach

| Expert approach | Coach approach |
| --- | --- |
| Authority | Partner |
| Educator | Facilitator of change |
| Define agenda | Elicit client's agenda |
| Feel responsible for client's health | Client is responsible for health |
| Solve problems | Foster possibilities |
| Focus on what's wrong | Focus on what's right |
| Have the answers | Co-discover the answers |
| Interrupt if off-topic | Learn from the client's story |
| Working harder than the client | Client working as hard as the coach |
| Wrestle with client | Dance with client |

*Source*: Moore and Jackson (2014: 317).

key ethical issue for the internal coach is to balance and prioritise, coaching conversations over the traditional (and habitual) approaches of offering direct instructions to patients on how to manage their condition. The differences between these traditional approaches and facilitative coaching conversations need to be reconciled, if coaching is to be effective and ethically grounded. However, it is important to emphasise here that we do not advocate one way or another; each of these approaches has a place and it depends on the intention. Is the intention of the clinician to coach, or is it to offer advice, even directive advice? In situations that are acute, it may be necessary to call on an *expert* approach. Conversely, supporting people in the self-management of living with long-term conditions calls for the more *collaborative* approach that coaching offers.

This brings us back to the key ethical issues relating to professional backgrounds and contexts that we discussed in Chapter 7. In essence, coaches need to be consciously aware of the professional expertise with which they approach and work with patients. Do they work with the patient as the expert who has the answer to the problem, or do they facilitate the patient's self-management of her condition and health? Against this view of coaching in healthcare, we consider some further ethical issues for internal coaches:

- *Capacity building and training*: Internal coaches who are increasingly encouraged to employ coaching approaches in dealing with patients are not always adequately trained to do so. As such, the transition from the traditional and direct medical model towards a more facilitative coaching approach poses a challenge.
- *Competing perceptions of the professional role*: Internal coaches (e.g. clinicians) must be clear about the approach they are expected to

use in relation to patients' expectations. This is necessary to ensure clear boundaries between offering advice and enabling the self-management of long-term conditions and/or supporting lifestyle and behaviour change for improved health and well-being. As we already discussed above, this will depend on context.

- *Managing expectations*: Following from the above issues, internal coaches should be able to clearly communicate to patients the way they will be working with them. This is particularly important for patients who expect to be told what to do in order to manage their health.

These are some of the primary ethical issues facing internal coaches in healthcare, especially those who, in one way or another, coach patients, as well as staff. But what about ethical issues facing external coaches and the wider coaching community? There seems to be an assumption that staff who receive informal coaching in the healthcare sector – such as healthcare assistants and porters, as we mentioned above – are somehow aware and capable of using those facilitative coaching conversations that can help foster a culture of coaching within the NHS. This is most certainly not the case. External coaches have an important role to play in this. By raising awareness of the enabling nature of coaching conversations and the significance of acknowledging that the coachee is capable of taking ownership of personal issues, external coaches can disseminate this coaching mindset to their coachees and, through them, towards the wider healthcare workforce. In essence, coaching can create a ripple that can enable coaching conversations to develop across the organisation, for staff and for patients. Viewed from this light, external coaches become 'capacity builders', who can contribute to the cultural shift in healthcare. They can do so in a variety of ways: through their one-to-one coaching with their coachees (who, in turn, may be asked to coach other members of staff); through delivering training; through participation in professional networks; and through disseminating ideas in conferences and other such initiatives.

We believe that, regardless of professional background and context, both external and internal coaches have a role to play in anticipating and dealing with ethical issues in healthcare. The ways in which we think about 'coaching', 'health' and 'context' will determine how we might think about coaching in healthcare. As we already discussed in Chapter 7, being conscious of the needs and boundaries of professional contexts is key. Within a healthcare context, our personal and professional values may clash with institutional values and priorities. This clash engenders significant ethical issues for coaches. How can we recognise and manage these tensions in our practice? We can do so by consciously understanding *who* we are when we coach, *where* we are when we coach, and *how* we coach, as we discussed in Chapter 7. The starting point, however, is understanding our personal and professional values and how they are congruent, or clash, with the institutional values and priorities of the healthcare system.

Ultimately, ethical coaching in healthcare entails understanding the impact of our work on the whole system; not only directly on our coachee but indirectly and more widely on healthcare. We therefore need to think beyond the immediate role of building and sustaining coaching relationships in this setting. Our introduction to these key ethical issues is only dipping a toe into the ocean. A book chapter is not enough to allow us to immerse ourselves deeply into the complex ethical issues that emerge in coaching within this context. We hope, however, that these introductory reflections will offer some ideas and direction for further exploration of these issues, beyond this chapter and beyond this book.

---

## Pause for reflection

Think about your own experience of healthcare (it doesn't matter whether you coach in healthcare or not):

- What ethical issues first enter your thoughts?

Now imagine that you are answering this question wearing a different hat:

- Firstly, as an external coach (independent coach), coaching within the healthcare sector.
- Secondly, as an internal coach (health professional or health worker).

What do you notice? How do your perspectives vary depending on the hat you wear?

---

Just as ethics and healthcare are inextricably bound together, so too are our personal and professional perspectives of the kind of ethical issues that arise for coaching in this context. One of the interesting aspects of these kinds of ethical explorations is that there is no truly right or wrong way. However, exploring this complex terrain from these different perspectives can help us to better understand these issues and find practical ways to address them.

## What can the coaching community do to address these ethical issues?

Throughout this chapter, we have tried to illuminate some of the key ethical issues and considerations for coaching in a healthcare context.

**Table 11.2**  Core factors for addressing ethical issues
for coaching in healthcare

| | |
|---|---|
| **Coaching culture** | Why are we doing this? Have we got the right mindset? |
| **Capacity** | What steps can be taken to build the necessary capacity, capability and confidence for working in this way? |
| **Impact** | How do we know coaching is making a difference? Are we taking account of both financial and social impact? |

One of the features that distinguishes coaching in healthcare from other contexts is the direct influence of government health policy and the regulation of how coaching is evolving within this context. We believe that ethical coaching in healthcare is dependent on the engagement of the wider coaching community. The factors shown in Table 11.2 can be a starting point for beginning to consider how the coaching community can help anticipate and address ethical issues for coaching in this context. We encourage you to take some time to consider these factors from the perspective of the coach, the patient and the healthcare organisation.

Although we have only introduced these issues briefly, there are some principles for practice that speak to these ethical concerns. We discuss these below. In agreement with Bond (2015: 20), we view ethical frameworks as a form of metaphorical scaffolding that enables practitioners to become more ethically mindful and confident. In this way, coaches in a variety of settings (formal and informal) can harness the potential for achieving a shared understanding of ethical issues and an ethical commitment. Such frameworks do not provide moral shortcuts towards a single answer to our ethical dilemmas; there is neither one way nor one single answer. Rather, they constitute rich sources of ethical information, acting as a valuable point of reference for any coach navigating this complex ethical terrain.

Still, in order to address ethical issues for coaching in healthcare, we need to consider approaches that allow everyone involved in coaching in this setting – or indeed anyone using healthcare services – to share stories, experiences and perceptions of ethical issues for collective learning. This will help guide future coaching development and practice. To be able to achieve this, it is important to understand that ethical coaching in healthcare (and beyond) is not simply the product of a set of skills. Rather, it is the mixture of attributes that emerge from character, commitment, personal integrity and authenticity. Modelling the attributes of ethical coaching engages, empowers and liberates ethical ways of being in everyone. It takes courage, self-trust and resilience. Whatever your position as a coach (external coach, internal coach, indeed, as we move further to the future, a patient coach), the starting point is having the willingness to learn and a mindset to model ethical behaviour. This kind of learning is not simply about coaching skills. Engaging in formal or informal programmes of learning enriches our knowledge and experiences. But ethical coaching goes beyond training; it is about developing an ethical way of being. For an internal coach this may mean re-crafting conversations that help navigate the shift from 'expert practitioner' towards 'coaching facilitator': from 'doing to' patients, to 'doing with' patients.

But how can the coach 're-craft' conversations that take place in healthcare settings, in order to move from 'expert practitioner' to 'coaching facilitator'? We believe that one way of achieving this is through the philosophy and approach of 'making every conversation count' (Hawley, 2012, 2015). This philosophy is the outcome of a piece of qualitative research that looked at the role of informal coaching (and mentoring) in the NHS, in order to address apparent inequities (Hawley, 2012). The research findings showed that, in order to harness the potential for ethical coaching in healthcare, we need to move beyond traditional perspectives of formal coaching. Moreover, the more informal types of coaching that take place in healthcare need to be elevated and capitalised upon, in order to bring those unrecognised coaching conversations into consciousness.

So, what exactly does the philosophy of 'making every conversation count' entail? In essence, 'making every conversation count' involves embracing the notion of an 'anytime, anywhere, any place' kind of learning that emerges through facilitative coaching conversations. Table 11.3 shows in detail what the key elements of this philosophy are. It provides a starting point for how we might think about ethical coaching, valuing lived experience as much as the qualification.

**Table 11.3**  A process for introducing coaching

| | |
|---|---|
| **Level 1**<br>*Readiness* | Readiness for engaging in these kinds of conversations |
| **Level 2**<br>*Getting started* | All staff (clinical and non-clinical) are able to recognise opportunities for making every conversation count by using basic coaching skills in every interaction with patients |
| **Level 3**<br>*Getting going* | Staff are able to select and use a range of professional, behavioural change and coaching techniques (e.g. GROW) to provide support to individual patients |
| **Level 4**<br>*Making every conversation count* | Staff are able to harness the potential for coaching patients from the individual conversations to the wider conversations across the health system as a whole |

Our development as coaches is much like an actual journey. Some of the landmarks on this journey will represent formal learning with a linear progression. This may span from short workshops and accredited courses, to undergraduate and postgraduate qualifications. Abridged with these are the more informal approaches that we described earlier in the book, such as developing reflective practice (see Chapter 2). This kind of learning, wonderfully described by Alred et al. as *'Pas de deux*: Learning in Conversation' (1998: 308), 'occurs through revisiting and re-examining recurring issues in working life to arrive at new perspectives and new commitments to act in new ways'. Enabling and encouraging such conversations, therefore, offers the opportunity for learning for both coaches and patients.

## From principles to practice: practitioner's reflection

### Andrew McDowell, Director of Health Coaching, The Performance Coach

I believe that if we want people to be more activated and self-managing, we need to also focus on supporting health practitioners to be more activated. The way we have conversations in healthcare needs to change. We need practitioners who are conscious of their consultation style, thoughtful about how they structure their conversations, and ready to use every opportunity to engage and work in partnership with the people who use health services.

Many clinicians see the need to adapt their approach, using a coaching approach to support the transition from expert provider of knowledge, towards more equal relationships with their patients that enable person-centred care. This approach is often characterised as supporting a conversation between two experts: the clinician who is expert in diagnosis, aetiology and treatment approaches; and the patient who is the expert in their own life and ultimately responsible for how they manage their health.

The movement from practice based in a biomedical model towards a biopsychosocial approach characterised by coaching style interactions is clearly a step in the right direction, but it brings a new series of ethical and values-based challenges. Professionals using coaching in healthcare bring different skills and mindsets to their role that can conflict with existing assumptions, relationships and systems. The task is to use coaching in a way that aligns with clinical roles and responsibilities, walking the line between using expertise and managing risk while encouraging people to generate their own solutions and trusting them to make decisions for themselves. Equally, external coaches interacting with the health system need to be mindful of the assumptions they bring, and how their approach to coaching aligns with a system in transition.

This reflection summarises why the coaching community should be involved in fostering a more collaborative culture in the NHS, and why 'making every conversation count' is an approach that can facilitate this process. Below we offer some further reflections on practical ways in which the coaching community can address the ethical issues that we have highlighted in this chapter, acting as a conduit for ethical practice. These are the following:

- Bringing ethical issues to the surface of our consciousness.
- Sharing conversations about ethical issues with other coaches as a way of everyday practice.
- Giving consideration to the role of external coach as capacity builder for ethical coaching for others, through both one-to-one coaching and through training, networks, conference attendance, etc.
- Clarifying roles through formal and informal contracting, anticipating potential ethical issues and addressing these.
- Seeing supervision as a place where these kinds of ethical issues can be explored, in a safe and trusting space.

Ultimately, the golden thread that binds together approaches for ethical coaching is simply modelling good practice. Modelling the attributes of ethical coaching engages, empowers and liberates ethical ways of being in everyone. As outlined earlier, it takes courage, self-trust and resilience. In this way we can, perhaps, make every conversation count, in order to enhance the use of coaching in a healthcare context.

## Conclusion

The changes in UK healthcare policy that have taken place over the last decade mark a paradigm shift away from traditional approaches of 'doing to' patients, towards more collaborative approaches of 'doing with' patients. In essence, there has been a shift of focus from illness to wellness that requires greater collaboration between healthcare staff and patients. This move towards greater collaboration in healthcare resonates with the core principles of coaching. Due to the inherent complexities of the healthcare system, coaching ethically in this context requires moving beyond a set of prescribed skills and capabilities; it entails acknowledging the significance of context and modelling ethical behaviours. The dominant narrative created by organisations has favoured top-down strategies in order to develop coaching cultures. However, ethical coaching in healthcare entails harnessing the less-used systemic approaches, which require 'a reflexive rationality that suspends assumptions from a number of perspectives' (Clutterbuck and Megginson, 2005: 78). The concept of 'making every conversation count' (Hawley, 2012, 2015) carries with it implications for developing ethical coaching practice. Embracing this notion of an 'anytime, anywhere, any place kind of learning' opens up opportunities for everyone; external coaches, internal coaches, patients and the wider public who use healthcare services.

## Chapter summary

- Coaching is congruent with a shift in UK healthcare away from 'doing to' people, towards 'doing with' people.
- Coaches have an important role in harnessing the potential for the paradigm shift that we described above, towards more collaborative relationships between health professionals and people who use healthcare services.
- Ethical coaching in healthcare is not about finding solutions but, rather, creating the conditions, through coaching conversations, that underlying ethical issues to the surface.
- Ethical coaching in the context of healthcare is not simply an outcome of a set of skills and competencies; rather, it entails embracing a coaching approach that is congruent with the changing nature of the healthcare system.
- The concept of 'making every conversation count' carries with it implications for developing an ethical coaching practice; valuing professional knowledge and experience in equal measure.

## Suggestions for further reading

For a deeper exploration of values and ethics across the helping professions, take a look at:

Seedhouse, D. (2009) *Ethics: The Heart of Healthcare*, 3rd edn. West Chichester: Wiley.

For a practical application of personal values across professional contexts, we recommend:

Lennard, D. (2010) *Coaching Models: A Cultural Perspective: A Guide to Model Development for Practitioners and Students of Coaching*. New York: Routledge.

*(Continued)*

*(Continued)*

For inspiring reflections on perspectives of coaching patients, we recommend:
Bennett, H., Coleman, E., Parry, C., Bodenheimer, T. and Chen, E. (2010) 'Health coaching for patients with chronic illness: Does your practice "give patients a fish" or "teach patients to fish"?', *Family Practice Management*, 17(5): 24–9.

And also:
Hawley, R. (2015) 'Coaching patients', in C. van Nieuwerburgh (ed.), *Coaching in Professional Contexts*. London: Sage Publishing, pp. 115–30.

# Conclusion: Towards a Shared Understanding of Ethical Standards

Over the past two decades, coaching has seen exponential growth on a global level; it has started to mature as a professional activity; and it is steadily developing a sense of collective identity, despite the diverse contexts in which coaches operate. Yet, notwithstanding this development, coaching is still not recognised as a legitimate, stand-alone profession. Indeed, recently scholars have gone so far as to suggest that a unified field of coaching may not even be possible (see, for instance, Drake, 2008). There are several reasons for this, including the lack of systematic regulation of coaching by an independent authority, either internal or exogenous to the profession. This does not mean that coaching is premised on superficial incentives with no regard for ethical standards. Instead, the relative quality assurance of the service is achieved through voluntary accredited registration with one of the several professional coaching bodies. As we have already seen, these bodies do not have any power of legal sanction in case of misconduct of the coach. In consequence, in the UK, as in most countries of the Anglosphere and continental Europe, the professional title (and role) of the coach remains legally unprotected. This can be detrimental to the credibility of the profession and its professionals.

To address this issue, many coaches consciously strive to increase their professional credibility by investing their personal time and resources on professional development and accreditation, which entails the adoption of a prescriptive code of ethics that is imposed by the chosen professional body. Although this is a worthy pursuit that we applaud, one of the powerful lessons we learnt during the writing of this book is to exercise caution on the usefulness and value of prescriptive codes of ethics. This is because, while ethical codes can provide the platform on which to build an ethical practice, there lies a paradox within them. At times, they can be too complex for practitioners to embrace and adopt, yet too simplistic to offer clear guidance on the intrinsically complex issues that coaches are faced with in their professional practice. In other words, codes can provide some moral shortcuts for ethical behaviour rather than the impetus for critical reflection on our beliefs, assumptions, behaviours and actions, as coaches.

Moreover, a collectively accepted code of ethics may be insufficient to support the great range of individual, cultural and professional values that coaches about the world bring into the coaching practice on a daily basis. This pluralism of values does not absolve coaches from their ethical responsibility towards the social and collective imperatives of contemporary life. Yet, the existence of normative and prescriptive codes of ethics that attempt some degree of pervasiveness are likely to compromise the mere reality of genuine ethical dilemmas that naturally arise during the coaching practice (Garvey et al., 2014: 226–7).

Indeed, while codes of ethics are designed to ring-fence coaching from poor practice or ill behaviour, they cannot and do not exempt us from difficult decisions. And of course, ethical decisions that are premised on moral principles are not always easy to make. This is because doing the right thing may not always feel right. This feeling of 'wrong-ness' – what Passmore and Mortimer (2011: 212) call cognitive dissonance, echoing Festinger's (1957) seminal theory – becomes the basis of the coach's trustworthiness and personal accountability to clients, colleagues and any other relevant stakeholders who are involved in the coaching process. To be sure, most coaches enter the profession with genuine intentions of helping their clients to achieve intended changes and goals. The best of intentions, however, cannot guarantee good judgement and practice. Challenging circumstances that call for difficult decisions may lead to poor judgement or inability to prevent substandard practice in a timely manner. A series of recent scandals in relevant professions within the realm of health and social care are testament to this (Bond, 2015: 297–8).

What then can guarantee the coach's ethical commitment, if established codes of ethics or the coach's professional idealism are inadequate? We believe that the starting point should be the development of a professional culture that prioritises a shared understanding of ethical standards, regardless of prescribed recipes for best practice. To be able to achieve this, we invite the coaching community to consider developing and maintaining a common ethical mindset that is geared towards social and collective requirements; the starting point is with our self. In practice, this means capitalising on the ethical strategies we already have in place: clear contracting; conscious reflection and reflexivity through critical enquiry; regular supervision; continuing professional development; and, importantly, open and shared communication between colleagues and relevant stakeholders, even inviting the input of clients. These are some of the strategies that will enable us to bring (and keep) our professional values and ethics to the forefront rather than the background of our coaching practice. In other words, these strategies will help us enhance our ethical mindfulness and maturity.

Here we feel that we must clarify what we mean by 'social and collective requirements and imperatives'. Bond (2015: 296) pertinently reminds us that the 'primary purpose of professional ethics is to put the client first in the competing claims for any professional's attention'. Most coaches, indeed, would agree that it is their ethical responsibility to place the client at the heart of their practice. Yet, as this book has illuminated repeatedly, this is not always as straightforward as it sounds. This is because the client is usually part of a social unit, a greater whole, such as an organisation or a family. What is our ethical responsibility to the wider system then? Consider for instance a scenario where, as part of the coaching you offer to an individual, they come to the decision to leave the organisation that sponsors the coaching or the spouse who subsidises it. What is your ethical accountability to this greater whole and how can you manage such conflicting ethical responsibilities? As these are not straightforward questions to answer or easy decisions to make, the coach's professional idealism may be inadequate to guarantee consistent ethical standards, regardless of codes of ethics or independent regulation.

The debate over who, if anyone, ought to regulate coaching, then, becomes secondary in importance. Why? Because there is a more pressing question: who should be responsible for assessing, reviewing and even developing coaches as ethical practitioners? While coaching scholarship and practice have not yet provided a clear answer to this question, we see the evolving nature of the coaching profession, which has so far remained unblemished by scandals or severe accusations of dishonour, as a wonderful opportunity to create a professional culture that is premised on ethical standards by situating ethics at the forefront of professional practice. Designing and integrating professional ethics courses in coach training and education; consciously discussing ethical issues in professional meetings and conferences; and adopting a 'research-informed' mindset that embraces evidence-based practice are some of the ways we can create a common ethical mindset and, by extension, enhance our ethical mindfulness and maturity as coaches.

Whether we are traversing a postprofessional era for coaching (Drake, 2008) or the road to acceptance as a genuine profession, which is still unfolding before us, one thing is certain: our conscious and collective efforts to maintain an active ethical mindset (by reinforcing our use of tried and tested ethical strategies) can pave the way for the establishment of coaching as a legitimate and reliable service. While this is not necessarily every coach's end goal, it is our belief that a conscious (rather than idealistic) ethical coaching practice is our individual ethical responsibility to our clients, our colleagues, our associates and the coaching service as a whole. It is a means to creating a positive professional culture that is driven by integrity and commitment to embrace the complexities of the continually changing nature of contemporary life. The focus, therefore, should be cast not on solving ethical issues but, rather, on creating those conditions and conversations that will bring them to the surface. It is our systematic espousal of inclusive and generative values and ethics that will contribute to the development, advancement and dissemination of ethical coaching practices and, in consequence, the reliability of the discipline of coaching.

---

## A final pause for reflection

- What are the key lessons you have learnt from reading *Values and Ethics in Coaching*?
- What are the next steps that you will take in your effort to enhance and maintain your ethical coaching practice?

# References

Alred, G., Garvey, B. and Smith, R. (1998) '*Pas de deux*: Learning in conversation', *Career Development International*, 3(7): 308–13.

American College of Preventive Medicine (ACPM) (2009) *Lifestyle Medicine: Evidence Review*. Washington, DC: ACPM. Available at: http://c.ymcdn.com/sites/www.acpm.org/resource/resmgr/lmi-files/lifestylemedicine-literature.pdf (accessed 4 April 2016).

American Management Association (AMA) (2008) *Coaching: A Global Study of Successful Practice*. New York: AMA.

Argyris, C. (1982) *Reasoning, Learning, and Action: Individual and Organizational*. San Francisco, CA: Jossey-Bass.

Asay, T.P. and Lambert, M.J. (2001) 'Therapist relational variables', in D. Cain and J. Seeman (eds), *Humanistic Psychotherapies: Handbook of Research and Practice*. Washington, DC: American Psychological Association, pp. 531–58.

Association for Coaching (AC) (undated *a*) 'Association for Coaching Code of Ethics and Good Practice'. Available at: www.associationforcoaching.com/media/uploads/AC_Code_of_Ethics_and_Good_Practice.pdf (accessed 12 April 2016).

Association for Coaching (AC) (undated *b*) 'AC Coach Training Accreditation'. Available at: www.associationforcoaching.com/pages/accreditation/ac-coach-training-accreditation (accessed 23 March 2016).

AC (2008) 'Shared Values Statement'. Available at: www.associationforcoaching.com/media/uploads/press_releases/M80221.pdf (accessed 28 April 2015).

AC (2016) 'Global Code of Ethics for Coaches and Mentors'. Available at: www.associationforcoaching.com/pages/about/code-ethics-good-practice (accessed 15 March 2016).

Association of Coach Training Organizations (ACTO) (undated) Available at: actoonline.org (accessed 30 March 2016).

Austin, M.W. (2013) 'Sports as a moral practice: An Aristotelian approach', *Royal Institute of Philosophy*, Supplement, 73: 29–43.

Bachkirova, T. (2007) 'Role of coaching psychology in defining boundaries between counseling and coaching', in S. Palmer and A. Whybrow (eds), *Handbook of Coaching Psychology: A Guide for Practitioners*. London: Routledge, pp. 351–66.

Bachkirova, T., Cox, E. and Clutterbuck, D. (2014) 'Introduction', in E. Cox, T. Bachkirova and D. Clutterbuck (eds), *The Complete Handbook of Coaching*, 2nd edn. London: Sage Publishing, pp. 1–18.

Bachkirova, T., Jackson P. and Clutterbuck, D. (2011) *Coaching and Mentoring Supervision: Theory and Practice*. Maidenhead: Open University Press.

Bacon, F. (1597) *'Meditationes Sacrae'*, in J. Spedding, R.L. Ellis and D.D. Heath (eds), *The Works of Francis Bacon*, Vol. 7. London: Longman, 1859, pp. 227–54.

Bailey, D.M. and Schwartzberg, S.L. (1995) *Ethical and Legal Dilemmas in Occupational Therapy*. Philadelphia, PA: F.A. Davis.

Banks, S. (2009) 'From professional ethics to ethics in professional life: Implications for learning, teaching and study', *Ethics and Social Welfare*, 3(1): 55–63.

Banks, S. and Galagher, A. (2009) *Ethics in Professional Life*. Basingstoke: Palgrave Macmillan.

Bate, P. (2014) 'Context is everything', in *Perspectives on Context: A Selection of Essays Considering the Role of Context in Successful Quality Improvement*. London: Health Foundation.

Beckett, C. and Maynard, A. (2013) *Values and Ethics in Social Work*, 2nd edn. London: Sage Publishing.

Bennett, H., Coleman, E., Parry, C., Bodenheimer, T. and Chen, E. (2010) 'Health coaching for patients with chronic illness: Does your practice "give patients a fish" or "teach patients to fish"?', *Family Practice Management*, 17(5): 24–9.

Bennett, J.L. (2006) 'An agenda for coaching-related research: A challenge for researchers', *Coaching Psychology Journal: Practice and Research*, 58(4): 240–49.

Biswas-Diener, R. (2009) 'Personal coaching as a positive intervention', *Journal of Clinical Psychology*, 65(5): 544–53.

Black, R. (2005) 'Intersections of care: An analysis of culturally competent care, client-centered care, and the feminist ethics of care', *Work*, 24(4): 409–22.

Bluckert, P. (2004) 'The state of play in corporate coaching: Current and future trends', *Industrial and Commercial Training*, 32(2): 53–6.

Bluckert, P. (2006) *Psychological Dimensions of Executive Coaching*. Maidenhead: Open University Press.

Bochner, A. and Ellis, C. (2003) 'An introduction to the arts and narrative research: Arts as inquiry', *Qualitative Inquiry*, 9(4): 506–14.

Bogdan, R.C. and Biklen, S.K. (2006) *Qualitative Research for Education: An Introduction to Theories and Methods*, 5th edn. New York: Pearson Education.

Bohart, A., Elliott, R., Greenberg, L.S. and Watson, J.C. (2002) 'Empathy', in J.C. Norcross (ed.), *Psychotherapy Relationships that Work: Therapist Contributions and Responsiveness to Patients*. New York: Oxford University Press, pp. 89–108.

Bolton, G. (2014) *Reflective Practice: Writing and Professional Development*, 4th edn. London: Sage Publishing.

Bond, T. (2015) *Standards and Ethics for Counselling in Action*, 4th edn. London: Sage Publishing.

Bond, T. and Mitchels, B. (2015) *Confidentiality and Record Keeping in Counselling and Psychotherapy*, 2nd edn. London: Sage Publishing.

Bourdieu, P. and Passeron, J.C. (1977) *Reproduction*, trans. by R. Nice. London: Sage Publishing.

Boxill, J. (ed.) (2003) *Sport Ethics: An Anthology*. Oxford: Blackwell.

Boyle, D. and Harris, M. (2009) *The Challenge of Co-Production: How Equal Partnerships between Professionals and the Public are Crucial to Improving Public Sector Services*. London: National Endowment for Science, Technology and the Arts (NESTA).

Boyle, D., Slay, J. and Stephens, L. (2010) *Public Services Inside Out: Putting Co-production into Practice*. London: NESTA.

Brennan, D. and Wildflower, L. (2014) 'Ethics in coaching', in E. Cox, T. Bachkirova and D. Clutterbuck (eds), *The Complete Handbook of Coaching*, 2nd edn. London: Sage Publishing, pp. 430–44.

Bresser, F. and Wilson, C. (2010) 'What is coaching?', in J. Passmore (ed.), *Excellence in Coaching: The Industry Guide*, 2nd edn. London: Kogan Page, pp. 9–26.

Brock, V. (2006) 'Where do we align our ethical code? Learning from other professions', *Choice*, 4(3): 42–5.

Brockbank, A. and McGill, I. (2006) *Facilitating Reflective Learning through Mentoring and Coaching*. London: Kogan Page.

Brookfield, S. (1987) *Developing Critical Thinkers: Challenging Adults to Explore Alternative Ways of Thinking and Acting*. San Francisco, CA: Jossey-Bass.

Brooks, B. (2001) 'Ethics and standards in coaching', in L. West and M. Milan (eds), *The Reflecting Glass: Professional Coaching for Leadership Development*. Basingstoke: Palgrave Macmillan, pp. 95–101.

Brotman, L.E., Liberi, W.P. and Wasylishyn, K.M. (1998) 'Executive coaching: The need for standards of competence', *Consulting Psychology Journal: Practice and Research*, 50: 40–66.

Brown, K.W. and Holt, M. (2011) 'Experiential processing and the integration of bright and dark sides of the human psyche', in K.M. Sheldon, T.B. Kashdan and M.F. Steger (eds), *Designing Positive Psychology: Taking Stock and Moving Forward*. New York: Oxford University Press, pp. 147–58.

Bruner, J. (1985) *Actual Minds, Possible Worlds*. Cambridge, MA: Harvard University Press.

Bruner, J. (1990) *Acts of Meaning*. Cambridge, MA: Harvard University Press.

Buckley, A. and Buckley, C. (2006) *A Guide to Coaching and Mental Health: The Recognition and Management of Psychological Issues*. London: Routledge.

Cameron, F. (1994) *The Artist's Way: A Course in Discovering and Rediscovering your Creative Self*. Croydon: Souvenir Press.

Campone, F. (2011) 'Current research on coaching', in L. Wildflower and D. Brennan (eds), *The Handbook of Knowledge-Based Coaching: From Theory to Practice*. San Francisco, CA: Jossey-Bass, pp. 329–40.

Campone, F. and Awal, D. (2012) 'Life's thumbprint: The impact of significant life events on coaches and their coaching', *Coaching*, 5(1): 22–36.

Carlo, D.M. and Prior, D.M. (2003) 'Committing to an ethical framework: A powerful choice', *Choice*, 1(1): 30–3.

Caroll, M. (1996) *Counselling Supervision: Theory, Skills and Practice*. London: Cassells.

Carroll, L. (1954 [1865]) *Alice's Adventures in Wonderland*. London: Dent & Sons.

Carroll, M. and Shaw, E. (2013) *Ethical Maturity in the Helping Professions: Making Difficult Life and Work Decisions*. London: Jessica Kingsley.

Carter, A., Tamkin, P., Wilson, S. and Miller, L. (2015) *The Case for Health Coaching: Lessons Learnt from Implementing a Training and Development Intervention for Clinicians across the East of England*. Brighton: Institute of Employment Studies.

Cavanagh, M. and Buckley, A. (2014) 'Coaching and mental health', in E. Cox, T. Bachkirova and D. Clutterbuck (eds), *The Complete Handbook of Coaching*, 2nd edn. London: Sage Publishing, pp. 405–17.

Cavanagh, M. and Grant A.M. (2004) 'Executive coaching in organisations: The personal is the professional', *International Journal of Coaching in Organizations*, 2: 6–15.

Charted Institute of Personnel and Development (CIPD) (2012) *Learning and Talent Development Annual Survey*. London: CIPD.

Clutterbuck, D. (1998) *Learning Alliances: Tapping into Talent*. London: Chartered Institute of Personnel Management.

Clutterbuck, D. (2007) *Coaching the Team at Work*. London: Nicholas Brealey.

Clutterbuck, D. (2008) 'What's happening in coaching and mentoring and what is the difference between them?', *Development and Learning in Organizations*, 22(4): 8–10.

Clutterbuck, D. (2013) 'Step forward the ethical mentor'. Available at: www.davidclutterbuckpartnership.com/step-forward-the-ethical-mentor/ (accessed 25 March 2016).

Clutterbuck, D. and Megginson, D. (2005) *Making Coaching Work: Creating a Coaching Culture*. London: Chartered Institute of Personnel Management.

Cohen, L., Manion, L. and Morrison, K. (2007) *Research Methods in Education*, 6th edn. London: Routledge.

*Collins English Dictionary*. Available at: www.collinsdictionary.com (accessed 16 June 2015).

Copeland, W.D., Birmingham, C., de la Cruz, E. and Lewin, B. (1993) 'The reflective practitioner in teaching: Toward a research agenda', *Teaching and Teacher Education*, 9(4): 347–59.

Coulter, A. (2012) *Leadership for Patient and Public Engagement*. London: King's Fund.

Coulter, A., Roberts, S. and Dixon, A. (2013) *Delivering Better Services for People with Long-Term Conditions: Building the House of Care*. London: King's Fund.

Covey, S. (2004) *The 7 Habits of Highly Effective People: Powerful Lessons in Personal Change*. New York: Simon and Shuster.

Cox, E. (2010) 'Last things first: Ending well in the coaching relationship', in S. Palmer and A. McDowell (eds), *The Coaching Relationship: Putting People First*. London: Routledge, pp. 159–81.

Cox, E. (2013) *Coaching Understood: A Pragmatic Inquiry into the Coaching Process*. London: Sage Publishing.

Cox, E., Bachkirova T. and Clutterbuck, D. (eds) (2014) *The Complete Handbook of Coaching*, 2nd edn. London: Sage Publishing.

Creswell, J.W. (2012) *Qualitative Inquiry & Research Design: Choosing among Five Approaches*, 3rd edn. London: Sage Publishing.

Crisp, R. (ed.) (2013) *The Oxford Handbook of the History of Ethics*. Oxford: Oxford University Press.

Crisp, R. (ed.) (2014) *Aristotle: Nicomachean Ethics*, revd edn. Cambridge: Cambridge University Press.

Crotty, M. (1998) *The Foundations of Social Research: Meaning and Perspective in the Research Process*. London: Sage Publishing.

Cunliffe, A.L. (2004) 'On becoming a critically reflective practitioner', *Journal of Management Education*, 28(4): 407–26.

Cunliffe, A.L. (2009) 'The philosopher leader: On relationalism, ethics and reflexivity – A critical perspective to teaching leadership', *Management Learning*, 40(1): 87–101.

Dallos, R. and Stedmon, J. (2009) 'Flying over the swampy lowlands: Reflective and reflexive practice', in J. Stedmon and R. Dallos (eds), *Reflective Practice in Psychotherapy and Counselling*. Maidenhead: Open University Press, pp. 1–22.

Daloz, L.A. (1986) *Effective Teaching and Mentoring*. San Francisco, CA: Jossey-Bass.

Daloz, L.A. (1999) *Mentor: Guiding the Journey of Adult Learning*. San Francisco, CA: Jossey-Bass.

de Haan, E. (2008) *Relational Coaching: Journeys towards Mastering One-to-One Learning*. Chichester: John Wiley & Sons.

de Haan, E. (2012) *Supervision in Action: A Relational Approach to Coaching and Consulting Supervision*. Maidenhead: Open University Press.

de Jong, A. (2010) 'Coaching ethics: Integrity in the moment of choice', in J. Passmore (ed.), *Excellence in Coaching*. London: Association for Coaching, pp. 204–14.

Deigh, J. (2010) *An Introduction to Ethics*. Cambridge: Cambridge University Press.

Dembkowski, S. and Eldridge, F. (2004) 'The Achieve Coaching Model: Dispelling the secrets of the most successful executive coaches', *The Coaching and Mentoring Network*. Available at: www.coachingnetwork.

org.uk/information-portal/Articles/ViewArticle.asp?artId = 76 (accessed 2 April 2016).

Department for Culture, Media and Sport (DCMS) (2000) *A Sporting Future for All*. London: DCMS.

Department of Health (DH) (2003) *Confidentiality: NHS Code of Practice*. London: DH.

DH (2010) *Practical Approaches to Co-production: Building Effective Partnerships with People Using Services, Carers, Families and Citizens*. London: DH.

DH (2013) *The NHS Constitution: The NHS Belongs to Us All*. London: DH.

Devine, M., Meyers, R. and Houssemand, C. (2013) 'How can coaching make a positive impact within educational settings?', *Procedia: Social and Behavioral Sciences*, 93: 1382–9.

Drake, D.B. (2008) 'Finding our way home: Coaching's search for identity in a new era', *Coaching: An International Journal of Theory, Research and Practice*, 1(1): 15–26.

Drake, D.B. and Stober, D.R. (2005) 'The rise of the postprofessional: Lessons learned in thinking about coaching as an evidence-based practice'. Paper presented at the Second Australia Conference on Evidence-Based Coaching, 8–9 October, University of Sydney.

Duffy, M. and Passmore, J. (2010) 'Ethics in coaching: An ethical decision-making framework for coaching psychologists', *International Coaching Psychology Review*, 5(2): 140–51.

Eaton, W.W., Anthony, J.D., Mandel, W. and Garrison, R. (1990) 'Occupations and the prevalence of major depressive disorder', *Journal of Occupational Medicine*, 32: 1079–87.

Ellinger, A.D., Beattie, R.S. and Hamlin, R.G. (2014) 'The manager as coach', in E. Cox, T. Bachkirova and D. Clutterbuck (eds), *The Complete Handbook of Coaching*, 2nd edn. London: Sage Publishing, pp. 256–70.

Elliott, P. (1972) *The Sociology of the Professions*. London: Macmillan.

European Federation of Management Development (EFMD) (2009) 'The role of corporate coaching in business', *Global Focus: Magazine of the European Foundation for Management Development*, Special Supplement, 3: 1–20.

Evered, R.D. and Selman, J.C. (1989) 'Coaching and the art of management', *Organizational Dynamics*, 18(2): 16–32.

Festinger, L. (1957) *A Theory of Cognitive Dissonance*. Stanford, CA: Stanford University Press.

Fischer, M. and Ereaut, G. (2012) *When Doctors and Patients Talk: Making Sense of the Consultation*. London: Health Foundation.

Fonagy, P., Target, M., Cottrell, D. and Philips, J. (2005) *What Works for Whom? A Critical Review of Treatments for Children and Adolescents*. New York: Guilford Press.

Foucault, M. (1980) 'Truth and power', in M. Foucault, *Power/Knowledge: Selected Interviews and Other Writings 1972–1977*, ed. C. Gordon. Hemel Hempstead: Harvester Wheatsheaf.

French, J.R.P. and Raven, B. (1959) 'The bases of social power', in D. Cartwright (ed.), *Studies in Social Power*. Ann Arbor, MI: Institute for Social Research.

Gadamer, H.G. (1989) *Truth and Method*, 2nd edn. London: Sheed and Ward.

Gallwey, W.T. (2015 [1974]) *The Inner Game of Tennis: The Ultimate Guide to the Mental Side of Peak Performance*, 1st edn, 1974. London: Pan Books.

Garvey, B. (2004) 'The mentoring/counseling/coaching debate: Call a rose by any other name and perhaps it's a bramble?', *Development and Learning in Organisations*, 18(2): 6–8.

Garvey, B. and Williamson, B. (2002) *Beyond Knowledge Management: Dialogue, Creativity and the Corporate Curriculum*. Harlow: Pearson.

Garvey, B., Stokes, P. and Megginson, D. (2014) *Coaching and Mentoring: Theory and Practice*, 2nd edn. London: Sage Publishing.

Gert, B. (1988) *Morality: A New Justification of the Moral Rules*. New York: Oxford University Press.

Gilley, A., Gilley, J.W. and Kouider, E. (2010) 'Characteristics of managerial coaching', *Performance Review Quarterly*, 23(1): 53–70.

Gilligan, C. (1993) *In a Different Voice*. Cambridge, MA: Harvard University Press.

Gillon, R. (1985) 'Autonomy and consent', in M. Lockwood (ed.), *Moral Dilemmas in Modern Medicine*. Oxford: Oxford University Press, pp. 7–22.

Goleman, D. (1995) *Emotional Intelligence*. New York: Bantam Books.

Global Coaching Community (GCC) (2008) *Dublin Declaration on Coaching*. Paper presented at the Global Convention on Coaching, Dublin, August.

Goleman, D. (2000) 'Leadership that gets results', *Harvard Business Review*, 78 (March–April): 78–90.

Goleman, D. (2001) 'An EI-based theory of performance', in D. Goleman and C. Cherniss (eds), *The Emotionally Intelligent Workplace: How to Select for, Measure, and Improve Emotional intelligence for Individuals, Groups, and Organizations*. San Francisco, CA: Jossey-Bass, pp. 27–44.

Grant, A.M. (2003) 'Keeping up with the cheese! Research as a foundation for professional coaching of the future', in I.F. Stein and L.A. Belsten (eds.), *Proceeding of the First International Coach Federation Coaching Research Symposium*. Washington, DC: International Coach Federation, pp. 1–19.

Grant, A.M. and Cavanagh, M.J. (2004) 'Toward a profession of coaching: Sixty-five years of progress and challenges for the future', *International Journal of Evidence Based Coaching and Mentoring*, 2(1): 1–16.

Grant, A.M. and Stober, D.R. (2006) 'Introduction', in D.R. Stober and A.M. Grant (eds), *Evidence-Based Coaching Handbook: Putting Best Practices to Work for Your Clients*. New York: Wiley, pp. 1–14.

Grant, A.M., Passmore, J., Cavanagh, M.J. and Parker, H. (2010) 'The state of play in coaching today: A comprehensive review of the field', *International Review of Industrial and Organizational Psychology*, 25: 125–66.

Gray, D. (2014) *Doing Research in the Real World*. London: Sage Publishing.

Green, J. (2009) 'The deformation of professional formation: Managerial targets and the undermining of professional judgement', *Ethics and Social Welfare*, 3(2): 115–30.

Guba, E.G. (ed.) (1990) *The Paradigm Dialogue*. Newbury Park, CA: Sage Publishing.

Gyllensten, K. and Palmer, S. (2007) 'The coaching relationship: An interpretative phenomenological analysis', *International Coaching Psychology Review*, (2)2: 169–77.

Habermas, J. (1990) *Moral Consciousness and Communicative Action*. Cambridge, MA: MIT Press.

Hackman, J.R. and Wageman, R. (2005) 'A theory of team coaching', *Academy of Management Review*, 30(2): 269–87.

Hall, L. (2013) *Mindful Coaching: How Mindfulness Can Transform Coaching in Practice*. London: Kogan Page.

Hamersley, M. (2013) *What is Qualitative Research?* London: Bloomsbury.

Hamlin, R.G., Ellinger, A.D. and Beattie, R.S. (2006) 'Coaching at the heart of managerial effectiveness: A cross-cultural study of managerial behaviours', *Human Resource Development International*, 9(3): 305–31.

Hardman, A., Jones, C. and Jones, R. (2010) 'Sports coaching, virtue ethics and emulation', *Physical Education and Sport Pedagogy*, 15(4): 345–59.

Hawkins, P. (2014) 'Coaching supervision', in E. Cox, T. Bachkirova and D. Clutterbuck (eds), *The Complete Handbook of Coaching*, 2nd edn. London: Sage Publishing, pp. 391–404.

Hawkins, P. and Shohet, R. (2006) *Supervision in the Helping Professions*, 3rd edn. Maidenhead: Open University Press.

Hawkins, P. and Smith, N. (2006) *Coaching, Mentoring and Organizational Consultancy: Supervision and Development*. Maidenhead: Open University Press.

Hawley, R. (2012) 'Making every conversation count: The role of informal coaching in the NHS', in P. Lindvall and D. Megginson (eds), *Developing Mentoring and Coaching Practice: Papers from the 2nd EMCC Research Conference*. Marlborough: European Mentoring and Coaching Council (EMCC).

Hawley, R. (2015) 'Coaching patients', in C. van Nieuwerburgh (ed.), *Coaching in Professional Contexts*. London: Sage Publishing, pp. 115–30.

Hay, J. (2007) *Reflective Practice and Supervision for Coaches*. New York: Wiley.

Health and Care Professions Council (HCPC) (undated) Available at: www.hcpc-uk.org. (accessed 25 March 2016).

Heidegger, M. (1962) *Being and Time*, trans. by J. Macquarrie and E. Robinson. Oxford: Blackwell.

Heslin, P.A., Vandewalle, D. and Latham, G.P. (2006) 'Keen to help? Managers' implicit person theories and their subsequent employee coaching', *Personnel Psychology*, 59(4): 871–902.

Hibbard, J. and Gilburt, H. (2014) *Supporting People to Manage their Health: An Introduction to Patient Activation*. London: King's Fund.

Hume, D. (2007 [1739]) *A Treatise of Human Nature*. Sioux Falls, SD: Nuvision.

Hunt, J.M. and Weintraub, J.R. (2002a) 'How coaching can enhance your brand as manager', *Journal of Organizational Excellence*, 21(2): 39–44.

Hunt, J.M. and Weintraub, J.R. (2002b) *The Coaching Manager: Developing Top Talent in Business*. Thousand Oaks, CA: Sage Publishing.

Hunt, J.M. and Weintraub, J.R. (2011) *The Coaching Manager: Developing Top Talent in Business*, 2nd edn. Thousand Oaks, CA: Sage Publishing.

Hursthouse, R. (1999) *On Virtue Ethics*. Oxford: Oxford University Press.

Iordanou, I. and Hawley, R. (2015) 'A snapshot on the findings from an investigation into the gap between coaching and mentoring practice and research'. Unpublished report for the European Mentoring and Coaching Council (EMCC).

Iordanou, I. and Williams, P. (2016, in print) 'Developing ethical capabilities for coaches', in T. Bachkirova, G. Spence and D.B. Drake (eds), *The Sage Handbook of Coaching*. London: Sage Publishing.

Iordanou, I., Leach, A. and Barnes, V. (2015) 'Coaching in higher education', in C. van Nieuwerburgh (ed.), *Coaching in Professional Contexts*. London: Sage Publishing, pp. 145–58.

Ives, I. and Cox, E. (2014) *Relationship Coaching: The Theory and Practice of Coaching with Singles, Couples and Parents*. London: Routledge.

Jarvis, J. (2006) *Coaching and Buying Coaching Services: A CIPD Guide*. Available at: www.cipd.co.uk/NR/rdonlyres/C31A728E-7411-4754-9644-46A84EC 9CFEE/0/2995coachbuyingservs.pdf (accessed 12 November 2015).

Jarvis, P. (1997) *Ethics and Education for Adults in a Late Modern Society*. Leicester: National Institute of Adult Continuing Education.

Johns, C. (2013) *Becoming a Reflective Practitioner*, 4th edn. Chichester: John Wiley & Sons.

Jones, R.L. (2009) 'Coaching as caring (the smiling gallery): Accessing hidden knowledge', *Physical Education and Sport Pedagogy*, 14(4): 377–90.

Jones-Devitt, S. and Smith, L. (2007) *Critical Thinking in Health and Social Care*. London: Sage Publishing.

Jowett, S. (2005) 'The coach–athlete partnership', *The Psychologist*, 18: 412–15.

Jowett, S. and Cockerill, I.M. (2002) 'Incompatibility in the coach–athlete relationship', in I.M. Cockerill (ed.), *Solutions in Sport Psychology*. London: Thomson Learning, pp. 16–31.

Jowett, S., Kanakoglou, K. and Passmore, J. (2012) 'The application of the 3 + 1 Cs relationship model in executive coaching', *Consulting Psychology Journal*, 64(3): 183–97.

Kabat-Zinn, J. (1994) *Wherever you Go, There you Are: Mindfulness Meditation in Everyday Life*. New York: Hyperion.

Kabat-Zinn, J. (2003) 'Mindfulness-based interventions in context: Past, present and future', *Clinical Psychology: Science and Practice*, 10(2): 144–56.

Kadushin, A. (2002) *Supervision in Social Work*, 4th edn. New York: Columbia University Press.

Kauffman, C. (2005) 'De-mystifying research: An introduction for coaches', in I.F. Stein, F. Campone and L.J. Page (eds), *Proceedings of the Second ICF Coaching Research Symposium*. Washington, DC: International Coach Federation, pp. 161–8.

Kauffman, C. and Coutu, D. (2009) '*Harvard Business Review* research report: The realities of executive coaching'. Available at: www.carolkauffman.com/images/pdfs/kauffman_coutu_hrb_survey_report.pdf (accessed 20 August 2015).

Kegan, R. (1982) *The Evolving Self: Problems and Process in Human Development*. Cambridge, MA: Harvard University Press.

Keller, J. (2007) *Attitude is Everything: Change Your Attitude and You Change Your Life*. Tampa, FL: INTI Publishing & Resource Books.

Kemp, M. (2001) 'Fictioning identities: A course on narrative and fictional approaches to educational practice', *Reflective Practice*, 2(3): 345–55.

Kets de Vries, M.F.R. (2005) 'Leadership group coaching in action: The Zen of creating high-performance teams', *Academy of Management Executive*, 19(1): 61–76.

Khurana, R. and Nohria, N. (2008) 'It's time to make management a true profession', *Harvard Business Review*, 86(10): 70–7.

Kilburg, R.R. (2000) *Executive Coaching: Developing Managerial Wisdom in a World of Chaos*. Washington, DC: American Psychological Association.

Kipling, R. (1902) *Just So Stories*. Toronto: George S. Morang & Co.

Knight, J. (2011) *Unmistakable Impact: A Partnership Approach for Dramatically Improving Instruction*. Thousand Oaks, CA: Corwin.

Knights, A. (2008) *Developing Coaching Capabilities in Organisations*. London: Chartered Institute of Personnel and Development.

Koggel, C. and Orme, J. (2010) Editorial: 'Care ethics: New theories and applications', *Ethics and Social Welfare*, 4(2): 109–14.

Kohlberg, L. (1981) *Essays on Moral Development, Vol. 1: The Philosophy of Moral Development*. San Francisco, CA: Harper and Row.

Kolb, D.A. (1984) *Experiential Learning*. Englewood Cliffs, NJ: Prentice Hall.

Kraut, A.I., Pedigo, P.R., McKenna, D.D. and Dunnette, M.D. (1989) 'The role of the manager: What's really important in different management roles?', *Academy of Management Executive*, 3(4): 286–93.

Lago, C. and Smith, B. (2010) *Anti-discriminatory Practice in Counselling and Psychotherapy*. London: Sage Publishing.

Lane, D.A. (2011) 'Ethics and professional standards in supervision', in T. Bachkirova, P. Jackson and D. Clutterbuck (eds), *Coaching and Mentoring Supervision: Theory and Practice*. Maidenhead: Open University Press, pp. 91–104.

Lane, D.A. and Corrie, S. (2006) *The Modern Scientist-Practitioner: A Guide to Practice in Psychology*. London: Routledge.

Lane, D.A., Stelter R. and Stout-Rostron, S. (2014) 'The future of coaching as a profession', in E. Cox, T. Bachkirova and D. Clutterbuck (eds), *The Complete Handbook of Coaching*, 2nd edn. London: Sage Publishing, pp. 377–90.

Laske, O. (2006) 'Why does your maturity matter?', *Choice*, 4(3): 10–12.

Latner, J. (2000) 'The theory of gestalt therapy', in E.C. Nevis (ed.), *Gestalt Therapy: Perspectives and Applications*. Cambridge, MA: Gestalt Press, pp. 13–56.

Law, H., Ireland, S. and Hussain, Z. (2007) *The Psychology of Coaching, Mentoring and Learning*. Chichester: John Wiley & Sons.

Lennard, D. (2010) *Coaching Models: A Cultural Perspective: A Guide to Model Development for Practitioners and Students of Coaching*. New York: Routledge.

Lynch, M. (2000) 'Against reflexivity as an academic virtue and source of privileged knowledge', *Theory, Culture & Society*, 17(3): 26–54.

Machin, S. (2010) 'The nature of the internal coaching relationship', *International Journal of Evidence Based Coaching and Mentoring*, Special Issue, 4: 37–52.

MacKensie, H. (2007) 'Stepping off the treadmill: A study of coaching on the RCN Clinical Leadership Programme', *International Journal of Evidence Based Coaching and Mentoring*, 5(2): 22–33.

Megginson, D. and Whitaker, V. (2003) *Continuing Professional Development*. London: Charted Institute of Personnel and Development.

Mink, O.G., Owen, K.Q. and Mink, B.P. (1993) *Developing High-Performance People: The Art of Coaching*. Reading, MA: Addison-Wesley.

Mintzberg, H., Ahlstrand, B. and Lampel, J. (2008) *Strategy Safari: The Complete Guide through the Wilds of Strategic Management*. Harlow: Prentice Hall.

Moore, M. and Jackson, E. (2014) 'Health and wellness coaching', in E. Cox, T. Bachkirova and D. Clutterbuck (eds), *The Complete Handbook of Coaching*, 2nd edn. London: Sage Publishing, pp. 313–28.

Morse, J.J. and Wagner, F.R. (1978) 'Measuring the process of managerial effectiveness', *Academy of Management Journal*, 21(1): 23–35.

Mumford, A. (1993) *How Managers can Develop Managers*, 2nd edn. Adlershot: Gower.

Nelson, E. and Hogan, R. (2009) 'Coaching on the dark side', *International Coaching Psychology Review*, 4(1): 9–22.

Newton, A.Z. (1997) *Narrative Ethics*. Cambridge, MA: Harvard University Press.

O'Connor, J. and Lages, A. (2007) *How Coaching Works: The Essential Guide to the History and Practice of Effective Coaching*. London: A & C Black.

Orlinsky, D.E. and Howard, K.I. (1986) 'Process and outcome in psychotherapy', in S.L. Garfielf and A.E. Gergin (eds), *Handbook of Psychotherapy and Behaviour Change*, 3rd edn. New York: John Wiley & Sons, pp. 152–211.

Orlinsky, D.E, Grawe, K. and Parks, B.K. (1994) 'Process and outcome in therapy', in E. Bergin and S.L. Garfiel (eds), *Handbook of Psychotherapy and Behavior Change*, 4th edn. New York: Wiley, pp. 270–376.

*Oxford Dictionary* [Online]. Available at: www.oxforddictionaries.com (accessed 15 June 2015).

Page, L.J. (2005) 'Research as "expertising": A reading guide for practising coaches', in I.F. Stein, F. Campone and L.J. Page (eds), *Proceedings of the Second ICF Coaching Research Symposium*. Washington, DC: International Coach Federation, pp. 152–211.

Palmer, S. and McDowall, A. (eds) (2010) *The Coaching Relationship: Putting People First*. London: Routledge.

Passmore, J. (2009) 'Coaching ethics: Making ethical decisions – novices and experts', *Coaching Psychologist*, 5(1): 6–10.

Passmore, J. and Brown, A. (2009) 'Coaching non-adult students for enhanced examination performance', *Coaching: An International Journal of Theory, Research and Practice*, 2(1): 54–64.

Passmore, J. and Mortimer, L. (2011) 'Ethics in coaching', in L. Boyce and G. Hernez-Broome (eds), *Advancing Executive Coaching: Setting the Course for Successful Leadership Coaching*. San Francisco, CA: Jossey-Bass, pp. 205–28.

Passmore, J. (ed.) (2011) *Supervision in Coaching: Supervision, Ethics and Continuous Professional Development*. London: Kogan Page.

Paul, R. and Elder, L. (2005) *A Guide for Educators to Critical Thinking Competency Standards*. Tomales, CA: Foundation for Critical Thinking.

Pearn, M. and Downs, S. (1989) 'Developing skilled learners: A strategy for coping with new technology', *Industrial and Commercial Training*, 89(3): 9–16.

Pelham, G. (2016) *The Coaching Relationship in Practice*. London: Sage Publishing.

Peltier, B. (2010) *The Psychology of Executive Coaching: Theory and Application*, 2nd edn. New York: Routledge.

Pitt-Aikens, T. and Thomas Ellis, A. (1990) *Loss of the Good Authority: Cause of Delinquency*. London: Penguin.

Polanyi, M. (1962) *Personal Knowledge*. Chicago, IL: University of Chicago Press.

Ponte, P.R., Gross, A.H., Galante, A. and Glazer, G. (2006) 'Using an executive coach to increase leadership effectiveness', *Journal of Nursing Administration*, 36(6): 319–24.

Poole, R. (1972) *Towards Deep Subjectivity*. London: Allen Lane.

Price, A. (2004) 'Encouraging reflection and critical thinking in practice', *Nursing Standard*, 18(47): 46–52.

PricewaterhouseCoopers (PwC) (2012) *International Coach Federation Global Coaching Study*. Lexington, KY: International Coach Federation.

Proctor, G. (2014) *Values and Ethics in Counselling and Psychotherapy*. London: Sage Publishing.

Redshaw, B. (2000) 'Do we really understand coaching? How can we make it work better?', *Industrial and Commercial Training*, 32(3): 106–8.

Reynolds, M. (1998) 'Reflection and critical reflection in management learning', *Management Learning*, 29(2): 183–200.

Rogers, C. (1951) *Client-centered Therapy: Its Current Practice, Implications and Theory*. London: Constable.

Rogers, C. (1961) *On Becoming a Person: A Therapist's View of Psychotherapy*. London: Constable.

Rogers, C. (1980) *A Way of Being*. Boston, MA: Houghton Mifflin.

Rogers, J. (2012) *Coaching Skills: A Handbook*, 3rd edn. Maidenhead: Open University Press.

Rose, N. (1999) *Governing Soul: Shaping of the Private Self*, 2nd edn. London: Free Association Books.

Rosinski, P. (2003) *Coaching across Cultures: New Tools for Leveraging National, Corporate and Professional Differences*. London: Nicholas Brealey.

Rowland, N. and Goss, S. (2000) *Evidenced-Based Counselling and Psychological Therapies*. London: Routledge.

Rowling, E. (ed.) (2012) *Leadership and Engagement for Improvement in the NHS: Together we Can*. London: King's Fund.

Sagar, T., Jones, D., Symons, K. and Bowring, J. (2015) *The Student Sex Work Project Research Summary*. Swansea: Swansea University.

Scheg, A. (2014) *Critical Examinations of Distance Education Transformation across Disciplines*. Hershey, PA: Information Science Reference.

Schön, D.A. (1984) *The Reflective Practitioner: How Professionals Think in Action*. New York: Basic Books.

Schön, D.A. (1987) *Educating the Reflective Practitioner*. San Francisco, CA: Jossey-Bass.

Scoular, A. (2011) *Financial Times Guides: Business Coaching*. Harlow: Prentice Hall.

Seedhouse, D. (2009) *Ethics: The Heart of Healthcare*, 3rd edn. West Chichester: Wiley.

Segers, J. and Vloeberghs, D. (2009) 'Do theory and techniques in executive coaching matter more than in therapy?', *Industrial and Organizational Psychology*, 2: 280–3.

Segers, J., Vloeberghs, D., Henderickx, E. and Inceoglu, I. (2011) 'Structuring and understanding the coaching industry: The coaching cube', *Academy of Management Learning & Education*, 10(2): 204–21.

Senge, P. (2006) *The Fifth Discipline: The Art and Practice of the Learning Organisation*. London: Random House.

Shaw, P. and Linnecar, R. (2007) *Business Coaching*. Chichester: Capstone.

Sills, C. (2012) 'The coaching contract: A mutual commitment', in E. de Haan and C. Sills (eds), *Coaching Relationships: The Relational Coaching Field Book*. Faringdon: Libri, pp. 93–110.

Slife, B.D. and Williams, R.N. (1995) *What's Behind the Research: Discovering the Hidden Assumptions in Behavioural Science*. London: Sage Publishing.

Soltis, J. (1986) 'Teaching professionals ethics', *Journal of Teacher Education*, 37(3): 2–4.

Spence, G.B. (2007) 'Future development of evidence-based coaching: Lessons from the rise and fall of the human potential movement', *Australian Psychologist*, 42(4): 255–65.

Spence, G.B. (2015) 'Coaching for optimal functioning', in C. van Nieuwerburgh (ed.), *Coaching in Professional Contexts*. London: Sage Publishing, pp. 11–28.

Spence, G.B., Cavanagh, M. and Grant, A.M. (2006) 'Duty of care in an unregulated industry: Initial findings on the diversity and practices of Australian coaches', *International Coaching Psychology Review*, 1(1): 71–85.

sports coach UK (undated) Available at: www.sportscoach.org (accessed 10 November 2015).

Steare, R. (2009) *Ethicability: How to Decide What's Right and Find the Courage to Do It*. London: Roger Steare Consulting.

Stedmon, J. and Dallos, R. (eds) (2009) *Reflective Practice in Psychotherapy and Counselling*. Maidenhead: Open University Press.

Stiles, W.B., Honos-Webb, L. and Suko, M. (1998) 'Responsiveness in psychotherapy', *Clinical Psychology: Science and Practice*, 5(4): 439–58.

Stober, D.R. (2014) 'Continuing professional development for coaches', in E. Cox, T. Bachkirova and D. Clutterbuck (eds), *The Complete Handbook of Coaching*, 2nd edn. London: Sage Publishing, pp. 418–30.

Stober, D.R. and Grant, A.M. (eds) *Evidence-Based Coaching Handbook: Putting Best Practices to Work for Your Clients*. New York: Wiley.

Stokes, J. and Jolly, R. (2014) 'Executive and leadership coaching', in E. Cox, T. Bachkirova and D. Clutterbuck (eds), *The Complete Handbook of Coaching*, 2nd edn. London: Sage Publishing, pp. 244–55.

Stokes, P. (2007) 'The skilled coachee'. Paper presented at the 14th European Mentoring and Coaching Council Conference, 11–13 October, Stockholm.

Stokes, P. (2014) 'Two important ways coachees can influence their own progress'. Available at: http://extra.shu.ac.uk/sbsblog/2014/03/two-important-ways-coachees-can-influence-their-own-progress/ (accessed 1 March 2016).

*The Economist* (2003) 'Coaching: Corporate therapy', 13 November. Available at: www.economist.com/node/2212916 (accessed 16 July 2015).

Taylor, S. and Ladkin, D. (2009) 'Understanding arts-based methods in managerial development', *Academy of Management Learning & Education*, 8(1): 55–69.

Thomson, B. (2009) *Don't Just Do Something, Sit There: An Introduction to Non-directive Coaching*. Oxford: Chandos.

Thomson, B. (2014) *First Steps in Coaching*. London: Sage Publishing.

Thorpe, S. and Clifford, J. (2007) *The Coaching Handbook: An Action Kit for Trainers and Managers*. London: Kogan Page.

United Nations Educational, Scientific and Cultural Organization (UNESCO) Available at: www.unesco.org (accessed 15 June 2015).

University Forum for Human Resources and Development (UFHRD) (2015) HRD Postgraduate Programmes in the UK. Available at: www.ufhrd.co.uk/wordpress/wp-content/uploads/2015/10/Database-HEI-programmes-Final-October-20151.pdf (accessed 28 March 2016).

van Nieuwerburgh, C. (ed.) (2012) *Coaching in Education: Getting Better Results for Students, Educators, and Parents*. London: Karnac.

van Nieuwerburgh, C. (2014) *An Introduction to Coaching Skills: A Practical Guide*. London: Sage Publishing.

van Nieuwerburgh, C. (ed.) (2015) *Coaching in Professional Contexts*. London: Sage Publishing.

van Nieuwerburgh, C. (2015) 'The importance of understanding professional contexts', in C. van Nieuwerburgh (ed.), *Coaching in Professional Contexts*. London: Sage Publishing, pp. 1–9.

Vogel, M. (2012) 'Story matters: An inquiry into the role of narrative in coaching', *International Journal of Evidence Based Coaching and Mentoring*, 10(1): 1–13.

Waddington, I. (1975) 'The development of medical ethics: A sociological analysis', *Medical History*, 19(1): 36–51.

Wang, J. and Zhang, L. (2015) 'Psychological consultations for Olympic athletes' peak performance', *Journal of Sport Psychology in Action*, 6(2): 59–72.

Watson, J.C. and Greenberg, L.S. (1994) 'The working alliance in experiential therapy: Enacting the relationship conditions', in A. Horvath and L. Greenberg (eds), *The Working Alliance: Theory, Research and Practice*. New York: John Wiley & Sons, pp. 153–72.

Wax, R. (2006) *A Mindfulness Guide for the Frazzled*. London: Penguin.

Webster, J. (2008) 'Establishing the "truth" of the matter: Confessional reflexivity as introspection and avowal', *Psychology and Society*, 1(1): 65–76.

Welman, P. and Bachkirova, T. (2010) 'The issue of power in the coaching relationship', in S. Palmer and A. McDowall (eds), *The Coaching Relationship: Putting People First*. London: Routledge, pp. 139–58.

Western, S. (2012) *Coaching and Mentoring: A Critical Text*. London: Sage Publishing.

Whitaker, V. and Rhodes, T. (2004) 'Transforming our shadow side: The masks of mentoring'. Paper presented at the 11th European Mentoring and Coaching Council Conference, 18–19 November, Brussels.

Whitmore, J. (2002) *Coaching for Performance: GROWing People, Performance and Purpose*, 3rd edn. London: Nicholas Brealey.

Wildflower, L. (2013) *The Hidden History of Coaching*. Maidenhead: Open University Press.

Wildflower, L. and Brennan, D. (2011) *The Handbook of Knowledge-Based Coaching: From Theory to Practice*. San Francisco: Jossey-Bass.

Williams, M. and Kabat-Zinn, J. (2013) *Mindfulness: Diverse Perspectives on its Meaning, Origin and Application*. London: Routledge.

Williams, P. and Anderson, K.S. (2006) *Law and Ethics in Coaching: How to Solve – and Avoid – Difficult Problems in Your Practice*. Hoboken, NJ: John Wiley & Sons.

Williams, P., Lindberg, W.H. and Anderson, S.K. (2006) 'Coaching to come', in P. Williams and K.S. Anderson (eds), *Law and Ethics in Coaching: How to Solve – and Avoid – Difficult Problems in Your Practice*. Hoboken, NJ: John Wiley & Sons, pp. 245–56.

Williamson, C. (2009) 'Using life coaching techniques to enhance leadership skills in nursing', *Nursing Times*, 105(8): 20–3.

Wolever, R.Q., Simmons, L.A., Sforzo, G.A., Dill, D., Kaye, M., Bechard, E.M., Southard, M.E., Kennedy, M., Vosloo, J. and Yang, N. (2013) 'A systematic review of the literature on health and wellness coaching: Defining a key behavioural intervention in healthcare', *Global Advances in Health & Medicine*, 2(4): 35–53.

Woodhead, V. (2011) 'How does coaching help to support team working? A case study in the NHS', *International Journal of Evidenced Based Coaching and Mentoring*, Special Issue, 5: 102–19.

Wright, J. (2012) *Reflective Writing in Counselling and Psychotherapy*. London: Sage Publishing.

Yanow, D. and Tsoukas, H. (2009) 'What is reflection-in-action? A phenomenological account', *Journal of Management Studies*, 46(8): 1339–64.

Yukl, G. (1994) *Leadership in Organizations*, 3rd edn. Upper Saddle River, NJ: Prentice Hall.

# Index

Note: Page numbers in *italic* refer to "stories from practice".